Digital Material

Digital Material

Tracing New Media in Everyday Life and Technology

Edited by
Marianne van den Boomen, Sybille Lammes,
Ann-Sophie Lehmann, Joost Raessens,
and Mirko Tobias Schäfer

Amsterdam University Press

MediaMatters is a new series published by Amsterdam University Press on current debates about media technology and practices. International scholars critically analyze and theorize the materiality and performativity, as well as spatial practices of 'old' and 'new' media in contributions that engage with today's digital media culture.
For more information about the series, please visit: www.aup.nl

The publication of this book was made possible with the financial support of the GATE project, funded by the Netherlands Organisation for Scientific Research (NWO) and the Netherlands ICT Research and Innovation Authority (ICT Regie), the Transformations in Art and Culture programme (NWO) and the Innovational Research Incentives Scheme (NWO). We would also like to express our thanks to the Research Institute for History and Culture (OCG) and the Department of Media and Culture Studies at Utrecht University for their kind support.

Cover illustration: Goos Bronkhorst
Cover design: Suzan de Beijer, Weesp
Lay out: JAPES, Amsterdam

ISBN   978 90 8964 068 0
e-ISBN   978 90 4850 666 8
NUR   670

Table of contents

Introduction

From the virtual to matters of fact and concern

All that is solid melts into air
Karl Marx and Friedrich Engels, 1848

Technology is society made durable
Bruno Latour, 1991

The 1982 Time magazine's 'Man of the Year' election was a special one. For the first time in the history of this traditional annual event, a non-human was celebrated: the computer was declared 'Machine of the Year 1982'. The cover displayed a table with a personal computer on it, and a man sitting passively next to it and looking rather puzzled. On the 2006 Time's election cover once again a computer was shown, now basically a screen reflecting the 'Person of the Year': 'YOU. Yes, you. You control the Information Age. Welcome to your world.'

Within 24 years the computer seemed to have changed from an exciting, mysterious machine with unknown capabilities into a transparent mirror, reflecting you, your desires and your activities. Apparently, digital machines embody no unsolved puzzles any more. At the beginning of the 21st century, they are so widely distributed and used that we take them for granted – though we still call them 'new media'. Computers, e-mail, the Internet, mobile phones, digital photo albums, and computer games have become common artefacts in our daily lives. Part of the initial spell has worn off, yet new spells have been cast as well, and some of the old spells still haunt the discourse about the so-called new media.

Three decades of societal and cultural alignment of digital machinery yielded a host of innovations, trials, failures, and problems, accompanied by hype-hopping popular and academic discourse. Meanwhile, new media studies crystallized internationally into an established academic discipline, especially when the first academic bachelor and master programs were institutionalized ten years ago, including the Utrecht program, New Media and Digital Culture.[1] A decade of unfolding the field implores us to reflect on where we stand now. Which new questions emerge when new media are taken for granted, and which puzzles are still unsolved? Is contemporary digital culture indeed all about 'you', or do we still not really fathom the digital machinery and how it constitutes us as 'you'? The contributors to the present book, all teaching and researching new media and digital culture, and all involved in the Utrecht Media Research group, assembled their 'digital material' into an anthology to celebrate the tenth anniversary of the Utrecht program. Together, the contributions provide a showcase of current state-of-the–art research in the field, from what we as editors have called a 'digital-materialist' perspective.

Immaterial, im/material, in-material

Popular discourse in the 1990s framed new media chiefly as possessing new and amazing qualities. They were believed to fundamentally transform the way we think, live, love, work, learn, and play. *Hypertext, virtual reality,* and *cyberspace* were the predominant buzzwords. They announced a new frontier of civilization, whether from an optimistic utopian perspective – pointing to the emergence of virtual communities, new democracy, and a new economy – or from a more pessimistic and dystopian angle – with warnings against the digital divide, information glut, and ubiquitous surveillance. Yet, both outlooks were rooted in the same idea: that new media marked a shift from the material to the immaterial, a general transformation of atoms into bits (Negroponte 1995) and of matter into mind (Barlow 1996). These lines of reasoning were characterized by what we may call *digital mysticism,* a special brand of technological determinism in which digitality and software are considered to be ontologically immaterial determinants of new media. New media and their effects were thus framed as being 'hyper', 'virtual', and 'cyber' – that is, outside of the known materiality, existing independently of the usual material constraints and determinants, such as material bodies, politics, and the economy. Though this kind of discourse was criticized right from the start as a specific ideology (Barbrook and Cameron 1995), it proved to be persistent, and traces of it can still be discerned in the current academic discourse.

When new media appeared on the radar of media and communication studies, the initial attempts to ground digitality consisted of remediating theories from the study of 'old' media, such as the performance arts (Laurel 1991), literature (Aarseth 1997; Ryan 1999), and cinema (Manovich 2001), or even taking 'remediation' itself as the regulative mechanism of digital media (Bolter and Grusin 1999). Over the years, new media studies gradually became emancipated from its remediating inspirers. The field claimed its own medium specificities, yet remained multidisciplinary, as it appropriated theoretical concepts and research methodologies from disciplines like media studies, cultural studies, philosophy, sociology, science and technology studies, and critical discourse analysis. This led to the emergence of subfields such as Internet studies, virtual ethnography (Hine 2000), game studies (Copier and Raessens 2003; Raessens and Goldstein 2005), and software studies (Fuller 2008).

During the past decade academic endeavors gradually left the initial speculative cyber-discourse behind. The focus shifted to the plurality of new media and digital cultures, and how they are embedded in society and everyday life (Lievrouw 2004; Bakardjieva 2005). New media were no longer considered as being 'out there' but rather as being 'here and amongst us'.

Still, this does not necessarily imply the complete dissolution of digital mysticism. The complexity of digital code is necessarily black boxed in user-friendly interfaces, and this makes assumptions of mysterious immateriality hard to exorcize. Even explicit attempts to foreground 'digital matters' in order to counter the relative underexposure of the material signifier speak of 'the paradox of im/materiality' (Taylor and Harris 2005) when addressing the issue of digital ontology. The solution of this paradox is usually to phrase it in the vein of Michael Heim's classic 'real and material in effect, not in fact' (Heim 1993), thus still presupposing an immaterial digital domain.

However, already in the early days of the digitization of culture and communication, the move beyond the seemingly insuperable dichotomy was attempted. In 1985 Jean-François Lyotard curated an exhibition at the Centre Georges Pompidou in Paris, entitled Les immatériaux (Lyotard 1985). This was the first public, experimental encounter with the cultural shift the computer was about to produce. The exhibition was accompanied by an interactive catalogue, written by various authors on the French Minitel system, thus representing one of the first pieces of collaborative electronic writing (Wunderlich 2008). While Lyotard and his co-authors – very much in tune with the predominant utopian fantasies of that period – mused about a future without material objects, the very title of the project already pointed towards the incorporation of the virtual into the material world. The simple use of the plural turned the immaterial, the realm of abstract thought, into palpable parts of something that is, although it cannot be touched, an inseparable part of the material world.

In a similar vein, the authors of this volume want to go a step further in recognizing digital materiality, not so much as 'im/material' but rather as 'in-material' – as software for instance cannot exist by itself but is intrinsically embedded in physical data carriers (Schäfer 2008). In other words, as stuff which may defy immediate physical contact, yet which is incorporated in materiality rather than floating as a metaphysical substance in virtual space. We consider digital cultures as material practices of appropriation, and new media objects as material assemblages of hardware, software, and wetware. As such, they are 'society made durable' (Latour 1991), that is, material artefacts and facts, configured by human actors, tools and technologies in an intricate web of mutually shaping relations.

This approach aligns with the 'material turn' that can be witnessed in cultural and media studies and has led to a renewed interest in anthropological and sociological theory in these fields. William J.T. Mitchell described the theoretical turn towards material aspects of everyday culture and the concern with objects or things (Brown 2004) as a reaction to immaterialization in a postcolonial world: 'The age of the disembodied, immaterial virtuality and cyberspace is upon us, and therefore we are compelled to think about material objects' (Mitchell 2004, 149). We would rather argue that this interest is a reaction to the myth of the immaterial, rather than pointing to an actual immaterialization of culture.

The material gatherings (Latour 2005; 1993) of new media that are explored in this book can take on many forms and formats, on various scales. They may be objects such as computer games, desktop icons, digitized archives, computer art, blog debates, or handheld gadgets, but also actions such as checking e-mail, uploading a movie to YouTube, online role-playing, listening to mp3 music, or using an e-learning environment. When it comes to digital material, the lines separating objects, actions, and actors are hard to draw, as they are hybridized in technological affordances, software configurations and user interfaces. Consequently, we aim to present an integrative approach in this book that takes into account 'technological' aspects as well as the social uses of media, including the accompanying discourses. Contrary to accounts that conceive digital artefacts as being immaterial, this book considers both the technological specificities as well as the sociopolitical relations and the effects on social realities as an inherent aspect of new media. The contributions cover different areas of digital culture, but they all endorse a material understanding of digital artefacts by situating their objects of research in a dispositif that comprehends the dynamic connections between discourses, social appropriation, and technological design (Kessler 2006).

Processor, memory, network, screen, keyboard

Together the chapters in this book will give an overview of, and at the same time develop a theoretical approach to, digital cultures as material practices – material practices as performed and experienced in daily life as well as configured in technology. They show how the idea of a digital materiality can be grasped and theorized within the field of new media studies, drawing on the diverse backgrounds and research objects, ranging from wireless technologies, software studies, computer graphics and digital subcultures to Internet metaphors and game-play.

To stay true to the digital-material approach that we envisage in this book, we have divided this book into five sections, each alluding to a material computer: PROCESSOR, MEMORY, NETWORK, SCREEN and KEYBOARD. While these concepts explicitly foreground technology, they should also be read as 'metaphorical concepts' (Lakoff and Johnson 1980), that is, as heuristic devices which highlight specific aspects of new media configurations. As computer components, they seem to refer primarily to hardware objects, yet it should be stressed that they all need software to work. Moreover, none of the components can function independently. Metaphorically, each component provides access to a different configuration of digital material, as each reflects another assemblage of the versatile research ground that new media studies entail. The PROCESSOR is the beating heart of a computer system; in this book it exemplifies the procedural inner workings of a machine, or better several machineries: technological, economical, and political. MEMORY refers to devices for storage and retrieval; metaphorically it stands for history, recurring patterns and persistent ideas. The NETWORK enables connections, transmissions, and extensions; as a metaphorical book section it interrogates how the social-cultural assemblages of contemporary machinery are connected to society and daily life. The last two sections – SCREEN and KEYBOARD – pertain to passage points: how users interact with digital machines through interfaces. The SCREEN represents how the machinery reflects and refracts its users, how their activities are channeled, and how hardware, software, and visual culture are related. And last but not least, the KEYBOARD foregrounds how users interact with the machinery; metaphorically it shows how users appropriate digital tools.

Inside the assemblage

The first three sections – PROCESSOR, MEMORY and NETWORK – stress the social-cultural assemblage of contemporary machinery. The PROCESSOR section consists of contributions that focus on questions pertaining to how digital machinery carries out certain cultural 'programs' or instructions. It specifically pays attention to how and by whom they are executed and created, whether in terms of ideology, participatory culture or design.

In his chapter *Serious games from an apparatus perspective*, Joost Raessens draws our attention to so-called serious gaming when he engages in a critical discussion about educational games that are meant to incite learning through playing. By approaching them as a ludic apparatus within the conceptual framework of the Lacanian philosopher Žižek, Raessens reveals the political-ideological tendencies that are inscribed in such games, through both design and play.

In *Empower yourself, defend freedom! Playing games during times of war*, David Nieborg takes us to quite another instance of 'serious gaming', as developed inside the military machine. Discussing the branding of the game *America's Army*, which was developed to recruit for the real American army, he examines how national propaganda can be effective in the context of global entertainment. Nieborg demonstrates that the global dissemination of this game among youth culture may weaken the purpose of recruitment, but at the same time endows it with a more implicit persuasive power that has its own ideological value.

In his contribution, *Formatted spaces of participation: Interactive television and the changing relationship between production and consumption*, Eggo Müller gives a historically comparative analysis of the television machinery by fleshing out the concept of participation in interactive television and how this has transformed associations between producing and consuming. By discussing three cases of interactive television and video sharing sites, Müller argues that participation can be best understood in terms of formatted spaces that are culturally determined.

The last chapter in this section returns to educational processing, now enabled not by games or entertainment but by the design of e-learning systems. In her contribution *Digital objects in e-learning environments: The case of WebCT*, Erna Kotkamp argues that a different approach to the design of e-learning environments such as WebCT and Blackboard is needed when educational tools change their objectives towards user interaction rather than content transference.

To function as a machine, a computer needs at very least a processor and MEMORY. The first is needed for execution and calculation, the second for storage and retrieval of data. In accordance, the MEMORY section of this book comprises chapters that deal with how digital machinery stores and retrieves data, thereby producing, reproducing and negotiating cultural artefacts. As Michel Serres famously noted in his conversation with Bruno Latour (Serres and Latour 1995), things are only contemporary by composition, and some parts are always related to memory and the past. Digital materials should correspondingly be seen as assemblages that hold various temporal references, tapping from previously stored and inscribed cultural resources. The chapters in this section examine in different ways how contemporary digital technologies relate to inscriptions of other times.

Imar de Vries draws our attention to a temporal dimension of new media when he discusses utopian discourses surrounding mobile devices. In *The vanishing points of mobile communication*, he ascertains that just like discussions in the early 1990s about the Internet, utopian visions about mobile communication embody an age-old quest for ideal communication. Yet, as De Vries shows, such utopian discourses of progress are incongruent in certain respects with how mobile technologies are experienced in everyday life. Hence, living in a connected culture entertains a paradoxical relationship with utopian ideals of perfect communication.

The MEMORY section takes on a more philosophical stance with Jos de Mul's discussion of Walter Benjamin. In *The work of art in the age of digital recombination*, De Mul contends that Benjamin's notion of 'exhibition value' should be replaced by that of 'manipulation value' to be able to understand art in the digital age. He claims that a 'database ontology' can serve as a suitable paradigmatic model to account for digital art, both by its technological affordances and its metaphorical power.

In *The design of world citizenship: A historical comparison between world exhibitions and the web*, Berteke Waaldijk examines historical dimensions of digital practices by comparing 19th-century world fairs with the Internet. She shows that the promise of seeing everything on the web bears clear similarities to the promise of seeing the world at world exhibitions. In both cases there is a disparity between ideological promises of seeing and the vulnerability of being watched and controlled as well as an oscillation between global and local positionings of citizenship.

In Isabella van Elferen's contribution 'And machine created music': Cybergothic music and the phantom voices of the technological uncanny, memory takes on yet another meaning by asserting that a fascination with the past is a constitutive part of cybergothic music cultures that celebrate the mixing of human and technological agency of past and present. Thus situated in a twilight zone, these subcultures replay and reshape sounds and voices from the past in a contemporary digital and technological setting.

The parts of our metaphorical computer can never function separately, but need to be connected to other parts to work properly. In the NETWORK section of this book, this facet is highlighted as attention shifts to how digital material should be conceived as being part of a more widespread network. How the participatory role of the user should be acknowledged as part of a network is addressed in the first two chapters of this section. William Uricchio relates the digital present to the analogue past when discussing in Moving beyond the artefact: Lessons from participatory culture how the 'digital turn', and the possibilities of participation as promised by Web 2.0 discourse, changed our concept of archiving historical data. He argues that the users' possibilities to add and alter content have changed our concept of archiving in old and new media.

In Participation inside? User activities between design and appropriation, Mirko Tobias Schäfer engages in a critical discussion about how the line between creation and consumption has blurred since the emergence of Internet applications like Napster. Though user appropriation of such file-sharing technologies challenges the established media industry whose business models rely on controlling the distribution of media objects, user activities should not be conceived as unequivocally subversive. Schäfer therefore calls for a critical analysis of how digital network technologies are appropriated, recreated and reassembled by various actors.

Marinka Copier plays up another dimension of networking technologies in describing how playing on-line games like World of Warcraft becomes a part of daily practice. In her contribution Challenging the magic circle: How online role-playing games are negotiated by everyday life, she argues that playing such games is so much interwoven with trivial daily activities that the idea of entering a 'magic circle' (Huizinga 1938) when playing a game no longer suffices. Instead, she proposes treating games like World of Warcraft as networks that are anchored in our everyday life.

In Douglas Rushkoff's chapter the digital world is understood as a network of stories in which the power of making stories is becoming more egalitarian. In Renaissance now! The gamers' perspective, he heralds a new generation of gamers who will generate a resurrection of participation in making stories. He foresees a new digitized world of playing in which we can be active agents in producing the stories that make the world go round, thus generating new narrative networks by controlling the buttons and breaking hegemonies.

Points of passage

The last two sections of the book concentrate less on the inside and more on the negotiations between the outside and inside of digital machinery, by respectively taking on the SCREEN and the KEYBOARD as perceptual interfaces and conceptual metaphors that serve as points of passage between user and machine. In the SCREEN section, contributions focus on how screens function as a membrane or locus of passage that hybridize and connect different realms and categories.

Frank Kessler undertakes a constructive comparison between analogue and digital photography and film in how they relate to 'the real' in *What you get is what you see: Digital images and the claim on the real*. He claims that debates about the real or authentic quality of recorded images has shifted since the emergence of new media, where an image is no longer necessarily pre-recorded and data become more mutable. He evaluates whether and how the Peircian term 'indexicality' (pertaining to a sign that points to a physical or existential relation) still holds validity for digital images.

Also in Eva Nieuwdorp's contribution *The pervasive interface: Tracing the magic circle*, matters of physicality and reality are addressed, here in relation to pervasive games rather than images. Pervasive games intentionally mingle with daily life and therefore need a theoretical framework that takes this into account. She argues that the notion of interface can serve as a central tool to recognize the 'liminal' character of such games that are not situated within a clearly delineated virtual game world. Hence Nieuwdorp calls for an interfacial approach to pervasive games that allows us to acknowledge the connection between its fantastical dimensions and daily life.

In the following chapter *Grasping the screen: Towards a conceptualization of touch, mobility and multiplicity*, Nanna Verhoeff analyzes the interface in another manner, when discussing the Nintendo DS as a particular new screen practice, that is at the same time mobile, tactile and making use of a double screen. Like Raessens, she proposes using the concept of dispositif. She appropriates this concept to show how the Nintendo DS, as a 'theoretical object', marks a rupture from the cinematic and televisual screen dispositif in terms of multiplicity of mobility and a shift from perception to tactile productivity.

In the last chapter of this section, Sybille Lammes analyzes cartographical screens in strategy games. In *Terra incognita: Computer games, cartography and spatial stories*, she discusses the use of cartography in such games. She particularly focuses on the mutable qualities of digital maps that are visible on the computer screen and how they are intertwined with landscapes that players have to master. Lammes shows that the distinction between tour and map as theorized by De Certeau (1984) needs to be revised in order to culturally comprehend the spatial functions of such games.

Lastly, in the KEYBOARD section, attention shifts to another interfacial aspect of new media, namely how users interact with digital material. Closely related to the section about screens, here the accent lies on how users have 'hands-on' contact with digital machinery. The main perspective changes here towards the user of the computer, whether writer, reader, player, or artist.

In the first chapter Thomas Poell discusses the user as reader and writer participating in public debates on the Internet. In *Conceptualizing forums and blogs as public sphere*, he explores whether and how the concepts of public sphere and multiple public spheres can be used to understand the role of web forums and blogs in public debate. Taking the heated debate that developed on the Internet after the assassination of Dutch critic and film director Theo van Gogh as his main case, he shows that even updated versions of Habermas's public sphere theory do not entirely cover the medium-specific dynamics of forums and blogs.

Marianne van den Boomen examines the user as a 'reader' and operator of material metaphors. In *Interfacing by material metaphors: How your mailbox may fool you*, she aims to yield insight into interface metaphors, such as the mail icon, which function as 'sign-tools'. She unravels these material metaphors as condensed icons that absorb and conceal their indexical relations to software and hardware processes. Similar to Kessler, she discusses computer icons as Peircian indexical signs, but also as Heideggerian tools.

While Van den Boomen discusses the user as an operator of sign-tools, Ann-Sophie Lehmann speaks about the user as artist. In *Hidden practice: The representation of artists' working spaces, tools and materials in digital visual culture*, she compares the way that painters' practices were represented in the pre-modern era with how the work of digital artists is presented in contemporary visual culture. She shows how media artists make use of similarly complex and custom-made tools as artists in the pre-industrial age, but contrary to representations of the painter at work, the practice of making digital art is rendered invisible.

Just like the parts of the metaphorical computer that structure this book, each chapter in this book highlights different constituents of the digital machine, mapping out how new media can be traced as digital material. One prevalent manner of doing so is by showing how technology is interwoven with culture and history. The Utrecht Media Research program has long been concerned with research into media's cultural construction, both diachronically and synchronically. This tradition stands in sharp contrast to definitions of media based solely upon a supposition of their technological, sociological, semiotic or aesthetic specificity. Our research is a quest for what may be termed the dynamics of media dispositifs, that is, tracing constellations of factors, including discursive formations, economic strategies, socio-cultural functions, as well as technological affordances and appropriation by users.

The contributions in this book all recognize that new media are not only embedded in but also generate and reassemble material cultures. This pertains to what Matthew Fuller has called the 'reality-forming nature of a medium' (Fuller 2005, 2). Contrary to views of new media as producing virtual experiences that lie outside everyday material realities, or as generating 'just representations', or 'just metaphors', this book emphasizes that they embody, assemble and reproduce gatherings that are always material – both in effect and as matters of fact. Or better, as matters of concern, since matters of fact should never be taken for granted. As Bruno Latour (2005, 114) writes: 'The discussion begins to shift for good when one introduces not matters of fact but what I now call *matters of concern*. While highly uncertain and loudly disputed, these real, objective, atypical, and above all, *interesting* agencies are taken not exactly as object but rather as *gatherings*.' New media and digital material are all about such interesting gatherings, as we hope to show in the present book.

Utrecht, December 2008

Marianne van den Boomen, Sybille Lammes, Ann-Sophie Lehmann, Joost Raessens, Mirko Tobias Schäfer

Note

1. For more information, see newmediastudies.nl

References

Aarseth, Espen J. 1997. *Cybertext: Perspectives on ergodic literature.* Baltimore: Johns Hopkins University Press.
Bakardjieva, Maria. 2005. *Internet society: The Internet in everyday life.* London: Sage.
Barbrook, Richard, and Andy Cameron. 1995. The Carlifornian ideology. *Mute* 1 (3).
Barlow, John Perry. 1996. A declaration of the independence of cyberspace. http://www.eff.org/~barlow/Declaration-Final.html.
Bolter, Jay David, and Richard Grusin. 1999. *Remediation: Understanding new media.* Cambridge, MA: MIT Press.
Brown, Bill, ed. 2004. *Things.* Chicago: University of Chicago Press.
Copier, Marinka, and Joost Raessens, eds. 2003. *Level up: Digital games research conference.* Utrecht: Utrecht University.
De Certeau, Michel. 1984. *The practice of everyday life.* Berkeley: University of California Press.
Fuller, Matthew. 2005. *Media ecologies: Materialist energies in art and technoculture.* Leonardo. Cambridge, MA: MIT Press.
—. 2008. *Software studies: A lexicon.* Cambridge, MA: MIT Press.
Heim, Michael. 1993. The essence of VR. In *The metaphysics of virtual reality*, 109-128. Oxford: Oxford University Press.

Hine, Christine. 2000. *Virtual ethnography*. London: Sage.

Huizinga, Johan. 1938. *Homo ludens: Proeve eener bepaling van het spel-element der cultuur*. Haarlem: Tjeenk Willink.

Kessler, Frank. 2006. Notes on dispositif. http://www.let.uu.nl/~Frank.Kessler/personal/notes%20on%20dispositif.PDF.

Lakoff, George, and Mark Johnson. 1980. *Metaphors we live by*. Chicago: University of Chicago Press.

Latour, Bruno. 1991. Technology is society made durable. In *A sociology of monsters: Essays on power, technology, and domination*, ed. John Law, 103-131. London: Routledge.

—. 1993. *We have never been modern*. London: Harvester Wheatsheaf.

—. 2005. *Reassembling the social: An introduction to actor-network-theory*. Oxford: Oxford University Press.

Laurel, Brenda. 1991. *Computers as theatre*. Reading: Addison-Wesley.

Lievrouw, Leah A. 2004. What's changed about new media? Introduction to the fifth anniversary issue of New Media & Society. *New Media & Society* 6 (1): 9-15.

Lyotard, Jean-François, ed. 1985. *Les Immatériaux*. Paris: Centre Georges Pompidou.

Manovich, Lev. 2001. *The language of new media*. Cambridge, MA: MIT Press.

Marx, Karl, and Friedrich Engels. 1848. *The communist manifesto*. Vol. 1. Marx/Engels selected works. Moscow: Progress Publishers.

Mitchell, William J.T. 2004. *What do pictures want? The lives and loves of images*. Chicago: University of Chicago Press.

Negroponte, Nicholas. 1995. *Being digital*. New York: Knopf.

Raessens, Joost, and Jeffrey Goldstein, eds. 2005. *Handbook of computer game studies*. Cambridge, MA: MIT Press.

Ryan, Marie-Laure, ed. 1999. *Cyberspace textuality: Computer technology and literary theory*. Bloomington: Indiana University Press.

Schäfer, Mirko Tobias. 2008. *Bastard culture! User participation and the extension of cultural industries*. Utrecht: Dissertation Faculty of Humanities Utrecht University.

Serres, Michel, and Bruno Latour. 1995. *Conversations on science, culture, and time*. Ann Arbor: University of Michigan Press.

Taylor, Paul A., and Jan L. Harris. 2005. *Digital matters: The theory and culture of the matrix*. New York: Routledge.

Wunderlich, Antonia. 2008. *Der Philosoph im Museum: Die Ausstellung 'Les Immatériaux' von Jean François Lyotard*. Bielefeld: Transcript.

Processor

Serious games from an apparatus perspective

Joost Raessens

According to the French philosopher Gilles Deleuze, concepts are meaningless unless they are helpful to the understanding and solution of significant contemporary problems (Deleuze and Parnet 1996).[1] In line with Deleuze, I will introduce the concept of the 'gaming apparatus' as a heuristic tool for the study of the political-ideological coloring of so-called serious games. These games have 'an explicit and carefully thought-out educational purpose and are not intended to be played primarily for amusement' (Michael and Chen 2006, 21). Such a tool is important because, to date, much of the debate on serious games has merely been framed in terms of effectiveness without paying attention to their political-ideological interest. And when theorists do pay attention to the political-ideological interest of games, they barely involve the game's medium specificity in their analyses.

In the first and second paragraph, I will define the concept of the gaming apparatus and discuss the possible political-ideological tendencies of the playing of serious games. In order to do so, I will refer to the work of the Slovenian philosopher Slavoj Žižek. In the third paragraph, I will interpret the possible political-ideological tendencies which Žižek refers to as 'virtual'. These tendencies may or may not be actualized, depending on the different ways in which the player of the game is positioned in or by the gaming apparatus. As I will argue in paragraph four and five, questions about the political-ideological meaning of a specific serious game can, thus, only be answered by taking into account all the elements of the gaming apparatus. We will see this in my analysis of Food Force (2005), a game I consider to be quintessentially serious.

The gaming apparatus

One of the founding fathers of the so-called 'apparatus theory' – a dominant theory within film studies during the 1970s – is the French psychoanalytic film theorist Jean-Louis Baudry (1986a, 1986b). Studying media from an apparatus perspective means studying them as configurations of technology and materiality, user positioning, unconscious desires, media text and context, and the production of meaning as an interplay between these elements.[2] Therefore, the analysis of serious games from an apparatus perspective pays attention to these five elements that contribute to their production of meaning: (1) The technical or material basis of serious games that help to shape (2) specific positionings of the player based upon (3) specific unconscious desires to which correspond (4) different game forms or texts with their specific modes of address and (5) different institutional and cultural contexts and playing situations. This multilayered model shows that the production of meaning emerges 'in new structures of political, material, and aesthetic combination' (Fuller, 2005, x). As a starting point I will analyze the political-ideological tendencies of the specific unconscious desires at play when playing serious games. I will do so by analyzing in this paragraph the conceptual framework of the Lacanian philosopher Žižek (1999) and in the next paragraph the ways in which his philosophical framework has been translated into the field of educational gaming.

Žižek starts his analysis of the range of unconscious desires by addressing the following question: 'What are the consequences of cyberspace for Oedipus – that is, for the mode of subjectivization that psychoanalysis conceptualized as the Oedipus complex and its dissolution?' (Žižek 1999, 110). What makes this question important to the study of serious games is that, framed within a Lacanian perspective, these kinds of games deal with the player's persuasion of or entry into the game's symbolic order.[3] Žižek himself advocates a third way, somewhere in between the two standard reactions toward cyberspace: that cyberspace involves the end of Oedipus (whether in a dystopian or utopian form) or, on the contrary, that cyberspace entails the continuation of Oedipus. This third way he defines as 'interpassivity'. These three reactions are charted in the following table.

Žižek	1 End of Oedipus		2 Continuation of Oedipus	3 In-between: interpassivity
	1A Dystopia	1B Utopia		

Table 1: Reactions toward cyberspace, from a Lacanian perspective

According to Žižek, the first standard reaction toward cyberspace is that it involves the end of Oedipus. According to some – Žižek is referring to Jean Baudrillard and Paul Virilio – this end of Oedipus is a dystopian development (1A, see Table 1):

Individuals regressing to pre-symbolic psychotic immersion, of losing the symbolic distance that sustains the minimum of critical/reflective attitude (the idea that the computer functions as a maternal Thing that swallows the subject, who entertains an attitude of incestuous fusion towards it) (Žižek 1999, 111).

On the other hand, there are theorists – here Žižek refers to Sandy Stone and Sherry Turkle – who emphasize the liberating potential of cyberspace (1B, see Table 1):

> Cyberspace opens up the domain of shifting multiple sexual and social identities, at least potentially liberating us from the hold of the patriarchal Law (...) In cyberspace, I am compelled to renounce any fixed symbolic identity, the legal/political fiction of a unique Self guaranteed by my place in the socio-symbolic structure (ibid., 112).

According to the second standard reaction toward cyberspace, the oedipal mode of subjectivization continues, albeit by other means:

> Yes, in cyberspace, 'you can be whatever you want', you're free to choose a symbolic identity (screen-persona), but you must choose *one* which in a way will always betray you, which will never be fully adequate; you must accept representation in cyberspace by a signifying element that runs around in the circuitry as your stand-in (ibid., 114).

Finally, Žižek argues that both standard reactions to cyberspace – as a break from or a continuation with Oedipus – are wrong and that we need to conceptualize a middle position. This 'in between' is described by Žižek as 'interpassivity'. 'Interactivity' and 'interpassivity' are two different ways in which digital technologies position people as responders. They are not oppositional, but mutually constitutive. According to Žižek, the term 'interactivity' is currently used in two senses: '(1) *interacting with* the medium – that is, not being just a passive consumer' (Žižek 1999, 105). This is the case when a player is clicking and moving a mouse, and tapping the keys of the keyboard. The second form of interactivity occurs when these actions lead to in-game actions: '(2) *acting through* another agent, so that my job is done, while I sit back and remain passive, just observing the game' (ibid., 105-106). This is the case when the player observes how an avatar on the screen acts. According to Žižek, interpassivity is a reversal of the second meaning of interactivity: 'the distinguishing feature of interpassivity is that, in it, the subject is incessantly – frenetically even – *active*, while displacing on to another the fundamental passivity of his or her being' (Žižek 1999, 106). We see this interpassive mechanism at work when the player is passionately clicking and tapping while his avatar is fulfilling the game's demands. Žižek's prime example of interpassivity is the Japanese electronic toy, the *Tamagotchi*. The Tamagotchi is a virtual pet that captivates those who take care of it by issuing orders:

> The interesting thing here is that we are dealing with a toy (...) that provides satisfaction precisely by behaving like a difficult child bombarding us with

demands. The satisfaction is provided by our being compelled to care for the object any time it wants – that is, by fulfilling its demands (...) The whole point of the game is that it *always has the initiative*, that the object controls the game and bombards us with demands (Žižek 1999, 107-108).

But, and this is crucial, those who take care of the Tamagotchi play this interpassive game under the condition of disavowal: '"I know very well that this is just an inanimate object, but nonetheless I act as if I believe this is a living being"' (Žižek 1999, 107). This moment of distancing means that we can follow the Other's orders while simultaneously having a critical, reflexive relation with them. Whether such a critical distance exists or needs to exist is a crucial question, as we will see in the next paragraph, in the debate about the political-ideological impact of serious games.

Political-ideological tendencies in serious games

These three 'virtual tendencies', reactions toward cyberspace as developed by Žižek (end of Oedipus, continuation of Oedipus, and in-between interpassivity), are 'translated' by game researcher Caroline Pelletier into the field of the educational sciences, as I have charted in Table 2. What makes Pelletier's approach important is that she traces these reactions in the literature about educational games. Although she specifically focuses on educational games, I would like to argue that her analysis is relevant to serious games because they have an 'explicit and carefully thought-out educational purpose' (Michael and Chen 2006, 21).

Žižek	1 End of Oedipus		2 Continuation of Oedipus	3 In-between: interpassivity
	1A Dystopia	1B Utopia		
Pelletier	Games as sensual temptations	Games as pain relievers	Games as replicas of non-virtual life	Games as dramatic stages for reality construction

Table 2: Reactions toward cyberspace and games

According to Pelletier, elements of the so-called 'end of Oedipus' reaction – either its dystopian or utopian mode – can be traced in those theories which define games as 'sensual temptations' or as 'pain relievers'. The games-as-sensual-temptations argument (see Table 2) goes like this: 'when using games as part of classroom teaching, teachers should interrupt the play process on a regular basis to prevent students immersing themselves in the game and losing sight of the learning objectives' (Pelletier 2005, 320). As Pelletier says, 'learning is seen to take place not through play but rather through reflection on the game's content' (ibid.). At first sight this argument seems to be contradicted by those studies which show that we can learn from playing games as such (Lieberman 2006; Ritterfeld and Weber 2006). But there are other examples that show that reflection on the game's content is an important component of learning as well (Raessens 2007).

Elements of the games-as-pain-relievers argument (see Table 2) can be traced back to the work of Mark Prensky (2001). His digital games-based learning approach defines 'active' learning in a two-fold way: as a pleasurable and liberating activity that (1) breaks with the traditional pain of learning, and (2) gives greater agency to learners. But as Pelletier rightly argues, Prensky's approach is misleading because he is 'challenging one form of authority in order to replace it with another – the global economy' (Pelletier 2005, 320). What Prensky does is simply reinstating authority elsewhere: 'So it is precisely Prensky's playful attitude towards learning which initiates the supremacy of a consumer-oriented and fast-paced brand of capitalism' (Pelletier 2005, 320).

The games-as-replicas-of-non-virtual-life argument (see Table 2) deals with those theories in which the Oedipal narrative is continued by other means. What this means becomes clear in James Paul Gee's comments on David Williamson Shaffer's How computer games help children learn (2006). In this book Shaffer 'shows how computer and video games can help students learn to think like engineers, urban planners, journalists, lawyers'. Gee's comments are in line with Pelletier's analysis when he characterizes Shaffer as having 'a deeply conservative vision (...) his goal is to put pressure on schools to prepare children to be productive workers, thoughtful members of society, and savvy citizens' (Shaffer 2006, xii). According to Gee and Shaffer, schools are 'not preparing children to be innovators at the highest technical levels – the levels that will pay off most in our modern, high-tech, science-driven, global economy' (Shaffer and Gee 2005). Their solution to 'our crisis' – the fact that the United States runs the risk of being overshadowed by countries like China and India – are 'epistemic games' (the term is Gee and Shaffer's). Epistemic games 'are about having students do things that matter in the world by immersing them in rigorous professional practices of innovation' (ibid.). In doing so, a game player is trained to become a member of a certain community and to adopt its epistemic frame: 'we call a community's distinctive ways of doing, valuing, and knowing its epistemic frame. We use this term because an epistemic frame 'frames' the way someone thinks about the world – like putting on a pair of colored glasses' (ibid.).

The meaning of the fourth argument – games-as-dramatic-stages-for-reality-construction (see Table 2) – becomes clear when we compare the playing of serious games to playing with a tamagotchi. When we play a serious game, according to Pelletier, the same two characteristics emerge as when we play with a Tamagotchi. On the one hand, the game captivates the player by issuing orders: 'Playing a game involves following orders; the game sets the objectives, the sequence in which they are to be completed, and usually the winning conditions' (Pelletier 2005, 322). On the other hand, playing serious games always incorporates a moment of disavowal – of distancing – specific to games. 'In playing games (...) we perform actions in the full knowledge that we are doing this within the constraints set by someone else' (ibid., 323). According to Pelletier, this is exactly the process on which gaming is based: 'Because the rules are already set, the goals already decided, we can be playful around them' (ibid.).

It is useful to translate the three standard reactions towards cyberspace into the field of educational/serious game studies as Pelletier does, because it makes us understand the different ways in which the player relates to the game's symbolic order. To decide which of these 'virtual' tendencies of the gaming apparatus become actualized in a specific situation, we have to analyze the different ways in which serious game players are positioned.

Positioning of the player

In the remains of this chapter I will focus on the four different forms of player positioning: the game's technical or material base, the game text itself, the institutional and the cultural environment in which serious games are made and played. In this paragraph I will give a short description of these different elements. In paragraph four I will analyze which of the four unconscious desires of the gaming apparatus are at the basis of Food Force. Finally, in paragraph five I will describe how these virtual dispositions become actualized by discussing the ways in which the game player is positioned by the game's technology, the game texts, its institutional contexts and cultural settings.

What is most striking about the technical basis of a serious game such as Food Force – a web-based, single-player PC game – is that the game player is immobilized yet highly active: she is sitting in a chair behind her PC with both hands occupied, one clicking and moving a mouse, the other tapping the keys of the keyboard. By using a keyboard and a mouse, the player controls the in-game actions. This clicking and tapping – referred to as a form of 'functional interactivity; or utilitarian participation' (Salen and Zimmerman 2004, 59) – is, as I will discuss later on, more or less complemented by three other forms of player participation: interpretation (including deconstruction), reconfiguration, and construction (Raessens 2005).

We also have to take into account how the player of the game is addressed or positioned both by the game text itself (Casetti) and the institutional context (Odin) in which the game is played. When we define a pragmatic approach as one that takes into account the role of the spectator (in film studies) or the player (in game studies), we can characterize textual positioning as an 'immanent' and contextual positioning as an 'extrinsic' form of pragmatics (Simons 1995, 210). The immanent film pragmatist Franceso Casetti develops three fundamental principles: 'that the film signals the *presence* of the spectator; that it assigns a *position* to him/her; that it makes him follow an *itinerary*' (cited in Buckland and Simons 1995, 115). Extrinsic film pragmatist Roger Odin, on the other hand, is of the opinion that a film spectator is primarily subjected to social institutions. A reading of a film 'does not result from an internal [textual] constraint, but from a cultural constraint' (Odin 1995, 213).

Last but not least, we also have to take into account the cultural settings in which games are made (Jenkins). Since they are mutually constitutive, the concept of 'interpassivity' runs the same risk as 'interactivity', namely that the cultural aspects of media are neglected. As Jenkins rightly argues, 'interactivity is a property of technologies; participation refers to what the culture does with these new media resources' (Jenkins 2007). So, serious games scholars should focus not only on how serious games bring about a critical, reflexive relation towards their content – as Pelletier suggests in her analysis of 'interpassivity' – but also on the two seemingly contradictory trends that are shaping the current media landscape:

> On the one hand, new media technologies have lowered production and distribution costs, expanded the range of available delivery channels, and enabled consumers to archive, annotate, appropriate, and re-circulate media content. At the same time, there has been an alarming concentration of the ownership of mainstream commercial media, with a small handful of multinational media conglomerates dominating all sectors of the entertainment industry (Jenkins 2007).

What makes Jenkins's position interesting is that he avoids both an attitude of refusal and an attitude of blind acceptance toward the cultural industries but opts for, as Žižek does, a position 'in-between': an open, negotiating relation in which consumers demand a share of popular culture by appropriating its content for their own purposes.

Virtual tendencies in Food Force

Food Force (2005, www.food-force.com) was released by the United Nations World Food Programme (WPF) with children aged eight to thirteen as its target group. The game, which takes approximately thirty minutes to play, tells the story of a food crisis on the fictitious island of Sheylan. When we look more closely at the four unconscious desires both Žižek and Pelletier refer to, it seems to be a *contradictio in terminis* to think that serious games in general, and *Food Force* in particular, would be able or willing to put an end to Oedipus, that is, keep the player from entering the symbolic order of the game. This means that both the games-as-sensual-temptation argument and the games-as-pain-reliever argument turn out to be foreign to the seriousness of these games. That does not mean, however, that Pelletier's reflections on both tendencies are useless here. The games-as-sensual-temptation argument makes clear that not only the playing of the game but also the reflection on the gaming experience are an important component of learning as well. I will discuss this element later on in this chapter. The games-as-pain-reliever argument makes us aware of the risks of what Vance Packard once labeled a 'hidden persuader' (1984). Claiming that the gamer is in control, as theorists often do, can hide a specific symbolic order from view in which the gamer is inscribed when playing the game, as is the case in Prensky's argument mentioned earlier. What we finally need to decide is whether the playing of serious games, such as Food Force, leads to a 'continuation of Oedipus' or to an interpassive relationship with it.

Let's first look at the 'continuation of Oedipus'. To analyze which symbolic order the player enters when playing Food Force, I recall Shaffer and Gee's reference to the game's epistemic frame that '"frames" the way someone thinks about the world – like putting on a pair of colored glasses' (Shaffer and Gee 2005). To understand how this process works, George Lakoff's concepts of 'framing' and 'metaphor' are useful here. According to Lakoff, metaphors frame our understanding of the world.

In order to increase our understanding of Food Force's symbolic order, it is productive to approach it from a 'family values' perspective. According to Lakoff, 'we all have a metaphor for the nation as a family (...) because we usually understand large social groups, like nations, in terms of small ones, like families or communities' (Lakoff 2004, 5). Food Force tries to persuade its players to adopt 'a [Democratic, progressive] nurturant parent family model' (ibid., 6). According to the metaphor of the nurturant parent, 'in foreign policy the role of the nation should be to promote cooperation and extend these values to the world' (ibid., 40) and to focus on 'international institutions and strong defensive and peacekeeping forces' (ibid., 63). Caring and responsibility equal 'caring about and acting responsibility for the world's people; world health, hunger, poverty (...) rights for women, children (...) refugees, and ethnic minorities' (ibid., 92). This metaphor goes against the metaphor of the [Republican, conservative] strict father family frame that, in foreign affairs, leads to the following: 'The government should maintain its sovereignty and impose its moral authority everywhere it can, while seeking its self-interest (the economic self-interest of corporations and military strength)' (ibid., 41). Because Food Force represents the United Nations World Food Programme as an organization able to – literally – 'nurture' its family members, this game expresses the values and lets the player enter the symbolic order of the nurturant parent family frame.

Secondly, to analyze the interpassive aspects of playing Food Force, we have to focus on the moment of disavowal – or distancing – that is specific to games, according to Pelletier. We need to answer the question of whether playing serious games entails a critical, reflexive relation towards these games. That means we must take a closer look at the three interpretative participatory strategies that may be activated in the player as a reaction to what Sherry Turkle calls the seduction of simulation (1996): players can surrender to the seduction of Food Force by interpreting the game more or less according to the encoded UN-ideological frames (simulation resignation). Or they may understand these frames by demystifying or deconstructing the assumptions or frames that are built into the simulation (simulation understanding). Or they can completely disavow the social and political importance of these kinds of games (simulation denial).

These three strategies do, indeed, determine the reactions of players and critics of both games. On the Water Cooler Games forum, for example, games critic and forum editor Gonzalo Frasca resigns to the seduction of Food Force when he writes: 'Finally! An educational game that rocks! Informative, well produced and very enjoyable to play with. Go United Nations! (...) Overall, I am extremely happy for this game, it is an excellent example of the way edutainment should be' (www. watercoolergames.org/archives/000381.shtml). Simulation denial and understanding are clearly in the minority. On the same forum, some players deny Food Force's importance by criticizing the UN for spending money on digital game development while thousands starve. Others criticize the built-in assumptions of Food Force because the game does not refer to forms of misconduct by UN personnel: 'How much like the real UN is it?'

What these reactions show is that it is, indeed, possible for players and critics to have the kind of critical, reflexive relation to these games described by Žižek and Pelletier. But looking through and exposing the hidden, naturalized, ideologically colored rules of serious games is, however, not commonplace. Players of Food Force seem to be more superficial than both Žižek and Pelletier hope for, at least when we define superficiality as the surface of the game's Oedipal, symbolic order as opposed to the in-depth process of deconstruction.

Player positioning by technology, text and context

Let's first look at player positioning by technology. Players of Food Force are positioned by the game's technology. We can think of the following assets: the game is accessible through the Internet; the game can be played for free; the game's website provides access to activist tools and offers the player all kinds of background information. Because Food Force is a web-based, single-player PC game, it does not offer multi-user environments in its game play, maybe because of financial restrictions. The game lacks a 'constructive' mode of participation in the sense that players are denied the possibility of game modification. The dominant mode of participation in Food Force is 'reconfiguration': 'the exploration of the unknown, in the computer game represented worlds' (Raessens 2005, 380).

Secondly, I would like to look at player positioning by text. Paraphrasing Casetti, the analysis of player positioning by the game itself must focus on three elements: how the game signals the *presence* of the player; how it assigns him a *position*; how it makes him follow an *itinerary*.

In the virtual world of *Food Force*, the player is assigned a position that can be described as a first-person point of view on the game's world: he is required to adopt a minimal degree of characterization, that is the young rookie addressed by the game as 'you'. In the beginning of the game, this young rookie is briefed by a man called Carlos on a humanitarian crisis on the fictitious island Sheylan in the Indian Ocean (see Figure 1).

Figure 1: Carlos's briefing

It is the player's mission to deliver food as quickly as possible to Sheylan's residents. Guided by a team of experts, in a race against the clock, the player has to accomplish six missions or mini-games in a linear order, delivering food to an area in crisis. In the first mission, for example, the player has to pilot a helicopter over a crisis zone in Sheylan to locate the hungry (see Figure 2).

The basic rule of *Food Force* is an ideologically motivated one: players win the game by completing the six missions and, in doing so, help to fight hunger. The goal of the game is directly conveyed to the player: 'You can learn to fight hunger (...) Millions of people are now depending on you for help. This is more than just a game. Good luck!' Players receive positive feedback on their performance from team members if their missions are successful. At those moments, the game signals the presence of the player. If the mission fails, the player is encouraged to try again. After playing the game, a player can summit his or her final score to a worldwide high score list on the game's website. Though the game does not have real-life consequences for the player, he is constantly reminded of the fact that in real life the WFP missions have huge consequences for these hungry people.

Figure 2: Mission 1, Air Surveillance

Next, the player positioning by context is important. In line with Odin's 'extrinsic' form of pragmatics and Jenkins's model of convergence culture, we have to take into account that players of Food Force are also addressed or positioned by the institutional context or cultural setting in which this game is played.

Three aspects of this institutional context or cultural setting are important. Firstly, the game is played in the context of a website that provides the player with background information about the social issues these games deal with. The Food Force website provides the player with information about the reality behind the game: 'In the world today hundreds of millions of people suffer from chronic hunger and malnutrition.' Furthermore, the player can learn about WPF's mission to fight hunger worldwide and learn how he can actively support the WFP activities outside the game world. Players can help by giving money to the WFP, by teaching others about famine, and by organizing fundraising activities at school or at home. Secondly, the game is often played in the context of a classroom situation. On the Food Force website, teachers can find all the information they need for the use of the game as a classroom tool for teaching about hunger. From a pragmatic perspective, both elements can be seen as a framework of cultural constraints that regulates the players' understanding of these games and thereby helps them entering the games' symbolic order. Thirdly, as part of today's media transformations, organizations are increasingly able to produce their own games outside the main gaming industry (also as a form of construction), and players are enabled to use the activist tools woven into the game's website. The fact that *Food Force* succeeds in raising issues that the mass-news media do not always consider newsworthy shows the relevance of this game.

Conclusions

In this chapter I have examined how the functioning and function of serious games are ideologically colored. The functioning of serious games concerns the different forms of player positioning that contribute to the production of meaning. To be able to study the functioning of serious games, I have introduced the concept of the gaming apparatus. The advantage or productivity of using this concept within game studies is that it helps to articulate the understanding of the production of meaning as deeply influenced by the ways in which configurations of technology, user positioning, desire, media text and context take shape in specific games.

I have questioned the function of serious games by analyzing the 'if' and 'how' of the player's entry into the game's symbolic order. I have described the four kinds of unconscious desires – 'virtual' tendencies in Žižek and Pelletier's use of the term – that may or may not become actualized, depending on how the player of a specific game is positioned or addressed in or by the gaming apparatus. In *Food Force*, the games-as-replicas-of-non-virtual-life argument seemed to be dominant. The ideologically colored construction seems not to be automatically revealed through the mere activity of play as Pelletier suggested. Furthermore, it turned out to be almost a *contradictio in terminis* to presume that serious games in general and *Food Force* in particular would be able or willing to put an end to Oedipus, that is, to keep the player from entering the symbolic order of the game. This would mean that there seems to be little room for a critical, reflective attitude towards the game's ideology while playing these games.

Whether such a critical distance needs to exist in the first place is up for discussion. It is of course a legitimate aspiration to teach children about hunger as *Food Force* intends to do. At the same time it is also legitimate to teach children how to understand the frames and values of which a specific serious game wants to convince its player. I agree with Turkle when she advocates the importance of an attitude of simulation understanding: 'Understanding the assumptions that underlie simulation is a key element of political power' (Turkle 1996, 71). It could be a task of media literacy education not only to teach children *through* but also *about* digital games. As Kurt Squire argues, 'students might be required to critique the game and explicitly address built-in simulation biases' (Squire 2002).

The fact that in the new media landscape children are becoming participants, and not only spectators or consumers, also means that they should be aware of their 'ethical responsibilities' (Jenkins 2007), for example by asking 'about the motives or accuracy of the ways games depict the world' (ibid.) or by asking what kind of (ideologically colored) games they would want to design themselves. Professional serious game designers as well as serious game theorists also have an ethical-political responsibility when they make decisions about the ways in which they want to design serious games and construct theories about them. Which of the 'virtual' tendencies become actualized is not directly inscribed in the game's technical properties. They are the 'possibilities opened up by cyberspace technology, so that, ultimately, the choice is ours, the stake in a politico-ideological struggle' (Žižek 1999, 123).

Notes

1. A longer and more elaborated version of this chapter is forthcoming in: Ritterfeld, Ute, Michael Cody and Peter Vorderer, eds. *Serious games: Mechanisms and effects.* New York: Routledge, Taylor and Francis (2009).
2. For a critical discussion of the Nintendo DS as mobile apparatus, see Nanna Verhoeff's chapter in this book.
3. For an extensive discussion of the processes of persuasion in war games, see David Nieborg's chapter.

Acknowledgements

This research has been supported by the GATE project, funded by the Netherlands Organization for Scientific Research (NWO) and the Netherlands ICT Research and Innovation Authority (ICT Regie). I would like to thank Christien Franken for editing this chapter.

References

Baudry, Jean-Louis. 1986a. Ideological effects of the basic cinematographic apparatus. In *Narrative, apparatus, ideology*, ed. Philip Rosen, 286-298. New York: Columbia University Press.

Baudry, Jean-Louis. 1986b. The apparatus: Metapsychological approaches to the impression of reality in the cinema. In *Narrative, apparatus, ideology*, ed. Philip Rosen, 299-318. New York: Columbia University Press.

Buckland, Warren and Jan Simons. 2005. Introduction. In *The film spectator: From sign to mind*, ed. Warren Buckland, 113-117. Amsterdam: Amsterdam University Press.

Deleuze, Gilles and Claire Parnet. 1996. H comme histoire de la philosophie. In *L'Abécédaire de Gilles Deleuze*. Paris: Vidéo Editions Montparnasse.

Fuller, Mathew. 2005. *Media ecologies: Materialist energies in art and technoculture.* Cambridge, MA: MIT Press.

Jenkins, Henri. 2007. Media literacy: Who needs it? http://www.projectnml.org/yoyogi.

Lakoff, George. 2004. *Don't think of an elephant! Know your values and frame the debate.* White River Junction, Vermont: Chelsea Green Publishing.

Lieberman, Debra. 2006. What can we learn from playing interactive games? In *Playing video games: Motives, responses, and consequences*, eds. Peter Vorderer and Jennings Bryant, 379-397. Mahwah, NJ: Lawrence Erlbaum Associates, Publishers.

Michael, David and Sande Chen. 2006. *Serious games: Games that educate, train, and inform.* Boston, MA: Thomson.

Odin, Roger. 1995. For a semio-pragmatics of film. In *The film spectator: From sign to mind*, ed. Warren Buckland, 213-226. Amsterdam: Amsterdam University Press.

Packard, Vance. 1984. *The Hidden Persuaders.* New York: Pocket.

Pelletier, Caroline. 2005. Reconfiguring interactivity, agency and pleasure in the education and computer games debate: Using Žižek's concept of interpassivity to analyse educational play. *E-Learning* (2) 4.

Prensky, Mark. 2001. *Digital game-based learning.* New York: McGraw-Hill.

Raessens, Joost. 2007. Playing history: Reflections on mobile and location-based learning. In *Didactics of micro-learning: Concepts, discourses, and examples*, ed. Theo Hug, 200-217. Münster: Waxmann Verlag.

— 2005. Computer games as participatory media culture. In *Handbook of Computer Game Studies*, eds. Joost Raessens and Jeffrey Goldstein, 373-388. Cambridge, MA: MIT Press.

Ritterfeld, Ute and René Weber. 2006. Video games for entertainment and education. In *Playing video games: Motives, responses, and consequences*, eds. Peter Vorderer and Jennings Bryant, 399-413. Mahwah, NJ: Lawrence Erlbaum Associates, Publishers.

Salen, Katie and Eric Zimmerman. 2004. *Rules of play: Game design fundamentals.* Cambridge, MA: MIT Press.

Shaffer, David. 2006. *How computer games help children learn.* New York: Palgrave MacMillan.

Shaffer, David and James Paul Gee. 2005. Before every child is left behind: How epistemic games can solve the coming crisis in education. http://epistemicgames.org.

Simons, Jan. 1995. Introduction. In *The film spectator: From sign to mind*, ed. Warren Buckland, 209-212. Amsterdam: Amsterdam University Press.

Squire, Kurt. 2002. Cultural framing of computer/video games. http://www.gamestudies.org/0102/squire.

Turkle, Sherry. 1996. *Life on the screen: Identity in the age of the internet.* London: Weidenfeld & Nicolson.

Žižek, Slavoj. 1999. Is it possible to traverse the fantasy in cyberspace? In *The Žižek reader*, eds. Elizabeth Wright and Edmond Wright, 102-124. Malden, MA: Blackwell Publishing.

Empower yourself, defend freedom!

Playing games during times of war

David B. Nieborg

The January 2008 edition of the popular Dutch game magazine *Power Unlimited* featured a two-page advertisement by the Koninklijke Landmacht (Royal Dutch Army). The full color advertisement on pages two and three carried the tagline: 'Fine leadership comes naturally.' The left page shows soldiers pointing at a map and discussing strategy, the right page packed a lot of reading. Interestingly, the ad shows no weaponry at all and is, compared to the showy marketing material for war games, quite considerate. The underlying recruiting motive here is professionalism – accepting a ranking job in the Royal Dutch Army primarily asks for management and leadership skills. Putting an ad in a game magazine is an obvious move, considering the shared target demographic (16- to 26-year-old boys) of both gaming magazines and army recruiters. Despite 'a disappearing audience for war' (Carruthers 2008), the First Person Shooter (FPS) game *Call of Duty 4: Modern Warfare* topped the all important 2008 holiday sales charts and has sold over nine million copies.

Despite the hunger of many 'hardcore' gamers to experience mediated warfare, as the stunning success of *Call of Duty 4* shows, the outlook for the Dutch Army, in terms of new recruits, is not at all favorable. For one thing, the Dutch involvement in the war in Afghanistan led to a number of fatal casualties, lowering the propensity of Dutch youngsters to consider an army career. To aid recruiting efforts, the Dutch Army is seeking recruits at increasingly lower ages and is directly tapping into the fabric of game culture. At the annual Army open door days and at industry events such as game conventions, the Army set up Xbox 360 demo pods to lure gamers into their recruiting booth to play the war game *Tom Clancy's Ghost Recon Advanced Warfighter 2*. However, it is with a mix of envy and esteem that ranking Dutch service members look at their allies in the west.

In 2006 the US Army had a whopping 3.9 billion dollar recruiting budget to spend on: 'slick ads that reach students before they set foot on campus – in fashion and music magazines, free iPod downloads, MySpace campaigns, on television and hip-hop radio stations, and through concert and sporting even sponsorships' (Allison and Solnit 2007, 46). During informal interviews with Dutch service members, most of them gamers themselves, I was told that Dutch recruiters are particularly envious of one specific recruiting project: America's Army. This game can be seen as the first state-produced, highly visible and popular game with an overt persuasive agenda (cf. Løvlie 2007). To label the America's Army project as successful would be an understatement. In direct ways, by projecting the US Army brand deeply into game culture at minimal costs, and indirectly by getting into 'the consideration set' of US high school students, the project is said to have saved hundreds of millions of marketing and recruiting dollars (Nieborg 2005).

The aim of this chapter is to deepen the understanding of the representation and simulation of modern war in games vis-à-vis government propaganda. Therefore, a short discussion on the Global War on Terror as a war on ideas follows first. Next, to contextualize the use of propaganda in games, the argument will be made that the theme of modern warfare is already a familiar commoditized intertext, thereby aiding the acceptance of pro-military themes. The militarization of society and of popular culture has a long history, and war has been a familiar theme in television, movies, toys and digital and non-digital games (Regan 1994; Hall 2003). The usage of games, and America's Army in particular, as part of wider US strategic communication efforts signals the usefulness of game culture for the dissemination of state-produced propaganda via military-operated game communities (Nieborg 2006).

The America's Army platform

The America's Army development team cleverly mixed various educational, marketing and propaganda mechanisms at their disposal to offer a free game which on the one hand fits perfectly into the FPS genre while at the same time reinforcing a highly politicized recruiting agenda (cf. Allison and Solnit 2007).[1] The best-known version of America's Army is its freely downloadable public version, or as version 2.8.2.1 (2008) is called America's Army: Special Forces (Overmatch). 'The Official US Army Game', as it is labelled by the US Army itself, is best described as an online, multiplayer, squad-based, tactical FPS PC game. The game is distributed via various game websites and was developed under the auspices and with material and immaterial input of the US Army. The goal of the game is to inform popular culture rather than to persuade, and to raise awareness of the US Army brand rather than to recruit directly, which is done by a large group of dedicated US Army recruiters. A key component in building and maintaining both the US Army and America's Army brand identities is the Goarmy.com website, and one of the main goals of the America's Army project is to raise traffic to the dedicated recruiting website. Primarily an advanced online recruiting station, the website offers a virtual insight into an Army career. Whereas before the game launched a large number of leads to the website stemming from TV and radio advertisements, today a significant number comes from the *America's Army* website and from within the game itself.

Similar to the Goarmy.com website, the US Army as a possible future career is a central theme to the game's design. Having commerce at the core of its brand identity, the PC game exemplifies the linkage of commercial goals with a cultural text through creating an engaging (brand) experience (Van der Graaf and Nieborg 2003). Along with a PC version, the *America's Army* brand has been expanded since its introduction on 4 July 2002 by publishing the Xbox game *America's Army: Rise of a Soldier* (2005), a Xbox 360 version called *America's Army: True Soldiers* (2007), and the mobile phone game *America's Army: Special Operations* (2007). In addition, dedicated fans can buy *America's Army* action figures, apparel or other knickknacks on armygamegear.com, or seek out an *America's Army* cabinet in an arcade hall.

Over the years the PC version of *America's Army* has become more of a platform than one single and stable game within the US Army. Or as the official website explains: 'The America's Army "Platform" (AAP) is a government-owned core technology and content infrastructure designed to support existing warfighters, instructors & students through a new generation of low cost, PC-based, web-deployable, interactive training' (US Army 2005). This set of non-public governmental applications was built by specialized sub-groups of in-house game developers in cooperation with commercial game studios and US Army researchers. Together they use advanced, commercial, off-the-shelf game technology to develop various training tools (e.g. for land navigation), and modeling and simulation applications (e.g. weapon testing), used by various US governmental organizations, such as the US Secret Service. The proprietary *Unreal* game engine, developed by the US-based Epic Games game development company, affords the Army a perpetually updated and versatile platform to provide high-fidelity simulations.

By analyzing the production, distribution, and use of both the governmental and public version of *America's Army*, four different dimensions can be distinguished. The *America's Army Platform* can be seen as an advergame, an edugame, a test bed and tool, and a propaganda game.[2] The edugame and test tool dimension are most apparent in several governmental applications, while the public version encompasses all four dimensions. Hereafter only the public use of the PC version of *America's Army* will be discussed. The adaptive character of contemporary game technology enables game developers to design multidimensional PC games, such as *America's Army*, moving beyond 'mere entertainment'. This begs the question: Is *America's Army* a form of propaganda? If so, how does it function as a propaganda tool within the vast US military complex? And, how does its propaganda message manifest itself in the representation and simulation of war in the game? Whether or not *America's Army* 'works' as intended, or whether it is, in the eyes of its players, a symbol of rampant American imperialism or a new form of camp is a highly relevant question, but falls outside the scope of this chapter. Next, the notion of soft power is introduced to expand upon the interplay between popular culture and propaganda.

Digital games as soft power

That infamous September morning in New York, the world changed the moment the first airplane hit the Twin Towers. The US was at war. Les Brownlee, former Acting Secretary of the Army, and General Peter J. Schoomaker, Chief of Staff of the US Army, emphasize the long-term character of the current war:

> This is not simply a fight against terror – terror is a tactic. This is not simply a fight against al Qaeda, its affiliates, and adherents – they are foot soldiers. This is not simply a fight to bring democracy to the Middle East – that is a strategic objective. This is a fight for the very ideas at the foundation of our society, the ways of life those ideas enable, and the freedoms we enjoy (Brownlee and Schoomaker, 2004).

According to US government officials, such as former US Defense Secretary Rumsfeld, the Global War on Terror (or GWOT) is not only a war on 'stateless criminals' but also a seemingly endless war on ideas (Taylor 2008). It is a war to spread freedom and liberty – i.e. values appropriated by and associated with the United States (Nye 2004). The handling of the ongoing wars in Afghanistan and Iraq, however, has had devastating results for the image of US foreign policy: 'The war has increased mistrust of America in Europe, weakened support for the War on Terrorism, and undermined US credibility worldwide' (Defense Science Board 2004, 15). This trend of the US's slipping global image and dwindling support for the GWOT is backed by the polling data of the Pew Research Center (2006). They conclude that although the values such as freedom and democracy, as well as free market capitalism, are shared around the world, the Bush-Cheney White House's handling of the war effort is seen as the main reason for the decreasing support of the US-led GWOT (Hersh 2004; Woodward 2006).

The question is then, how? How are anti-American attitudes to be altered? In his book *Power, terror, peace, and war: America's grand strategy in a world at risk*, foreign relations expert Walter Russell Mead (2004) reflects on this question and discusses the changing role of the US as a superpower. In his opening chapter he addresses the almost messianic role of American grand strategy, to spread peace, freedom and liberty around the world using various forms of power. Mead builds on Joseph Nye's (2002) distinction between hard and soft power, offering two sub-categories for both. Hard (military and economical) power is split up into sharp (military) and sticky (economical) power, and soft power (cultural power) is split up in hegemonic and sweet power.[3] As comic books and Coca-Cola are part of the US's sweet power, so are games, movies and television series. According to Mead and Nye the GWOT cannot be won by hard power alone, you need soft power as well: 'In any case, American sweet power, though limited and variable, clearly plays an important role in winning sympathy and support for American foreign policy around the world' (Mead 2004, 39-40). Soft power is not under government control like propaganda is, and has limits, just as military power does. But, as I will argue hereafter, *America's Army* is not only a propaganda tool, it is a powerful example of the ability of the US to successfully wield soft power by directly tapping into popular culture.

The military entertainment arcade

If foreign relations experts are to be believed, anti-American attitudes are not only a direct threat to US national security, they also undermine the sole surviving superpower's soft power. Since soft power is mostly manufactured by commercial enterprises, it will be no surprise that the US military is eager to appropriate such valuable practices. The Defense Science Board (2004) directly points to the private sector with its expert knowledge when it comes to successfully getting across messages with an agenda. One way to do this is by using 'interactive and mediated channels', because 'pervasive telecommunications technology permits the cost effective engagement of target audiences in sustained two-way interactions using electronic mail, interactive dialogue, virtual communication, interactive video games, and interactive Internet games' (ibid, 57-8). As such, online games are to be used for the US effort. And why not, the sweet power of many military themed games seems stronger than anything else. Think of recent examples such as *Battlefield* 2 (2006), *Call of Duty 4: Modern Warfare* (2007), and *Tom Clancy's Ghost Recon Advanced Warfighter* 2 (2007). How has this come to be?

The US military and the global game culture are profoundly interlinked on a technical, cultural and social-economic level, and the representation and simulation of modern war in computer games are at the same time a result as well as a catalyst of this bond (Halter 2006). The technological symbiosis between games for entertainment and military simulations has a long shared history. With the end of the Cold War, the structure of the US military and the way US forces would wage future wars changed dramatically (Toffler and Toffler 1995). Simultaneously, the research and development into modelling and simulation techniques flourished in the commercial entertainment industries. The booming innovation of commercial simulation technology did not go unnoticed by the US military, and the vast and influential military-industrial complex transformed into the military-entertainment complex. The reach of the military-entertainment complex is beyond the technical realm of simulation technology. Co-developed films, television series, toys, and various other entertainment products are direct outputs of the complex (Hall 2003; Robb 2004).

The representation and simulation of modern warfare in games demonstrate that there is already a common understanding about digital war (Nieborg 2005). Think of the many conventions in the FPS genre such as the fetishism of weaponry and the focus on combat (at close quarters). The US Army does not have to make an expensive movie or produce their own television series; they are able to directly tap into existing technological and socio-economical frameworks of the military-entertainment complex, and above all the military masculinity of certain parts of game culture. The Army can harness the collaborative nature of online game communities and use them to their advantage: spreading the Army's symbolic capital (Van der Graaf and Nieborg 2003). Gamers are familiar or at least not surprised by another Army game, since military advisers decorated the box shots of commercial games for over a long time. Modern warfare, similar to the *Harry Potter* or *Lord of the Rings* franchises for example, has become an intertextual experiential commodity, and the need for simulations of war is omnipresent in today's youth popular culture. A global gaming culture, with its military origins of interactive play, is entertained by games primarily based on conflict, eagerly developed by young males for young males (Kline, Dyer-Witheford and De Peuter 2003).

Empower yourself! Defend freedom

Short and simple, *America's Army* is a form of propaganda. At least, following the definition in the *Department of Defense Dictionary of Military and Associated Terms* in which propaganda is defined as: 'Any form of communication in support of national objectives designed to influence the opinions, emotions, attitudes, or behavior of any group in order to benefit the sponsor, either directly or indirectly' (Department of Defense 2004, 427). Propaganda is thus a message with a clear intention, known in advance by its sender, meant to influence behavior. As stated, *America's Army*'s four dimensions make it a fairly unique game. Three of its four dimensions show an interesting overlap, as propaganda, advertisement and education have much in common. The multidimensional approach of the *America's Army* project leads to two coinciding 'persuasive goals' (Bogost 2007). The first and most vivid is its recruiting agenda. The second rhetorical goal concerns the game's opaque ideology of war: 'as a manifestation of the ideology that propels the U.S. Army, the game encourages players to consider the logic of duty, honor, and singular global political truth as a desirable worldview' (Bogost 2007, 79). While *America's Army* is first and foremost a sophisticated marketing tool, it also (literally) teaches gamers what it means, or at least should mean, to be a US soldier.

America's Army's main design principle is to create a virtual replica of certain aspects of life in the US Army, mainly those involving combat. As an important institution in the American society, the US Army directly and indirectly represents the values of this society and its government. And as a copy of the US Army, the game reflects US foreign policy. The loading screen of the game features the Soldier's Creed and before joining any online round, players get to see the creed telling them: 'I am a Warrior and a member of a team. I serve the people of the United States and live the Army Values,' culminating in, 'I stand ready to deploy, engage, and destroy the enemies of the United States of America in close combat. I am a guardian of freedom and the American way of life. I am an American Soldier.' It seems almost like a virtual contract. When the game is ready, the loading screen disappears, and the player temporarily joins the virtual US Army.

Propaganda does not equal lying or deceiving. Far from it, the most effective forms of propaganda are factually accurate for the greater part. It is the context of a message which turns opinions and world views into information (Taylor 1998). As with the above-mentioned Royal Dutch Army's advertisement, *America's Army's* rhetorical strategies actually accentuate modesty and responsibility and are based on the US Army's take on morality. Drawing on computer game theory, Løvlie (2007) emphasizes three rhetorical strategies underlying America's Army's persuasive agenda: the strategy of identification, that of authenticity, and that of legitimization (cf. Nieborg, 2005). Let's consider these strategies more in depth.

One of the ways *America's Army* aims to influence the attitudes of gamers is by showing that the use of violence by the US Army is justified because freedom has to be defended. In addition, players are taught that the US Army is a professional organization, based on the US Army values – Loyalty, Duty, Respect, Selfless Service, Honor, Integrity, and Personal Courage (LDRSHIP). To put these values into context, *America's Army* appropriates the format of the FPS genre and recontextualizes common in-game player actions previously devoid of any political or ideological connotation. For many gamers the sheer joy of playing tactical FPS games comes from playing as a team. The US Army skilfully refurbishes conventional player actions such as teamplaying by labeling them as value-laden expressions. By offering an 'authentic' combat simulation, the Army provides a game space where Army values become more explicit. A vivid example of this mechanism comes from the first lecture during 'medic training', part of the single player edugame dimension. Sitting behind a desk in a classroom, the player watches a virtual drill sergeant boom:

> In many cases, you will be risking your own life in a selfless way to provide first-aid. You are doing what's right, and showing personal courage, both physically and morally. By performing first aid, we are living up to the Army value of honor, because saving a human life brings honor to yourselves and to the United States Army.

In his critique of the many 'myths of war' Hedges argues: 'The hijacking of language is fundamental to war' (2002, 34). Common in-game actions, such as nur-turing, self-sacrifice and acts of heroism, are assigned a new purpose in the game by designating Army values to them, such as 'loyalty', 'selfless-service' and 'personal courage'. *America's Army* propagates the US Army ethos and through this, the rationale and legitimation of US foreign policy.

An abrupt break with FPS design conventions is the change in point of view. The game's point of view is, by means of a software trick, limited to that of an American soldier, setting the game apart from all other, that is commercial, FPS games. Whereas you can choose to be a German, British, American or Russian soldier in the multiplayer segments of almost every World War Two shooter out there, you cannot play one of the 'Opposing Forces' in *America's Army*. Just as news reporters used 'we' and 'us' to bend the complex logic of war into the more streamlined ideology of 'good-versus-evil' (Taylor 1998), 'we' and 'us' in *America's Army* always stands for the US Army. Make no mistake, in *America's Army* you are always 'with us/US'. It is one of the oldest and most common propaganda tricks in the book, limiting the point of view in order to vilify and obscure the enemy (Toffler and Toffler 1995).

The acceptance of the role as an US soldier is never really questioned on the game's official forum, and debates asking for different roles – i.e. to play a terrorist – are virtually nonexistent. Many gamers are aware of the fact that they perform two roles – i.e. functioning as 'double-bound warriors'. An American soldier towards oneself and towards your team, you see your own hands holding an American weapon. At the same time you are, in the eyes of your opponent, one of the opposing forces. The 'terrorist' perspective from popular FPS games such as *Counter-Strike* is lost to reinstate the only 'right' point of view.

In short, the game shows how the US Army fights and why. The 'Why?' question is made explicit offline in the official 224-page *America's Army* game manual stating: 'while tactical movement and communications are often essential to the success of a mission, the US Army exists to defend freedom, and employing force in combat is an important element of their job' (Tran 2003, 36). In this case, lethal force is justified as a legitimate state action: 'The rules and definitions of violent force are dangerously fluid and arbitrary. By mediating the definitions of violence, nation states have the ability to shield their own uses of force from censure and, furthermore, to manipulate representations of their uses of force to inspire citizens' (Hall 2003, 27). In *America's Army* the sole justification to use lethal force is to empower oneself in order to defend freedom.

The role of strategic communication

The ongoing GWOT calls for more soldiers and thus more recruits. The second Gulf War in particular has put heavy strains on the available manpower of the Army. However, while *America's Army* may be a legitimate branding tool and recruiting aid within the US, being available worldwide conflicts with the games' recruitment goals. The FAQ section on the official website explains why someone outside the US can play *America's Army* for free: 'We want the whole world to know how great the US Army is' (US Army 2007). Deliberately choosing to make the game accessible for gamers worldwide challenges the original goal of recruitment. Which other national army has the financial means to develop and distribute a free high-tech PC game? Being a free, highly advanced, and frequently updated game with the simulation of hard power, *America's Army* becomes part of the US' soft power.

How then, as a form of sweet power, does *America's Army* fit in the overall strategic media use of the US government? The developers do not explicitly frame the game as a recruiting tool or an advergame, but as a 'strategic communication tool' (Davis 2004). In this paragraph the concept of strategic communication as it is used within the US military will be linked to *America's Army*. Although the next definition does not directly include *America's Army*, or any other video game in particular, it gives a valuable insight into the rationale of using strategic communication:

> (...) strategic communication describes a variety of instruments used by governments for generations to understand global attitudes and cultures, engage in a dialogue of ideas between people and institutions, advise policymakers, diplomats, and military leaders on the public opinion implications of policy choices, and influence attitudes and behavior through communications strategies (Defense Science Board 2004, 11).

The emphasis on influencing attitudes and behavior aligns strategic communication with propaganda. The renewed attention to the role of strategic communication within the US defense community is a direct result of the GWOT.

The US Government uses four instruments to deploy strategic communication: public diplomacy, public affairs, international broadcasting services, and information operations. Toffler and Toffler discuss the different levels of strategy 'at which the military propaganda game', i.e. strategic communication, 'is played' (1995, 194). Information Operations, also known within the US military as Psychological Operations (PSYOPS), are used at the tactical level of strategy through radio transmissions, leaflets, or television broadcasts aimed at foreigners in order to influence their behavior. In an advice to the former US Secretary of Defense regarding 'the creation and dissemination of all forms of information in support of [PSYOPS] in time of military conflict', the Defense Science Board discusses the use of 'other media types' for PSYOPS:

> A number of other media types, and means of dissemination, are also widely popular. Video games are perhaps the most popular. They can be disseminated by a number of techniques, ranging from diskettes to web downloads. Internet

games allow a number of geographically dispersed players to participate in a large, shared virtual space. (...) All are suitable for PSYOP in some situations (2004, 43).

While currently *America's Army* is not directly used on the battlefield as a tactical PSYOPS tool, it just may become one in the future as public opinion will become an increasingly important factor in 'The Long Information War' (Taylor 2008).

Two other components of strategic communication, public diplomacy and public affairs, are two aspects of strategic communication which are more directly related to the use of *America's Army*. Public diplomacy is an interactive way to inform foreigners about US culture, values and policy (e.g. by offering scholarships, official websites in various languages, and televised interviews with ambassadors and military commanders). As discussed before, *America's Army* explicitly communicates various values, policies and views on US (military) culture. By doing so, *America's Army* has become so much more than just a free downloadable game, it forms part of the US public diplomacy effort. In times where the US's international public standing is in disarray, the success of *America's Army* justifies the expansion of the *America's Army* brand into global popular culture. In its role as a strategic communication tool, the game and its many spinoffs may turn out to be the cheapest weapon in the US arsenal ever conceived. As with any weapon of war, however, there is 'collateral damage'. In this case it is the subsequent militarization of popular culture and the politization of game culture.

Conclusion

America's Army goes beyond branding and marketing when it disseminates US Army ideology and thus indirectly US foreign policy into a global popular culture. By showing a global audience why and how the US Army fights, the game has become an example of public diplomacy through the exchange of 'ideas to build lasting relationships and receptivity to a nation's culture, values, and policies' (Defense Science Board 2004, 12). It even may be classified as a psychological operation, being a 'military activity' using selected information and indicators 'to influence the attitudes and behavior' of 'groups, and individuals in support of military and national security objectives' (ibid, 13). Media have become instruments of war; an army may win a battle on the tactical level, but lose on the strategic level, and thus lose the entire war by a lack of public support: 'Wars that lose their mythic stature for the public, such as Korea and Vietnam, are doomed to failure, for war is exposed for what it is – organized murder' (Hedges 2002, 21). In the wake of the ubiquitously criticized war in Iraq, *America's Army*'s simple slogans and cliché good-versus-evil dichotomy reifies the 'myth of war' as a historical inevitable and justified state operation.

In a similar vein Toffler and Toffler argue that future warfare 'will take place on the media battlefield' (1995, 194). However, various news media are still wary of direct Pentagon intrusion (Taylor 1998). In this light, games such as *America's Army* seem like highly suitable propaganda tools. In the end, rather than embedding a camera crew or censoring Hollywood scripts, the highly sanitized view on war in *America's Army* is constructed by the US Army itself. *America's Army* shows non-US citizens that the US Army is a highly trained, professional force, willing to fight against 'those who oppose freedom' and does so in an interactive dialogue with gamers through both the game and its community. In addition, as a byproduct of using the format of a technologically advanced free FPS game, *America's Army* adds to the US' soft power as a strategic communication tool.

By employing a discourse of authenticity in its marketing efforts, the US Army uses/misuses its institutional discursive power to market their game to a group of gamers who have never experienced real combat – i.e. teens. From a skilfully designed first-person viewpoint, a specific ideological perspective on the GWOT reaches the hearts and minds of a global youth culture. Entertainment has always been an indispensable element in the propagandist's toolbox. For many, *America's Army* is a legitimate model of how to use soft power to win a war on ideas. The Defense Science Board (2004) is clear about the role for the wider military-entertainment complex; its many military contractors should be ordered to develop even more vehicles, that is military games, for the dissemination of US soft power. As such, the unrelenting success of *America's Army* has serious implications for thinking about the use of games for advertisement, education, and most of all, state-produced propaganda.

Notes

1. For a critical discussion of the ideological implications of educational games, see the chapter by Joost Raessens in this book.
2. See Nieborg (2005) for an overview and a detailed analysis of *America's Army's* four dimensions.
3. Hegemonic power is the interplay of sharp, sticky, and sweet power making: 'Something as artificial and arbitrary, historically speaking, as the American world system since World War II looks natural, desirable, inevitable and permanent. So, at least, we hope' (Mead 2004, 25).

References

Allison, Aimee, and David Solnit. 2007. *Army of none: Strategies to counter military recruitment, end war and build a better world.* New York: Seven Stories Press.

Bogost, Ian. 2007. *Persuasive games: The expressive power of videogames.* Cambridge, MA: MIT Press.

Brownlee, Les, and Peter J. Schoomaker. 2004. Serving a nation at war: A campaign quality army with joint and expeditionary capabilities. *Parameters* 34 (2).

Carruthers, Susan L. 2008. No one's looking: The disappearing audience for war. *Media, War & Conflict* 1 (1): 70-76.

Davis, Margaret, ed. 2004. *America's Army pc game vision and realization.* San Francisco: US Army and the Moves Institute.

Defense Science Board. 2004. *Report of the defense science board task force on strategic communication.* Washington, DC: Office of the Under Secretary of Defense For Acquisition, Technology, and Logistics.

Department of Defense. 2004. *Department of defense dictionary of military and associated terms.* Washington DC: Department of Defense.

Hall, Karen J. 2003. War games and imperial postures: Spectacles of combat in US popular culture, 1942-2001. PhD Thesis. Syracuse University.

Halter, Ed. 2006. *From Sun Tzu to xbox: War and video games.* New York: Thunder's Mouth Press.

Hedges, Chris. 2002. *War is a force that gives us meaning.* New York: PublicAffairs.

Hersh, Seymour. 2004. *Chain of command: The road from 9/11 to Abu Ghraib.* London: HarperCollins.

Kline, Stephen, Nick Dyer-Witheford and Greig de Peuter. 2003. *Digital play: The interaction of technology, culture, and marketing.* Montreal: McGill-Queen's University Press.

Løvlie, Anders Sundnes. 2007. The rhetoric of persuasive games: Freedom and discipline in America's Army. Master thesis. University of Oslo.

Mead, Walter Russell. 2004. *Power, terror, peace and war: America's grand strategy in a world at risk.* New York: Alfred A. Knopf.

Nieborg, David B. 2005. Changing the rules of engagement: Tapping into the popular culture of America's Army, the official US army computer game. Master thesis. Utrecht University. http://www.gamespace.nl/thesis.

Nieborg, David B. 2006. Mods, nay! Tournaments, yay! The appropriation of contemporary game culture by the US military. *Fibreculture Journal* 4 (8). http://journal.fibreculture.org/issue8/issue8_nieborg.html.

Nye, Joseph S. 2002. *The paradox of American power: Why the world's only superpower can't go it alone.* Oxford: Oxford University Press.

Nye, Joseph S. 2004. *Soft power: The means to success in world politics.* New York: PublicAffairs.

Pew Research Center for the People & the Press. 2006. *No global warming alarm in the U.S., China: America's image slips, but allies share U.S. concerns over Iran, Hamas.* Washington, DC.

Regan, Patrick. M. 1994. War toys, war movies, and the militarization of the United States, 1900-85. *Journal of Peace Research* 31 (1): 45-58.

Robb, David. 2004. *Operation Hollywood: How the Pentagon shapes and censors the movies.* Amherst, NY: Prometheus Books.

Taylor, Philip M. 1998. *War and the media – Propaganda and persuasion in the Gulf War.* 2nd ed. Manchester: Manchester University Press.

Taylor, Philip M. 2008. Can the information war on terror be won? A polemical essay. *Media, War & Conflict* 1 (1): 118-124.

Toffler, Alvin, and Heidi Toffler. 1995. *War and anti-war (Making sense of today's global chaos).* New York: Warner Books.

Tran, Nam 'DocNartman'. 2003. *America's Army version 2.0 Training manual.* Army Game Project.

US Army. 2005. *America's Army platform: Technology*. http://info.americasarmy.com/technology.php.

US Army. 2007. *America's Army: Special Forces – Support – Frequently Asked Questions*. 2007. Americasarmy.com. http://www.americasarmy.com/support/faqs.php?t=3&z=12#12.

US Army. 2008. *America's Army: Special Forces (Overmatch)*. US Army.

Van der Graaf, Shenja, and David Nieborg. 2003. Together we brand: America's Army. In *Level up: Digital games research conference*, eds. Marinka Copier and Joost Raessens. Utrecht: Utrecht University: 324-38.

Woodward, Bob. 2006. *State of denial: Bush at war, part III*. New York: Simon & Schuster.

Formatted spaces of participation

Interactive television and the changing relationship between production and consumption

Eggo Müller

As has occurred before within the history of emerging media, the advent of digital media and the World Wide Web generated two opposing discourses on the social and cultural effects of the new media: one utopian and one dystopian. The more prevalent utopian discourse proclaims the revolutionary transformation of mass media into a truly democratic mediascape: one in which old and new media converge; where users do not merely consume pre-fabricated media content passively, but themselves become interactive producers and distributors of media content; and a location where creative ideas and knowledge are mutually shared online by ordinary people: '[T]he interactive revolution (...) is about using powerful tools to create our own educational and entertainment experiences rather than passively accepting that which is fed to us by so-called experts. It is about the dissolution of boundaries and the translation of all thought into a common vocabulary. Binary code is the digital Esperanto that is leading concurrently to individual empowerment and worldwide unity' (Pierce 1997, xvii).

This McLuhanian approach to New Media, though rather extreme in its wording, remains characteristic of much contemporary theorizing about digital media's 'participatory culture'. The differences between 'old' and 'new' media are exaggerated in order to praise digital technology's ability to overcome modernity's separation between the realms of production and consumption, and thus to create empowering forms of communication and cultural participation. Whereas industrial and economic discourses describe this process as the advent of the 'prosumer' (Toffler 1980, 282ff.; Tapscott 1996, 62f.; Tapscott/Williams 2006, 124ff.), the scholarly discourse declaims a 'participatory turn in culture' and 'the blurring of boundaries between the categories of production and consumption' (Uricchio 2004, 139). Online networks such as Napster, Slashdot, or Wikipedia serve as the chief witnesses of this 'participatory turn' in our media culture, in which the consumer gains control over the production and distribution of media content.[1]

In opposition to this approach and less prominent, the dystopian discourse on the social and cultural effects of digital media focuses on corporate industry's ability to exploit the interactive potential of participatory cultures. As Mark Andrejevic (2003; 2004) points out in his seminal, neo-Marxist critique of interactive reality television, digital media allow for a new economic format that redefines interactivity and participation in terms of an enforced capitalist exploitation of the interactive consumer:

> [T]he contemporary deployment of interactivity exploits participation as a form of labor. Consumers generate marketable commodities by submitting to comprehensive monitoring. They are not so much *participating*, in the progressive sense of collective self-determination, as they are *working* by submitting to interactive monitoring. The advent of digital interactivity does not challenge the social relations associated with capitalist rationalization, it reinforces them and expands the scale on which they operate (Andrejevic 2003, 197, emphasis original).

Andrejevic's critique aims at what I would call the naïve embrace of digital media's interactive potential and the uncritical assumption that any form of interactivity gives consumers more control over media and allows for culturally more valuable forms of participation. According to Andrejevic, television shows such as *Big Brother* and *American Idol*, or online video-sharing sites such as YouTube, are examples of how the corporate media industry invests in digital technologies to redefine the relationship between the spheres of production and consumption: by seducing the audience to contribute to a television show or website, new sources of revenue are created; users pay fees to participate in a television show or to gain access to encrypted live streaming; users contribute their own content without monetary compensation; and whenever they do go online and interact, users produce data valuable for targeted marketing and mass customization.

Both perspectives, the utopian and the dystopian, address relevant dimensions of the ongoing redefinition of the relationship between the realms of production and consumption in the digital mediascape, but neither can sufficiently grasp the current transformations. The opposition between these two perspectives seems to reiterate the 'annoying' debate between cultural studies' active audience approach and the critical political economy of media in the 1980s (see Garnham 1995; Grossberg 1995). While the utopian perspective highlights examples of participation that show exceptionally committed, often fan-based communities creating their own virtual spaces in order to contribute to the production or distribution of knowledge and culture, the dystopian perspective focuses on forums, in which the well-established media industry adopts digital technologies in order to open up new markets and to create even more sophisticated forms of consumer seduction and exploitation. While the utopian perspective draws on theories of the active audience and therefore tends to overestimate self-determined and subversive cultural practices, the dystopian perspective refers to critical theory and political economy and therefore tends to overestimate corporate industry's power to determine cultural production and the circulation of meaning. While the utopian perspective discusses interactive reception and production of media content on the level of micro politics, the dystopian perspective addresses institutional and economic transformations on the macro level. In other words, there is actually no debate between the two perspectives at all: in the course of their argument, both perspectives draw on different examples, theories and approaches, and thus create two different fields of study; however, at the same time, both generalize their claims and findings as characteristic of the new participatory culture (in the words of the utopian approach) or the new online economy (in the words of the dystopian approach).

More current accounts, such as Henry Jenkins's *Convergence culture* (2006), which acknowledges the competing top-down and bottom-up powers defining digital media's participatory culture, do not manage to cover both perspectives. Although Jenkins adequately states in the book's introduction that 'corporations (...) still exert greater power than any individual consumer or even the aggregate of consumers' (2006, 3), in his analysis he focuses specifically on subversive and resistant activities performed by dedicated fans. Simultaneously, in his analysis of user participation in television shows and online communities, he downplays the top-down powers that structure even fan-based participatory cultures. In contrast, Andrejevic's (2004) rather differentiated analysis of resistant cast behavior in the *Big Brother* house and of related fan practices ultimately comes to the conclusion that all of the cast's and fans' efforts to determine the outcome of the reality game show, according to their own self-created rules, merely served the producers' interests.

Against the background of the reversed blind spots apparent in these two different accounts of participatory media, I will discuss how three different examples of participation television – *America's Most Wanted* (Fox since 1988), *Big Brother* (CBS since 2000), and YouTube (after its acquisition by Google in October 2006) – institutionalize 'spaces of participation' and how participation becomes 'formatted' within these spaces. I call this process 'formatting' in reference to the adaptation of internationally circulating television programs, in which the format details how a program should be produced but at the same time allows producers to adapt it to the local culture. The term thus indicates a characteristic tension between the predefinition by conceptual structures and the redefinition by practices. In a similar manner, the concept of 'institutionalization' (Berger/Luckmann 1967) as 'socially constructed templates for actions, generated and maintained through ongoing interactions' (Barsley/Tolbert 1997, 94) helps to analyze the relation between the interface, as offered by a television program or website, and the routinized forms of user interaction. In the following, the term 'interaction' refers to actual, physical acts of interaction between a television program's or website's interface and users, whereas the term 'participation' will be used as a concept to address the social, political and cultural characteristics of what I call 'spaces of participation'.

I suggest a spatial metaphor to indicate that television programs or website interfaces form the frameworks within which users who access and 'inhabit' such a space perform their actions. Unlike ethnographic practice theory, which focuses on the observation of 'publicly accessible practices' (Swidler 2001, 76), I do not think that practices as such are the starting point for an individual's actions within real or virtual spaces. Rather, practices are structured by pre-existing socially and ideologically defined spaces within which actions are performed. These actions may negotiate and transform the very conventions and limits of a given, in this case mediated, space; however, the social power to construct such spaces and to define the frameworks for action is not shared equally within a society. Particularly in the realm of media, the power to create frameworks of communication is not distributed democratically, but instead is controlled by a multinational industry, and in this regard digital media are no exception (see also Resnick 1998). The crucial question remains how various powers structure such spaces of cultural participation, because the interconnected question about whether digital forms of interaction allow for more self-determined forms of participation will be determined in this manner.

Against this background, a comparative historical approach to different frameworks and spaces of participation is useful: it helps to avoid naive accounts that proclaim new forms of participation to be radically different when they are actually linked, to a much greater extent than the utopian perspective acknowledges, to traditional forms of culture and cultural conventions.

Aktenzeichen XY: participation as 'nation watching'

Television shows that invite members of the audience to participate in a program are not a new phenomenon in the history of television. Prior to the advent of digital media, there were very few shows that initiated audience interaction by implying the possibility for viewers' participation in the show while they were simultaneously watching at home. One of the earliest examples of participatory television shows was the West-German reality crime show, *Aktenzeichen XY... ungelöst* (ZDF, beginning in 1967), which became the prototype for *America's Most Wanted* (Fox, beginning in 1988) and can, therefore, be seen as a key forerunner for a certain brand of reality programming (see also Jermyn 2007; Pinseler 2007; Müller 2009). *Aktenzeichen XY* transformed the television studio into a stylized police department, presented reconstructions of real criminal cases as short filmic narratives, solicited the audience to call in live and thus to help in solving the cases.

This show's distinctive combination of dramaturgic elements made the program an immediate and long-lasting international success. In the US, as in many European countries, the program has been especially criticized for its power to address the national audience as police informers (see also Cavender 2004; Jermyn 2007). As the German psychoanalyst Claus-Dieter Rath (1985) commented furiously in an essay entitled *The invisible network*, this program is 'a perverse realization of Brecht's theory of radio, which called for the distribution system of radio to be turned into a communications apparatus in which everyone is involved. (...) The TV-citizen becomes a member of the police, the restorer of "law and order", the eye of the law. The state and the police force merge into the audience, into a community around the broadcast, made up of the invisible electronic network between isolated homes and dwellings which (...) serves to arrest the errant and the deviant. Thus the social arena functions as a hunting ground, the living room as a hunter's hide' (1985, 200).

This critique could be translated into the more optimistic language of the utopian approach to participatory media, which focuses on the 'blurring of boundaries' while neglecting questions of power: The 'hybrid combination' of television and telephony breaks down modernity's separation of public and private, of citizens and state authorities, of information and entertainment. It turns the passively consuming mass audience of traditional television programming into active users of the interactive possibilities of a multimedia environment that allows the 'collaborative intelligence' of broadcasters, the police and the audience to fight crime and make the world a safer place. This patently unreasonable translation of Rath's dystopian account misses the central question about power relations, which are implied in the program's specific setup and structure the interaction of the participating parties. *Aktenzeichen XY* and its international adaptations define a very narrow ideological space of participation: not only does this show allow for a very limited range and depth of interaction[2]; the broadcaster, in collaboration with the police, remains in control of the production of the television text, while the show forces the interacting audience to subscribe to the ideological position of the program, as defined by the conservative call for law and order.

This might explain the polarizing effect characteristic of this and subsequent forms of television programming that drew on actual audience participation: whereas the 'passive' viewer has the freedom to negotiate or resist the ideology of a program (as described in active audience theory), the interactive participant necessarily affirms the program's ideological stance: the interactive viewer engages in this televisual form of nationwide 'neighborhood watching'. *Aktenzeichen XY* and its international adaptations provoked two different, if not quite opposite, reactions: one can be described as the affirmation of citizenship, in a conservative sense, by those who were willing to interact and forward information to state authorities via television and telephone; the other, as embodied in a flood of critical commentaries and parodies, can be described as a progressive form of citizenship that questions the legitimacy of the collaboration between state authorities and public television in a civil society. Though one could argue that, for most viewers, the participatory potential of the program remains only virtual, the critical reception of the program teaches us to not only examine the technological interface of digitally enhanced forms of television and participatory websites, but also to critically analyze how their dramaturgical and ideological setups structure actual forms of interaction in any specific 'space of participation'.

Big Brother: participation in a cross-media spectacle

Although *Aktenzeichen XY* and its international adaptations made use of a hybrid media ensemble, they remain examples of how television structured the relationship between the spheres of production and consumption as developed by broadcast media in the 20th century: the range and depth of possible interactions were limited and ideologically defined. However, at the end of the 'century of broadcasting', another highly controversial television program redefined the genre of reality programming. For the first time in television history, the Dutch reality format *Big Brother* systematically employed a hybrid combination of television, telephony and the internet to create enhanced forms of audience participation. In addition to a daily episode, this cross-media spectacle made unedited live streaming from cameras in the house accessible, which covered the life of the cast 24 hours a day. In addition to this, *Big Brother* invited the audience to discuss the cast and the events on the program's official website and (in its original version as broadcast in 1999/2000[3]) to decide every other week which of the two nominated cast members should be expelled from the house. Any viewer with access to a phone or a networked computer could literally make his or her choice between the two options every other week, and it is well documented that many viewers did so and further attempted to define the program's development by communicating their vote.

While the 'traditional' audience used the old media, television and telephone, as a means for communication, a more media-savvy group of users began watching *Big Brother* on the Internet and employed this medium as a communicative space, which allowed for alternate means of relating to the development of the program and its reception (see also Mathijs/Jones 2004). Online, fans commented on contestants, speculated about future developments in the house or about the outcomes of nominations and votes, formed fan groups supporting individual contestants, and advised producers about possibilities for further development of the program. For this group of active fans, differences between the edited sixty-minute episodes on television and the live streaming on the Internet became crucial, as the live feed allowed this audience to watch life in the house independently of the producers' choices, and thus to accumulate knowledge and generate interpretations that were uninfluenced by the edited and dramatized narratives that were broadcast on television. According to comments by online fans, these edited episodes misrepresented the events in the house in order to manipulate the television audience's decisions and bring them into accordance with the producers' economic calculations (see Andrejevic 2004, 117-141; Tincknell/Raghuram 2004; Wilson 2004). The online fans' critique raised two crucial questions: who actually exercised editorial control over the program, and whether the range and depth of *Big Brother*'s interactivity were as meaningful as the producer's promotion for the program had claimed. As a cross-media platform, *Big Brother* created an enhanced, but at the same time still restricted, 'space of participation'.

In his neo-Marxist approach to reality television, Mark Andrejevic (2004) suggested that the space of participation, as created by *Big Brother*, can be described as 'a commodified example of procedural authorship: the producers craft the set of rules whereby cast members (and sometimes audiences) shape the show' (2004, 49). Compared to *Aktenzeichen XY*, this form of procedural authorship does allow for more complex contributions by the audience, particularly on the internet. Nevertheless, possible moments and the dramaturgical depth of potential contributions by the audience are still limited. Beyond that, the range of participation is formatted by the program's setup and is structured by the program's ideology. Therefore, Andrejevic in his analysis claims that 'the result has not been a transfer of power and control from the power elites of Hollywood to the masses, but rather a shift in the burden of labor from paid actors and writers to the viewers, from whose rank the cast is drawn and whose free labor of fan sites helps add value and interest in often lackluster performances' (2004, 89).

Andrejevic points to a problem that is characteristic of the intermediate step located between a merely consuming audience and the evolution of interactive users in the realm of digitally networked media: whenever the audience stops simply watching and consuming, whenever viewers start to interact with and contribute to a program or to a program's 'overflow' (Brooker 2001) on the Internet, whenever users share their views or content online, they perform unpaid labor and submit to extensive monitoring. This generates a surplus value that only the producers can control and exploit. Arguing within the tradition of critical theory and political economy, Andrejevic tends to equate any act of interaction in the cross-media space of participation with the economic rationale of the industry; however, his critical analysis of reality television highlights aspects of the new media economy that many of the utopian approaches neglect or downplay. In a more comprehensive approach, one could address this as the 'condition of participation'. On the one hand, active users do perform unpaid labor and produce exploitable data. At the same time, members of the *Big Brother* audience become active contributors to the program, and some of them do move, as fans, critical commentators and creative contributors on the Internet, beyond the limits of the space of participation as formatted by the producers.

YouTube: Participation in a digital bazaar

Compared with *Aktenzeichen XY* and *Big Brother*, which represent two different types of producer-formatted participation, video-sharing sites such as YouTube, Google Video or Revver create a completely different space of participation, one in which users maintain more control over the space. These sites allow users to upload and distribute any video file that does not show adult or offensive content, or violates copyrights. As *Wired* magazine has commented, 'any amateur can record a clip' and can, by following the six easy steps as recommend by *Wired*, 'look like a pro' (Feely 2006). Generally speaking, any one who owns the technological means to record and upload a video film can share his or her self-made clips online. The rapid increase in the number of video clips uploaded to and watched on YouTube, by far the most popular of all online video-sharing sites,[4] appears to prove the claim that the ease of access to digital means of production and distribution disrupts the traditional regimes of television production and distribution. This substantiates the aforementioned statements, which have indicated that the boundaries between the spaces of production and consumption are becoming increasingly blurred (e.g. Uricchio 2004; Anderson 2006; Jenkins 2006).

Nevertheless, video-sharing sites remain something distinctly unlike utopian spaces of communication that are free of any technological, legal, economic or cultural constraints. The first restrictions are posed by 'protocols' (Galloway/ Thacker 2007, 28ff.) and copyright regulations such as the *Terms of Use* and *End-User License Agreement*. In addition, Google's 1.85 billion dollar acquisition of YouTube in October 2006, and the subsequent adjustments to the site, demonstrate the new online economy has identified video-sharing sites such as YouTube as important markets for customized advertising. The corporate media industry has begun to incorporate and redefine the 'cooperative non-market production of information and culture' (Benkler 2006, 2). In sheer economic terms, video-sharing sites are not completely different from traditional systems of commercial broadcasting. As Dallas Smythe (1977) has expressed: commercial broadcast television is in the business of producing audiences for advertisers. Video-sharing sites offer not only content that attracts peers, because many clips are produced by peers, it also provides the advertisers with data that reveal any individual user's online activities, his or her cultural preferences, and the communities in which he or she participates. Therefore, online video-sharing sites may perform the economic function of television in the future, even more effectively than commercial television has in the past.

Beyond this still-developing economic framework, the interfaces of video-sharing sites and the routinized forms for accessing and using these sites have culturally transformed them into highly structured spaces of interaction and participation. In an attempt to characterize online video-sharing sites, José van Dijck (2007) suggests that their institutional form can be characterized as 'homecasting', in contrast to broadcasting and narrowcasting, and that the cultural form of user-generated videos clips can best be understood as 'snippets': 'prerecorded, rerecorded, tinkered, and self-produced audiovisual content' that is not finished like a traditional broadcast television program, but invites users to appropriate, tinker with and respond to it. This characterization of 'homecasting' and the 'snippet' highlights the differences between traditional television and online video-sharing sites. However, in terms of institutionalization and cultural forms, there are also many similarities between these two types of audiovisual content with regard to production, distribution and reception.

As a matter of fact, the traffic on YouTube demonstrates that the number of users and downloaded clips far outnumbers the quantity of individual contributors and uploaded clips. Figures as published in July 2006 might still be indicative of the ratio between incidental 'producers' and sheer 'consumers' of content on YouTube: whereas 65,000 clips were uploaded per day, a total of 100 million clips were watched, which represents a ratio of 1:1,538.[5] In other words, most YouTubers do not employ YouTube as a means for publishing and distributing their clips, but rather view it like traditional television, as 'consumers' of a 'tube of plenty' (Barnouw 1990).

At the same time, there are an extraordinary number of users who do contribute video clips to YouTube. Prior to uploading clips, users have to create an account where they can then post their videos. This account becomes visible as an identifiable 'channel' to which other users can subscribe. Even those who do not upload their own clips can still create a channel by choosing clips already available on YouTube. Thus, as in traditional broadcast television, the concept of 'channels' structures the way clips are distributed online, and many users actually try to brand their channel to attract a larger audience.

When uploading a video, the user is required to create a title and a description for the clip, enter keywords, and choose one category from a list of fourteen to characterize the clip's genre, such as 'education', 'how to & style', or 'people and blogs'. Although the sheer number of videos available on YouTube functionally prevents the exhaustive categorization of the content, handbooks such as *YouTube 4 You* (Miller 2007) and *YouTube for Dummies* (Botello/Sahlin 2007) reflect routinized methods for accessing and using YouTube. Miller differentiates between nine prototypes of users, namely the 'recorder/sharer', the 'historian/enthusiast', the 'home movie maker', the 'video blogger', the 'instructor', the 'reporter', the 'performer', the 'aspiring film director' and the 'online business' (2007, 76-86). Both the genre categories, as defined on YouTube, and the types of users, as described by Miller, indicate that tinkering with the 'snippets' of other contributors is actually not the first and foremost practice performed on YouTube.

Though it is true that there are many examples where the content of other users is reused and tinkered with, these still form the exception rather than the rule, which is that clips on YouTube, even if not well structured in terms of dramaturgy, are primarily meant to be watched. The interface offers no indication as to how often a clip has been reused, but instead how often it has been watched, and how it has been rated. As in any other mass medium, an implicit imperative of YouTube is to create so-called 'viral videos', which will themselves be embedded in many channels, blogs and websites, and thus will be watched by a larger audience.[6] Handbooks include sections such as: 'What makes a great YouTube video?', 'Sell product placement in your videos', or 'How to increase your YouTube ratings – and your potential profits' (Miller 2007, 87, 166, 172). Again, these remain approaches that are characteristic of commercial broadcast television and function to structure YouTube's space of participation according to its rationale.

However, as Van Dijck correctly points out, YouTube's interface in general, and many clips in particular, ask users to respond to the clips. The interface specifically invites users to post comments on clips; further, users can respond to the comments themselves, or users can post another video in response to a clip. As compared to traditional broadcast television, in which only a few formatted moments existed in specific programs when members of the audience can literally respond, a dialogic structure is characteristic of online video-sharing sites, which links YouTube to traditions of oral cultures. There is a huge diversity of the types of comments on YouTube: some commentators express that they share experiences or tastes; some tutor the maker of a clip and give tips on how to improve the quality; others articulate what a viewer of a regular television show might shout at his set when watching a program at home; some try to create attention for their own clips on YouTube; and there are myriad other responses. Characteristic of most such comments is their use of everyday language, as if users were just chatting in an informal context. On YouTube and other video-sharing sites, this appears to be the cultural norm, the routinized practice. Again, although different from broadcast television, YouTube and other video-sharing sites generate their own (as far as the interface is concerned) explicit and (as far as recurrent practices are concerned) implicit rules and conventions, which format the space of participation YouTube offers.

Both the framework and the rules and conventions that define this space of participation have to be analyzed in much more detail. My point here is that video-sharing sites are formatted by a cultural framework that defines a video-sharing site's space of participation. This framework is partly generated by the website's interface and partly by the users' recurrently performed and thus 'highly institutionalized actions' (Zucker 1977, 727). Regarding YouTube, concepts that are characteristic of broadcast television and conventions that are characteristic of oral cultures combine to format the space of participation. On the one hand, these concepts reveal the difference between producers and consumers, the construction of channels, the notion of genres as a framework for production and reception, the worship of high ratings and their implicit commercial potential. On the other hand, these conventions form the dialogic structure and traditions of oral culture define this space. This is, although video-sharing sites allow for far more diverse forms of participation than the examples of interactive television programs analyzed in sections one and two, even video-sharing sites structure possible acts of participation, and they do so by drawing on well established conventions that then may become transformed and redefined.

A user who decides to upload clips to a video-sharing site subscribes to participating in what could best be described as a 'bazaar',[7] in which television is redefined as part of an amateur culture. This non-professional approach to television draws on dialogic structures and oral traditions, but at the same time is geared to its professional and commercial form, which formats this specific space of participation. Although YouTube and other video-sharing sites differ from broadcast television; broadcast television and online video-sharing sites do not embody diametrically opposed concepts, but different institutionalizations of television on a spectrum of cultural forms of television that mutually define each other.[8] Therefore, one should not underestimate broadcast television's power to shape what I call the participatory space of video-sharing sites.

Formatted spaces of participation

In the past decade, it appears as though we have witnessed what Bruno Felix and Femke Wolting titled *The end of television as we know it* (2000), in their documentary on the emerging online economy. Television 'as we know it' will remain powerful in shaping participatory practices on cross-media and digital platforms. As Henry Jenkins in *Convergence culture* has correctly argued, we have to consider 'ever more complex relations between top-down corporate media and bottom-up participatory culture' (2006, 243). However, I doubt that his romanticizing vision of top-down vs. bottom-up forces provides an adequate account of the economic, social, and cultural processes that are shaping and reshaping the relationship between the spheres of television production and consumption. The romantic metaphor of 'top-down versus bottom-up', very much like the opposition between the utopian and the dystopian account of digital media as discussed at the beginning, evokes a morally tinted opposition that characterizes non-professional and non-commercial media practices by definition as authentic, democratic and empowering, whereas professional and commercial media practices are marked as repressive and manipulative. As I have demonstrated in my historically comparative account of three different forms of interactive television and video-sharing sites, any of these forms creates institutionally and culturally structured spaces of participation. These are not merely imposed upon users by the industrially created interfaces. Particularly in cross-media and in digital setups, such as *Big Brother* and

YouTube, these spaces are co-created and shaped by the recurrent and thus routinized practices of users. Instead of simply praising the 'blurring of boundaries' between the spheres of production and consumption, the concept of 'formatted spaces of participation' allows for a more differentiated and adequate analysis of the technological, economic, social and cultural powers and conventions that structure the diverse participatory practices which these spaces allow for and also provoke. In this emerging field of research into interactive television, online video-sharing and participatory culture, the concept of 'formatted spaces of participation' helps to move beyond the technologically defined range and depth of interactivity. It asks us to critically address the routinized practices within these spaces that make these spaces into individualized institutions with their own specific, cultural conventions and ideologies.

Notes

1. In discourses on media and citizenship (e.g. Couldry, Livingstone and Markham 2007), cultural policy (e.g. Blokland 1997), and traditional art (e.g. Arns 2004), the word 'participation' refers to acts of engaging in culture and art by actively receiving culture, i.e. reading, attending performances, visiting exhibitions, etc. However, the meaning of the word 'participation' has changed: people characteristically 'participate' not only through active reception of culture and art but also, and primarily, through the active contribution of content to the culture in which they engage. See, for example, Ebare (2004) or Jenkins (2006; 2007).
2. I employ here Jenssen's (1999) theoretical approach to interactive television, in which he favors a quantitative model of interactivity that allows for distinctions between different levels of interaction, which are allowed within a medium or application.
3. The rules for the format vary from season to season, not only to keep the format fresh and attractive for the audience, but also to redesign the possible forms of audience interaction. Generally speaking, the show's producers increasingly attempt to control the 'space of participation', which was much less restricted in the first season.
4. YouTube itself does not reveal exact data; however, data published by ComScore Media Matrix, for September 2007, demonstrate the consistent popularity of YouTube as one of the top ten overall websites: 75% of all internet users in the US watch streaming video online, 27.6% of all users log on to YouTube. As ComSocre Media Matrix reports, 'nearly 70 million people viewed more than 2.5 billion videos on YouTube.com. Online viewers watched an average of slightly more than three hours of online video during the month (181 minutes). The average online video duration was 2.7 minutes. The average online video viewer consumed 68 videos, or more than two per day' (http://www.com-score.com/press/release.asp?press=1929; April 2, 2008). Stelter (2008) reports more than 3.4 billion video downloads in February 2008.
5. USA Today, July 16, 2006 (http://www.usatoday.com/tech/news/2006-07-16-youtube-views_x.htm; April 2, 2008).
6. Success stories, like Apple buying and remaking 17-year-old British college student Nick Haley's self-made commercial for the iPod Touch (Elliot 2007), not only demonstrate that YouTube functions as a space where professional and amateur cultures meet, but also that acknowledgment by many viewers and professionals is an implicit objective on YouTube.

7. The metaphor 'bazaar' employed by Raymond (1999) for open source software development might serve as a metaphor for online video-sharing sites (as opposed to the 'cathedral' of broadcast TV), if one takes into account that a bazaar, although accessible to anyone who can walk, is an institutionally and culturally highly structured space where people not only meet to sell and buy, but additionally where there are different roles, hierarchical structures, and conventions of conduct, all of which remain more or less impregnated by the economic rationale of a bazaar.
8. Roepke (2006) shows that the boundaries between home moviemaking, amateur filmmaking and the professional film world have remained blurred ever since.

Acknowledgements

I am grateful to Johannes von Moltke and Martina Roepke for their advice and suggestions and to Rebecca L. Garber for her careful revision of this text.

References

Anderson, Chris. 2006. People power: Blogs, user reviews, photo-sharing – The peer production era has arrived. *Wired*, July 14, 2006. http://www.wired.com/wired/archive/14.07/people.html.

Andrejevic, Mark. 2003. The webcam subculture and the digital enclosure. In *MediaSpace: Place, scale and culture in a media age*, eds. Nick Couldry, and Anna McCarthy. London/New York: Routledge.

Andrejevic, Mark. 2004. *Reality TV: The work of being watched*. Lanham: Rowman, and Littlefield.

Arns, Inke. 2004. Interaction, participation, networking: Art and telecommunication. *Media Art Net*. http://www.mediaartnet.org/themes/overview_of_media_art/communication/1/.

Barsley, Stephen R., and Pamela S. Tolbert. 1997. Institutionalization and structuration: Studying the links between action and institution. *Organization Studies* 18 (1): 93-117.

Barnouw, Eric. 1990. *Tube of plenty: The evolution of American television*. Oxford: Oxford University Press.

Benkler, Yochai. 2006. *The wealth of networks: How social production transforms markets and freedom*. New York: Yale University Press.

Berger, Peter L., and Thomas Luckmann. 1967. *The social construction of reality*. New York: Doubleday.

Blokland, Hans. 1997. *Publiek gezocht: Essays over cultuur, markt en politiek*. Amsterdam: Boom.

Botello, Chis, and Doug Sahlin. 2007. *YouTube for dummies*. Hoboken: Wiley Publishing.

Brooker, Will. 2001. Living on *Dawson's Creek*. Teen viewers, cultural convergence, and television overflow. *International Journal of Cultural Studies* 4 (4): 456-472.

Cavender, Gray. 2004. In search of community in reality TV: *America's Most Wanted* and *Survivor*. In *Understanding Reality Television*, eds. Su Homes, and Deborah Jermyn, 154-172. London: Routledge.

Couldry, Nick, Sonja Livingstone and Tim Markham. 2007. *Media consumption and public engagement*. London: Palgrave.

Ebare, Sean. 2004. Digital music and subculture: Sharing files, sharing styles. *First Monday* 9 (2). http://firstmonday.org/issues/issue9_2/ebare/index.html.

Elliot, Stuart. 2007. Student's ad gets a remake and hits a big time. *New York Times*, October 26. http://www.nytimes.com/2007/10/26/business/media/26appleweb.html.

Feely, Jim. 2006. Lights! Camera! Vodcast! How to make your own viral hit. *Wired*, May 14. 2006. http://www.wired.com/wired/archive/14.05/howto.html.

Felix Bruno, and Femke Wolting. 2000. *It's the end of TV as we know it.* Video documentary. Hilversum: VPRO.

Garnham, Nicholas. 1995. Political economy and cultural studies: Reconciliation or divorce? *Critical Studies in Mass Communication* 12: 62-71.

Grossberg, Lawrence. 1995. Cultural studies vs. political economy: Is anyone else bored with this debate? *Critical Studies in Mass Communication* 12: 72-81.

Jenkins, Henry. 2006. *Convergence culture: Where old and new media collide.* New York: New York University Press.

Jenkins, Henry. 2007. *Confronting the challenges of participatory culture: Media education for the 21st century.* Chicago: MacArthur Foundation.

Jenssen, Jens F. 1999. The concept of 'interactivity' in 'interactive television' and 'interactive media'. In *Interactive television: tv of the future or the future of TV?* eds. Jens F. Jensen, and Cathy Toscan, 25-66. Aalborg: Aalborg University Press.

Jermyn, Deborah. 2007. *Watching 'Crimewatch UK'.* London: Clarendon Press.

Mathijs, Ernest, and Janet Jones, eds. 2004. *Big Brother international: Formats, critics and publics.* London, New York: Wallflower Press.

Miller, Michael. 2007. *YouTube 4 you.* Indianapolis: Que Publishing.

Müller, Eggo. 2009. Crime watch EU: Transnational circulation of formatted television. *Media History* 15 (3).

Pierce, Cecilia. 1997. *The interactive book: A guide to the interactive revolution.* Indianapolis: Macmillan.

Pinseler, Jan. 2007. *Fahndungssendungen im deutschsprachingen Fernsehen.* Cologne: Herbert von Halem Verlag.

Rath, Claus-Dieter. 1985. The invisible network: Television as an institution in everyday life. In *Television in transition: Papers from the first international television studies conference,* eds. by Phillip Drummond, and Richard Paterson, 199-204. London: BFI.

Raymond, Eric S. 1999. *The cathedral and the bazaar: Musings on Linux and open source.* Sebastopol: O'Reilly Media.

Resnick, David. 1998. Politics on the Internet: The normalization of cyberspace. In *The politics of cyberspace,* eds. Chis Toulousee, and Timothy W. Luke, 46-68. New York: Routledge.

Roepke, Martina. 2006. *Privat-Vorstellung: Heimkino in Deutschland vor 1945.* Hildesheim: Olms.

Smythe, Dallas. 1977. Communications: Blind spot of Western Marxism. *Canadian Journal of Political and Social Theory,* 1 (3): 1-28.

Stelter, Brian. 2008. You've seen the YouTube video; now try the documentary. *New York Times,* May 10, 2008. http://www.nytimes.com/2008/05/10/arts/television/10kruger.html?scp=1&sq=youtube&st=nyt.

Swidler, Ann. 2001. What anchors cultural practices? In *The practice turn in contemporary theory,* eds. Theodore R. Schatzki, Karin Knorr Cetina, Eike von Savigny, 74-92. New York: Routledge.

Tapscott, Don. 1996. *The digital economy: Promise and peril in the age of networked intelligence.* New York: McGraw-Hill.

Tapscott, Don; Williams, Anthony D. 2006. *Wikinomics: How mass collaboration changes everything.* New York: B&T.

Tincknell, Estella, and Parvati Raghuram. 2004. Big Brother: Reconfiguring the 'active' audience of cultural studies? In *Understanding reality television,* eds. Su Homes, and Deborah Jermyn, 252-269. London: Routledge.

Toffler, Alvin. 1980. *The third wave.* New York: William Morrow.

Uricchio, William. 2004. Cultural citizenship in the age of P2P networks. In *European Culture and the Media,* eds. Ib Bondebjerg, and Peter Golding, 139-164. Bristol: Intellect.

Van Dijck, José. 2007. Homecasting: The end of broadcasting? *Vodavone Receiver Magazine* 18. http://www.receiver.vodafone.com/18-homecasting-the-end-of-broadcasting.

Wilson, Pamela. 2004. Jamming *Big Brother*: Webcasting, audience intervention, and narrative activism. In *Reality TV: Remaking television culture,* eds. Susan Marray, and Laurie Ouellette, 323-343. New York: New York University Press.

Zucker, Lynne G. 1977. The role of institutionalization in cultural persistence. *American Sociological Review* 42: 726-743.

Digital objects in e-learning environments

The case of WebCT

Erna Kotkamp

Higher education in the 21st century is challenged by changes, many of them instigated by the promising potential of new technologies in teaching, especially the Internet and web-based tools. These web-based tools are often clustered in so-called e-learning environments, or Learning Management Systems, that aim to support and even improve learning. In these environments different components and tools like bulletin boards and online syllabi are put together into one application, usually set up so that these tools can be used in separate courses. Well-known and heavily used environments in higher education are WebCT, Blackboard, Moodle, FirstClass, N@tschool and Claroline. In higher education these environments are put to use in different ways, extending from supporting face-to-face teaching with an additional online component, to supporting full online courses where all learning activities take place within the e-learning environment (Kotkamp et al. 2005).

E-learning or web-based learning is heralded by some for being able to serve an important pedagogical function, especially supporting teaching and learning from a social-constructivist perspective (Littlejohn 2003; Jochems et al. 2004; Downes 2006). The rise of these environments is even considered by some to be the reason for the increase in popularity of a social-constructivist philosophy in debates on learning theories (Anderson and Garrison 2006). However, when looking at the actual use of these integrated e-learning environments, the most important function they seem to serve is an administrative one. Christaan Dalgaard argues that especially when teaching from a social-constructivist perspective, large, integrated e-learning environments can only play a minor role (Dalgaard 2006).

In this article I want to look at those aspects of social constructivism that are significant in this discussion on the pedagogical potential of e-learning environments. I will analyze and show how this potential is not yet being fulfilled, by using WebCT as a case in point. In the last part I will move on to various technical and design aspects of e-learning environments that might account for some of the observed discrepancies between the aim to design for a social-constructivist learning process and the actual outcome.

Social-constructivist philosophy

Much has been written about social constructivism and its meaning for learning processes. Ideas like collaborative learning, student-centered learning, self-governed learning, authentic learning, and peer review are associated with the discussion on social constructivism and e-learning. Many of these ideas can be traced back to the work of educational reformist John Dewey at the beginning of the 20th century. A central element of his work is the idea that learning will be improved by reflection. Reflective thought for Dewey meant 'active, persistent, and careful consideration of any belief or supposed form of knowledge in the light of the grounds that support it and the further conclusion to which it tends' (Dewey 1910, 6). Learning is not so much a process of transmitting information, but a process of recreation and giving meaning (Dewey 1938).

Hence, learning is considered a constructive process that will turn out different for every learner. This is related to the importance Dewey assigns to previous experience and prior knowledge. According to Dewey, 'all genuine education comes about through experience' (Dewey 1938, 13). In a classroom setting this means that the experience of a learner has to be incorporated in the teaching to improve the learning process. Dewey proposed a theory of experience, consisting of two principles: continuity and interaction. Continuity pertains to the importance of past experiences for a person's future, and to the need for continuous embedding in the learning experience. Interaction pertains to the influence of the context and the situation in which these experiences occur. It becomes the responsibility of the teacher to create space for the incorporation of continuity and interaction (Dewey 1938).

Dewey's theory of experience is still relevant today, as it provides the basis of the concept of authentic learning. Within authentic learning it is considered of great importance that learners link what they are learning to a context where this newly acquired knowledge actually has a function (Volman 2006). Learning has to reflect actual practice and meaning, and this can only be accomplished by including experience and adhering to the two principles of continuity and interaction.

Related to this notion of experience is the acknowledgment of power relations at work in knowledge production and teaching processes. Knowledge is not objectively 'discovered' but created in a power-charged social relation (Haraway 1988; Freire 1970/1996). Although not explicitly mentioned in Dewey's work, this principle is implicated in the social values and norms by which experiences are shaped and knowledge is constructed. Taking these power relations into account and including them in a learning experience enables reflection on the relation between teacher and student. A teacher is seen as an expert in her field but should also function as a coach of the learning process. The teacher should be pedagogically competent at both tasks (Garrison and Anderson 2006, 4). This also implies that, in some regards, the relation between teacher and student should be horizontal: a teacher can learn from a student, too. This becomes especially important when new media are being used in teaching and learning. In a traditional higher education setting, students are often more competent than their teachers in dealing with new media, and teachers could learn this from their students (Holm Sørensen 2006).

Another important element of Dewey's theory is the idea that thinking should be considered as 'a state of perplexity, hesitation, doubt' (Dewey 1910, 9). According to this principle, effective learning should be troublesome, should involve a phase of uncertainty and disturbance. Learning is not a stable process that starts and ends with clarity and security. According to Dewey and others after him, a certain amount of insecurity and chaos is crucial for an effective learning process.

The social aspect of social-constructivist thinking is also reflected in Dewey's work. He once stated, 'I believe that the individual who is to be educated is a social individual and that society is an organic union of individuals' (Dworkin 1959, 22). From this follows the current notion of the importance of collaborative learning. This can take many forms and can serve different goals. A small explorative study amongst higher education teachers I conducted at different faculties revealed that many teachers valued collaborative learning, but that they did so for different reasons. Some teachers saw it as an extra skill to be learned, a goal in itself; other teachers saw it as an inherent part of the knowledge construction process, by which students can learn from each other's knowledge and experience. The latter concurs with social-constructivist learning: in collaboration different experiences and social contexts can be combined to achieve a richer learning experience.

From these principles of a social-constructivist pedagogy, we can derive some requirements for an e-learning environment. It should cater to the *complexity* of learning processes and their contents, and it should create room for a *diversity* of learners and their prior experience and knowledge. This notion of *diversity* implies that *interactivity* occurs not only between learners and content, but also among the learners. All in all, this calls for an environment that is in itself *dynamic*, but also capable of facilitating *dynamic* and *complex* learning processes in which insecurity and doubt can have a place.

The case of WebCT

In the following section I will measure these notions of *complexity*, *diversity*, *interactivity* and *dynamics* against a concrete e-learning environment, WebCT, as it claims to accommodate these principles.

WebCT, one of the first large e-learning environments, came right out of a higher education teaching practice around 1995, instigated by computer-science instructor Murrey Goldberg at the University of British Columbia. Goldberg was a firm supporter of the idea that education would benefit from using online tools. In his opinion the greatest advantage and added value of such tools was communication independent of place and time. The possibility of asynchronous communication was thus at the heart of the first prototypes. As he stated, 'In the studies we have done, it is the communication tools that have the greatest impact on the educational experience, not the on-line content' (Goldberg 2000a). Though Goldberg did not elaborate on how these communication tools and the communication itself could influence the learning experience, we may assume that his emphasis on communication implies acknowledgment of interactivity, collaborative learning, and social context as beneficial for education.

Moreover, Goldberg developed the environment together with his students, as a learning experience for them but also in order to incorporate their ideas. In doing so, he in fact put into practice the idea that students are a source of knowledge themselves. As a teacher Goldberg opened himself to learning from his students, thereby establishing a more horizontal relation between teacher and students. Goldberg also pointed at the added value of self-reflection by the teacher: 'It requires you to reevaluate both the content you are teaching and the way in which you teach' (Goldberg 2000b). This implies that Goldberg saw teaching as a dynamic process that needs constant evaluation and adjustment.

By the end of the 1990s, WebCT became a commercial company. The e-learning environment gained popularity with the increase of web-based teaching in general. It was one of the few large integrated environments available, and its multitude of possibilities attracted many universities.[1] However, this multitude of possibilities was also at the core of the criticism that the product was difficult to use. WebCT company claimed that this was mostly due to the flexibility and the number of features. According to WebCT, other e-learning environments, such as Blackboard, were simpler as they only presented a single way of organizing course material. WebCT presented itself as a genuine attempt to offer more options, by which individual instructors could have more freedom to design the course environment. WebCT's vision claimed 'to support a broad range of pedagogical and learning styles'.[2]

Hence, WebCT was not intended to be used as just a repository for the course material, but should function as an environment where collaboration and interaction can play a crucial role in the e-learning experience, and where the environment itself can influence the learning process in a constructive manner. However, when scrutinizing the functionalities in WebCT, there seems to be a discrepancy between the underlying pedagogical views and the technological modeling of the environment.

Take for example the so-called roles available in WebCT: what functionalities and possibilities are implied in these roles, and what implications does this entail for the teaching process? WebCT Vista 3.0 offers role types that have been defined by the IMS Global Learning Consortium and are indicated in Table 1 (WebCT 2004).

Administrators	Manage settings, enrolment, files and templates
Help Desk User	Receives a subset of administrator permissions
Designers	Build courses or templates
Instructors	Deliver courses and assign grades
Teaching assistants	Assist instructors in delivering course and grading
Students	Take courses and receive a final grade
Auditors	Take courses but do not receive a final grade

Table 1: Roles in WebCT Vista 3.0

These different role types function in what WebCT calls different learning contexts (ibid.) (Table 2).

Learning Context	Includes These Role Types	Role Name for Your Installation
Server	administrator	Server Administrator
Domain	administrator	Domain Administrator
	designer	Domain Designer
Institution	administrator	Institution Administrator
	help desk	Institution Help Desk User Institution Designer
	designer	
Group	administrator	Group Administrator
	help desk	Group Help Desk User
	designer	Group Designer
Course	designer	Course Designer
	instructor	Course Instructor
Section	designer	Section Designer
	instructor	Section Instructor
	teaching assistant	Section Teaching Assistant
	student	Section Student
	auditor	Section Auditor

Table 2: Learning contexts in WebCT Vista 3.0

All of these roles have different forms of access to different tools and possibilities within their Learning Context. Traditional courses in this learning context are placed on the level of a Section. This is due to WebCT's decision that 'learner roles exist only within sections and get the student version of whatever the designers have designed for the section plus some of their own personal tools, like *My Progress* or *My Grades*' (ibid.).

This means learners in the Student role receive access only on the level of a section, and in a course-centered teaching setting this also applies to the roles of Instructor and Designer. The Designer is the role that can actually 'design' the course and the learning process: manage online content and determine which tools can be accessed by the other roles of Instructor, Teaching Assistant, Student and Auditor. It is the only role that can create assignments, assessments, weblinks and can upload files in a generally accessible area within the section. Remarkably, a Designer cannot interact with Students; this role has no access to the mail tool or the discussion forum. The Instructor does have that kind of access, but this role cannot remove or add tools, though it can edit some of the settings of the tools. The Student can only view the course material but cannot add or alter content. This role only grants access to assignments and assessments to hand them in, and allows for participation in the discussion forum and chat. Only the main Instructor can enroll users into roles. It is possible to combine the role of Instructor and Designer but not the role of Instructor and Student, nor Designer and Student. Functions cannot be separated from the roles; as Administrator it is not possible to assign specific functionalities to a role.

From the perspective of the aforementioned social-constructivist principles, this strict division into roles and attached functionalities is problematic. Though the roles of Instructor and Designer may be combined, a teacher who is seen as a guide and coach in a flexible learning process should have the ability to alter the design of the course throughout the course to ensure this flexibility. More importantly, the Student role is limited to only viewing what the Instructor or Designer has created. This is in sharp contrast to the different pedagogical visions WebCT claims to support. How can you embed previous knowledge and experience into the current learning process? The Student role is not allowed access to the File Manager, and thus cannot add content to the course environment except through attachments on forum postings. The same applies to the Media Library, where Instructors can upload content of different formats, and link them to other content. The Student role is not allowed to provide additions, nor to make connections to or from the Library.

With these limitations, learners assigned the Student role become restricted in their interaction with the content, as they lack adequate space for connecting previous knowledge and experience into the course. It furthermore limits the possibility of sharing their knowledge construction, obscuring insight into their learning process for both the teacher and other learners. This entails a partial loss of the social in social-constructivist education.

Roles and functionalities

As mentioned before, an obstacle to a social-constructivist use of WebCT is the inflexible one-to-one relation between role and functionality. It is not possible to separate access to certain functionalities from the roles they are connected to. Learners in the Student role cannot be given the right to add to or alter entries to the Media Library. Or to personalize or create their own learning space by giving them access to an Organizer Page, where course content can be clustered together on a single page. A management of specific functionalities detached from roles would enable a more flexible learning environment where students could have some or even all the rights and possibilities now restricted to the Instructor and Designer roles.

This division reveals and reinforces a hierarchical and binary structure between learner (Student role) and teacher (Designer/Instructor role). Again, this limits the use of the environment as a place for knowledge construction. A learner is not given the opportunity to create, produce, add or alter content, and the teacher is not allowed to grant the learner these rights. Neither linking to previously uploaded material nor connecting to other courses or resources is possible in the Student role. The principles of diversity of content and learners cannot be enacted; in fact, the principle of contextualized learning is disabled. Not being able to assign a diversity of rights and functionalities to a learner makes it difficult to dynamically construct knowledge and to have a learner be responsible for and in control of his/her own content and learning process. As there is little room to introduce and share previous knowledge, the continuity of the learning process runs the risk of being interrupted.

This also applies for the starting page of each course (called Section in the WebCT Learning Context). This is a fixed entity to which only predefined objects can be added. None of the roles can personalize this page to accommodate the individual learning process. The Designer role can add content here, but this content is limited to the objects available in WebCT, such as (links to) an Organizer Page, Content Module or communication tools like Discussion Forum and Mail. The starting page has a predefined layout format; neither images nor text can be placed on the main page. The more tech-savvy users in the Designer role discovered a workaround for this inflexibility: the header and footer of the main page appeared to be amenable by some basic HTML, and this made it possible to include other objects than the ones defined by WebCT.

These examples reveal WebCT's closed (and closeted) way of shaping and accommodating the learning process. After all, the design of WebCT seems to be aimed at serving as a repository of information with only very limited possibilities of interaction with the material and each other. There is a severe lack of flexibility, which is necessary to create a dynamic learning environment that does justice to the complexity of a learning process supporting a diversity of learners and learning styles. This is surprising in the light of WebCT's history and the reply to the criticism of user-unfriendliness. Indeed, a high degree of functionalities and choices renders the environment complex, but this does not make the environment automatically more suitable for a diversity in pedagogy and learning styles.

Since WebCT does claim to have this intention, the loss may be due to the technical translation of these aims, that is, to choices made in the early stages of developing the application. At least, there seems to be a tension in the conceptualization of what an environment might support and the technical output of this. In the next section[3] I will explore this tension by addressing how human interaction is conceived within computer science, and what this entails for the technological translations.

Computer science and object orientation

Since the beginning of computation and computer science, the focus has been on data and the processing of data between machines. This means that information is translated into mathematical expressions and procedures that are understood by machines. From this perspective, interactions between software and hardware are modeled as causal procedures linking senders to receivers. The actions (messages) of the sender are the impulses for the actions/reactions of the receivers. The important element in this structure is the clear and unambiguous relation between these impulses and their reactions. Interaction, then, is fully structured and planned in these systems.

By the end of the last century, a shift had taken place from the processing of information between hardware systems to offering ready-made interactions with humans. These actions were aimed at automating and/or enhancing human action; first focused on calculating, later on text and image editing, and in an even later stage learning.

However, within computer science the way of dealing with interaction remained the same as when dealing with machine-machine interaction. Interaction is handled in a clear and formalized manner, excluding any ambiguity. As pointed out by several technology theorists, the modeling of complex interaction patterns between humans is still based on the transmission model used for the representation of data-exchange between artificial senders and receivers (Crutzen 2001; Suchman 1994; Leigh Star 1991; Laurel 1991). In other words, the modeling of software applications aimed at human interaction is based on the generalization of information, communication and interaction.

This generalization has increased with the paradigm of object orientation (OO). The development of object-oriented programming (OOP) started out in the beginning of the 1960s with the programming language Simula developed by Dahl and Nygaard (2001). In OOP, predefined objects make up the basic structure of the software. Software is seen as a collection of objects that work together. These objects relate to and act upon each other, and the interaction between these objects in the form of passing messages is the core of this programming paradigm.

The difference between OOP and other paradigms is that within OOP, data and the operations that can manipulate these data are placed in one object instead of being separated. This meant a break with the paradigm of procedural programming. Within procedural programming software behavior is defined by procedures, functions, and subroutines. In OOP these behaviors are contained as methods in the object itself. A method is a foundational element of an object class and is inextricably merged with the object itself. Methods can only be invoked by sending an appropriate message to the object (Weisfeld 2004). The object thus becomes the basis and starting point of the interaction.

To illustrate this OO principle, let's look again at the roles in WebCT. These roles function as predefined object classes. These classes are the highest level within OOP. In WebCT it is likely that a class is created for 'student'. In this class general properties and methods are defined, and relations to other classes are established. When a class is instantiated, an object emerges in which these properties are built in. Basically, a class can be seen as an empty form with predefined form fields; an object comes into existence when filling in or activating this form. The class 'student' then becomes an object with a name and other specific properties, such as a student number. Within the class the object 'student' could be defined to have different methods at its disposal, for example ViewPage() or RetrieveMediaLibraryObject(). It is also possible that the class 'student' may not have many methods itself but can be used as the basis for invoking methods of other classes such as the class 'discussionforum', in which methods like AddPosting(), DeletePosting(), etc. can be defined.

By combining objects and methods, an inseparable assemblage is made between an object (in this case ironically a human subject) and its possible interactions. This implies that there is only room for preplanned actions. Humans or other entities (objects) can only act if a preprogrammed plan exists and its execution conditions are being met. Data and the manipulation of data are contained within the object itself, and changes in interactions are only possible when preprogrammed within the object. Interaction and the representation of interaction is located within the objects, and not on a procedural level. In doing so the behavior of humans can only be represented as fixed. Ad hoc interactions are usually not represented and thus become excluded.

In software like WebCT, where flexibility in the form of the possibility for unplanned interactions is of great importance, this way of programming creates tension, to put it mildly. Moreover, this tension is not limited to the actual programming. As several scholars have shown, this is already at stake in the first stages of conceptualizing and modeling the software. As argued by Cecile Crutzen for example, OOP has grown from a programming paradigm towards a broader field: an object-oriented approach and methodology for the interpretation, representation and analysis of human interaction in computer science (Crutzen 2001). This extended object-oriented approach (OOA) has gained popularity since the early 1990s, as shown by numerous publications on the topic and its use in computer science education (Booch 1993; Jacobson, Jonsson and Övergaard 1992; Rumbaugh et al. 1991). As Crutzen points out, the OO approach transferred the fear of doubt, as opposed to security, to the designed interaction model (Crutzen 2001). Dominant ideas in software engineering are that software should be unambiguous and should have mastered complexity. When transferring this to a real world analysis, as it is called in computer science, complexity and ambiguity appear as problems which have to be tamed by abstraction.

Abstraction techniques, such as generalization, classification, specialization, division, and separation, are fundamental for most modeling methods. According to Jacobson, such techniques are used to 'decrease complexity on the object level' (Jacobson et al. 1992, 254). Abstraction is seen as unavoidable when projecting and representing dynamic real world processes into modeling structures, but this implies a loss. Jacobson mapped out different (human) interaction diagrams, and showed how the use of abstraction techniques yields to ignoring dynamic aspects of the world. Hoare suggested, 'Abstraction arises from recognition of similarities between certain objects, situations or processes in the real world and the decision to concentrate upon these similarities and to ignore for the time being the differences' (Hoare 1972, cited in Booch 1992, 39). In other words, these modeling methods force a search for similarities between human actors and processes, while ignoring the differences. Differences thus are downplayed, since they are technically hard to handle, especially when they tend to ambiguity. Ambiguity is precisely what has to be reduced in technical modeling. As Alan Davis puts it,

> As systems become more complex however, it becomes increasingly difficult to explain behavior in an unambiguous manner. (...) A model simply provides us with a richer, higher level, and more semantically precise set of constructs than the underlying natural language. Using such a model reduces ambiguity, makes it easier to check for incompleteness, and may at times improve understandability (Davis 1993, 213-214).

Hence, models based on the OO approach as the methodology for interpreting and analyzing human behavior are aimed at dissolving any doubt and ambiguity. In this approach, models appropriate for interaction analysis on a technical level are used for constructing planned interaction by humans, without proper consideration of the differences. From the OO perspective, the ambiguities that come with human interaction are inconveniences that have to be straightened out on the technical level.

This fear of the ambiguity, complexity, and unpredictability of human behavior is at odds with a flexible learning environment that accommodates social-constructivist learning. While the acknowledgment of complexity and unpredictability is of great importance, precisely these aspects are being abstracted and reduced, at the expense of being able to cater to a social complexity. To return to the examples of roles in WebCT: once you are assigned a role, you will not be able to take on another role, or use methods (interactions) from other roles. There is no possibility for interactions that are not preconceived during the modeling stage of the environment and its objects. One may wonder whether a meaningful learning environment along the lines of social constructivism can be created at all, if this environment already presupposes what and how we learn in a very specific and static way, with predefined actions and objects.

It would be interesting to get access to the actual process of how WebCT has been conceptualized and modeled, how the objects came to be defined, and which methods are contained in which objects with what consequences. How was the action/interaction planned, what pedagogical-based choices were made, and how did this influence both the programming paradigm and the modeling approach? An in-depth analysis of these issues could advance a next generation of learning environments beyond the sole use as course administration and repository. It may then eventually live up to its potential to transform learning processes in higher education.

Notes

1. Blackboard was at that time working on their first release of Blackboard CourseInfo, later renamed the Blackboard Learning System.
2. See the archived website of WebCT 1999 at http://web.archive.org/web/19991012032600 /http://www.webct.com/vision.
3. Parts of this section are a reworking of the article 'Object Orientation' by Cecile Crutzen and Erna Kotkamp (2008), in *Software studies: A lexicon*, edited by Matthew Fuller (Cambridge, MA: MIT Press).

References

Alexander, Dey. 2006. An accessibility audit of WebCT. *Ausweb 08: The Fourteenth Australasian World Wide Web Conference*. http://ausweb.scu.edu.au/aw02/papers/refereed/alexander/paper.html.

Booch, Grady. 1994. *Object-oriented analysis and design, with applications*. Second edition. Redwood City: Benjamin/Cummings.

Chandler, Daniel. 1995. *The act of writing: A media theory approach*. Aberystwyth: University of Wales.

Crutzen, Cecile. 2001. *Interactie, een wereld van verschillen: Een visie op informatica vanuit het perspectief genderstudies*. Dissertatie Open Universiteit Nederland, Heerlen.

Crutzen, Cecile, and Erna Kotkamp. 2008. Object orientation. In *Software studies: A Lexicon*, ed. Matthew Fuller. Cambridge, MA: MIT Press.

Dahl, Ole-Johan. 2001. *The birth of object orientation: The Simula languages.* http://heim.ifi.uio.no/~olejohan/papers/Birth-of-S.pdf.

Davis, Alan M. 1993. *Software requirements: Objects, functions and states.* Englewood Cliffs, NJ: Prentice Hall.

Dalgaard, Christiaan. 2006. Social software: E-learning beyond learning management systems. *European Journal of Open, Distance and E-Learning* 9 (2). http://www.eurodl.org/materials/contrib/2006/Christian_Dalsgaard.htm.

Dewey, John. 1910. *How we think.* Boston: D.C. Heath.

Dewey, John. 1938/1998. *Experience and education: The 60th anniversary edition.* West Lafayette, India: Kappa Delta PI.

Dworkin, M.S. 1959. *Dewey on education.* New York: Teachers College Press.

Garrison, D.R., and Terry Anderson. 2003. *E-learning in the 21st century: A framework for research and practice.* London: Routledge Falmer.

Goldberg, Murray. 2000a. Modest beginnings. http://www.webct.com/service/ViewContent?contentID=2339374.

Goldberg, Murray. 2000b. Alternative beginnings.
http://www.webct.com/service/ViewContent?contentID=2339414.

Freire, Paulo. 1972. *Pedagogy of the oppressed.* Harmondsworth: Penguin.

Illinois Center for Information Technology Accessibility. 2008. WebCT Accessibility Interest Group. http://cita.disability.uiuc.edu/collaborate/webct/evaluations.php.

Jacobson, Ivar, Magnus Christerson, Patrik Jonsson and Gunnar Övergaard. 1992. *Object-oriented software engineering: A use case driven approach.* Reading, MA: Addison-Wesley Publishing Company.

Kirkup, Gill. 2003. Cyborg teaching. In *ICT's in teaching and learning women's studies: Perspectives and practices in Europe*, eds. Sara Goodman, Gill Kirkup and Magda Michielsens. ATHENA/Universiteit Utrecht/Centre for Gender Studies, Lund University.

Kotkamp, Erna, Sandra ten Horst and Pierre van Eijl. 2005. *Online learning: (work) in progress. The case of European women's studies & feminist pedagogies.* Utrecht University/Athena/IVLOS.

Laurel, Brenda. 1991. *Computers as theatre.* Boston: Addison-Wesley.

Michielsens, Magda. 2003. Feminist pedagogy. In *ICT's in teaching and learning women's studies: Perspectives and practices in Europe*, eds. Sara Goodman, Gill Kirkup and Magda Michielsens. ATHENA/Universiteit Utrecht/Centre for Gender Studies, Lund University.

Oudshoorn, N. and T. Pinch, eds. 2003. *How users matter.* Cambridge, MA: MIT Press.

Richards, Jan. 2001. Conformance of WebCT v3.6 to W3C's authoring tool accessibility guidelines 1.0. *World Wide Web Consortium* http://www.w3.org/WAI/AU/2002/WebCT3_6.html.

Star, Susan Leigh. 1991. Invisible work and silenced dialogues in knowledge representation. In *Women, work and computerization: Understanding and overcoming bias in work and education*, eds. Inger V. Eriksson, Barbara A. Kitchenham, and Kea Tijdens. Amsterdam: Elsevier Science Publishers.

Sengers, Phoebe and Bill Gaver. 2005. Designing for interpretation. *Proceedings of Human-Computer Interaction International.* http://cemcom.infosci.cornell.edu/papers/sengers-gaver.design-for-interpretation.pdf.

Simons, Robert-Jan. 1999. New learning: Three ways to learn in a new balance. *Lifelong Learning in Europe* 4 (1): 14-23.

Sørensen, Birgitte Holm. 2006. When teachers become knowledge leaders. *DPU Quarterly Newsletter: Knowledge, ideas, inspiration* http://www.dpu.dk/site.aspx?p=8649&newsid1=3965.

Suchman, Lucy. 1994. Working relations of technology production and use. *Computer Supported Cooperative Work (CSCW)* 2 (1-2): 21-39.

University of Tasmania. 2006. Is WebCT Vista Accessible?
http://www.utas.edu.au/accessibility/webct/is_webct_accessible.html.

Volman, Monique. 2006. *Jongleren tussen tradtie en toekomst*. Inaugural speech. Amsterdam, Free University.

WebCT. 2004. *Administrators' guide WebCT Vista™ 3.0: Technical communications*. April 8.

Weisfeld, Matt. 2004. Moving from procedural to object-oriented development. http://www.developer.com/design/article.php/3317571.

Memory

The vanishing points of mobile communication

Imar de Vries

At the beginning of the 21st century, mobile communication devices are virtually ubiquitous. The attraction of their ability to potentially connect anywhere, anytime, to anyone or anything in the informational network, combined with an ongoing emphasis of the individual as the nexus of communication and entertainment, has sculptured the apparatuses into vital cultural artefacts. Their pervasiveness has rendered them ordinary and, in a sense, invisible; they seamlessly blend into almost every social activity imaginable. As such, they represent the strangest breed of new media we have come to study in the past ten years: instead of being subject to initial feverish 'buzzification', mobile communication devices have steadfastly insinuated themselves among us, and in contrast to the widespread academic enthusiasm that for instance the Internet generated in the 1990s, they sparked very little scholarly interest.

However, in a remarkable reversal of the steps from hype to reality, mobile communication devices have increasingly been framed in utopian terms during the last few years. This is primarily visible in how dominant mobile communication discourses advance a very specific notion of the all-important place that mobile devices should take in the overall media landscape. A detailed analysis of such discourses would show that what is stressed are the potential gains to be made in productivity, sociability, efficiency, safety, reassurance, and mutual understanding; in other words, they stress communication improvement and its benefits, and present wireless communication technologies as the ultimate facilitator. In many ads, press releases, and expressions of popular culture, a similar reasoning process can be distinguished, one that is repeated as a guiding mantra: mobile communication devices are the self-evident technological expressions of a presumed 'natural' progression in the quest for perfected communication.

So, the pressing question that confronts us today is to what extent the infrastructures and everyday practices that co-construct the ways in which we experience mobile communication actually sustain idealized ideas of communication. In one rather straightforward sense, the adoption speed alone suggests that there is a large overlap between what dreams of ideal communication prescribe and what mobile communication devices can offer. A quick glance at their breakneck-paced integration into everyday life could easily lead to the conclusion that the age-old desire to bridge distances and instantaneously communicate with anyone and anywhere, which has expressed itself countless times in predictions and glorifications of new media, is now for many people more fulfilled than ever. But such an explanation would obscure the different reasons why people in various demographic categories adopt mobile communication technologies, and neglect the inevitable problems and challenges that arise out of a shift towards a radical wireless connectedness. Mobile communication devices may indeed facilitate the kinds of contact that fit idealized conceptions of the zenith of communication, but do we experience them as such? Where are the kinks in the ideals, what are the paradoxes in today's mobile communication condition?

In this chapter, it is therefore my aim to make an analytical cut along the discourses of what I perceive as three of the most striking characteristics of current-day mobile communication, namely those of facilitating ubiquitous connectivity, fluid sociability, and real-time relief of anxiety. In these analytical cuts I will describe how the various aspects of idealized communication run into paradoxes when confronted with everyday communication, and I will support my claims by using illustrative examples of research conducted by media and communication scholars who set out to empirically measure and gauge the impact of mobile communication devices. In the conclusion I will argue that the feverish embracement of mobile communication technologies forces both mobile telephone users and media scholars to realign their notions of concepts such as connectivity, privacy, accountability, and information flows, if they are to understand the latent consequences of the dreams that are deeply rooted in media evolution.

Ubiquitous connectivity

The obvious and single most defining characteristic of wireless communication technology, one that precedes and co-defines its other specific features, is that it renders space almost irrelevant as a variable in constituting mediated contact. And, due to contributing factors such as the standardisation of communication protocols, the ease of construction of basic technological frameworks, the portability of devices, the intuitive use of mobile telephones, and the high social and cultural value of personal communication devices, wireless services are steadfastly becoming truly ubiquitous indeed. What is significant about this process is that the supporting infrastructure is often made virtually invisible, as a conscious attempt to create and uphold the illusion that the wireless connection is 'just there', to be invoked at will to magically synchronise different space and time co-ordinates. As in early seventeenth-century fantasies of magnetised compass needles that would move in communicative rapport wherever they were, a certain sense of – and need for – telepathic immediacy pervades modern wireless communication technologies; just turn on the mobile device, and a connection will be guaranteed to exist almost instantly.

With their omnipresence, wireless communication technologies thus facilitate the further compression of geographical space into what Manuel Castells (1996) calls the *space of flows*. In the space of flows, people, goods, and information are in a constant state of flux, moving between physical locations while being part of a dynamic network that is linked together through the use of communication technologies. Because wireless communication devices radically alter the long-lasting relationship between communication nodes and fixed locations, in the space of flows, spatial vectors become increasingly heterogeneous, and thus simultaneous social interaction at a distance turns into a pervasive activity that can be engaged in anywhere, at any time. What follows is that we become more and more immersed in what Kenneth Gergen identifies as the 'relational net', in which everyone and everything can potentially link up (Gergen 2003, 111). Having a wireless communication device like a mobile telephone at one's disposal implies having access to ever-present, real-time communication channels, and thus to the means to engage in dialogue or to disseminate information whenever and wherever one wants. A mobile telephone therefore provides a very strong psychological fix by supplying the abundant availability of *communicative choice*, the freedom to electronically connect and mediate knowledge, opinions, and desires; it is an apparatus of opportunity, a potential-rich portal.

The tendency to depict mobile telephones as powerful devices that possess an unlimited connective potential is reflected by the strong emotional and cognitive investments that people make in wireless communication technologies. Mobile telephones have become considered as essential and vital extensions of the body, which is for instance vividly illustrated by their naming conventions. In many countries they are called 'hand phones', or their names refer to the fact that communication is 'always on' and can always be carried along on the body (Townsend 2002, 68-69). In one particular case, the name quite dramatically expresses the urge to attribute magical powers to the body extension: in Israel, a mobile telephone is called *pelephone*, after the name of Israel's first cellular communications company, which literally means 'wonder-phone' (Thompson 2005, 21). Also, mobile telephones and their invisible but potentially present connections have now become so intimately integrated into our being, that many people experience feelings of panic when they find they have not brought their mobile telephone with them, or think it is lost (Vincent 2003, 220). The severance of the Hertzian umbilical cord is felt like an amputation that many would like to avoid.[1]

There are some paradoxical ramifications, however. True, from a socio-psychological standpoint, wireless communication devices can be said to be perceived as the latest candidates to gratify the yearnings for wholeness and completeness that have continuously risen from our collective 'technological imaginary'. And indeed, at first, a perpetually connected state seems to be a perfect point of departure for establishing and managing all kinds of successful communication situations, and thus for reaching the ideal goal of a common understanding. But a closer inspection of what is at hand reveals that merely increasing the opportunities to connect might actually not help in bringing people closer together in a utopian fashion. George Myerson, for instance, comes to the conclusion that what he calls the process of 'mobilisation' is predominantly geared towards just making 'basic contacts' (Myerson 2001, 27). And indeed, there are research findings that can be interpreted as supporting Myerson's claim: people generally spend less time calling on mobile telephones than they do on fixed phones (Licoppe 2003, 175), they think of asynchronous text messaging as 'quicker and more convenient than voice telephony' (Ling 2004, 150), and they sometimes lock themselves in 'tele-cocoons' from which they only keep in touch with their most intimate friends, refraining from communicating with the outside world (Ito et al. 2005, 10-11). While some of these phenomena can be explained as user strategies aimed at managing billing systems and keeping costs low, the suggestion remains that mobile telephony and its infrastructure offer affordances that primarily invite what Christian Licoppe calls a 'connected' practice of interaction instead of a 'conversational' practice (2003, 174; 183). The 'anywhere, anytime' paradigm so much pervades interaction in everyday life, Licoppe found, that users prefer to think of their mobile communication practices mostly as intuitive whenever-you-feel-like events, which often primarily serve to acknowledge the connection that people share (ibid., 180-181).

While such short communicative gestures are important elements in the shaping and maintenance of what can be called a 'performative value' in social relationships (Green 2003, 207), they do add to swelling flows of information, messages, and data, all of which affirm one's connectedness up to a highly redundant level. If always being connected is what brings pure communication a step closer, it is also what foregrounds the communication paradox, and forces us to realize that pure communication is relentless in its intrusive nature. Studies have shown that when, for whatever reason, the times and places at which people can be contacted are extended to all possible environments, and those contacts become more frequent, a tension arises between on the one hand the desire and expectancy for immediate and unlimited access to others, and on the other hand the need to filter out and restrict incoming access requests in increasingly variable circumstances. Hence, the presence of a perpetual connection pressures users of wireless communication devices into managing all kinds of complicated communication schemes (Sherry and Salvador 2002, 114-115), into employing inventive ways to cope with awkward social situations caused by disruptive incoming calls (Ling 2004, 123-143), and even into being deprived of sleep when they are kept awake at night by calls or text messages (Turrettini 2007).

Discourses of wireless communication technologies, then, reflect how the compression of space by making connection nodes ubiquitous is of constitutive importance in the transformation of our understanding of communication. Across a wide range of demographic compositions, many social activities that used to rely on physical proximity or on the pre-arranged coordination of interaction are now reshaped into ad-hoc patterns of de-spatialised and heterogeneous contacts. With the shift towards more connectedness, we experience faster and more often than before that the desire for pure communication brings us both pleasure and discomfort. As Michael Arnold holds, the mobile telephone is Janus-faced, a socio-technical system that is 'not reducible to a direction or valence tipped with a single arrowhead, but better understood as a conflation of tangential implications, at least some of which can be read as ironically and paradoxically self-contradicting phenomena' (Arnold 2003, 234). Because of mobile telephony, the paradox hiding in the desire for ideal communication becomes more articulated than ever.

Fluid sociability

User accounts of reconfigurations of connectedness can provide a good view of how people seek to exploit the range of communicative affordances of wireless communication devices, and subsequently of how they experience what are presupposed to be idealized ideas of communication sparked by a desire for perpetual contact. This is especially visible in one particularly poignant theme that runs through these user accounts, which is the theme of social coordination, or rather what Richard Ling and Birgitte Yttri (2002) distinguish as a combination of 'micro- and hyper-coordination'. Micro-coordination is the type of nuanced instrumental coordination typical of a significant part of mobile telephone use: trips that have already started can be redirected, people can call or send a text message to say they will be late, and meetings can be scheduled at a rather loosely defined time or location, only to become more definite when those who want to meet call each other while they are on their way (Ling and Yttri 2002, 143-144). Hyper-coordination adds an expressive layer to this instrumental use, both in the form of social and emotional communication (chatting, gossiping) and in the form of mobile etiquettes telling where mobile telephones should not be used or which models are in fashion (ibid., 140). Both types, then, are specifically about how to manage increasingly connected social networks: micro-coordination in a logistical way that makes full use of enhanced communicative availability, and hyper-coordination in a cultural way that establishes the mobile telephone as today's *ne plus ultra* means to create, maintain, and express social bonds and values. In user accounts of both types, elements of ideas of fulfilment through improved communication seep through voiced expectations and desires.

First examining micro-coordination, Ling and Yttri find for instance that a strong need for connectedness is conveyed in many comments about the motives for using mobile telephones, aimed at making instrumental communication proceed as smoothly as possible. This instrumental approach to mobile telephony is widespread, if not constitutive. Ling and Yttri retrieved their data mainly from interviewing Norwegian teens, but similar attitudes towards the importance of being connected for instrumental reasons have already been registered in the earliest social analyses of the adoption of mobile telephones – most notably by Kopomaa (2000) – and have been identified as largely age-indifferent and cross-cultural phenomena (cf. Castells et al. 2007; Katz and Aakhus 2002) The emphasis in such mobile communication lies on orchestrating each other's movements and positions in the space of flows to the point where they ultimately overlap and merge. This is only possible, however, if permanent availability is guaranteed and is incorporated in the ideology of mobile communication. The main motivation for using wireless communication devices in such cases lies in the assumption that if there are more opportunities to connect, it means that there will be an improvement in how we arrange social interactions, and thus in how social groups function as a whole. Of course, this assumption only holds when there is an agreement on how social interactions should actually be arranged, but in the mobile vision – availability solves everything, together is good – the mere possibility to contact anyone from anywhere is enough to suggest that such problems can easily be dealt with, simply by making another call or sending another text message.

In hyper-coordination, the value of being connected is less related to efficient planning or dealing with practical issues, and more to achieving a certain status and maintaining intimate social bonds. Such communicative activities are about sharing experiences and confirming personal links, and can take the form of gossiping, catching up on each other's adventures, or exchanging symbolic gifts (see Johnsen 2003). These practices have been around for a long time, but the ubiquitous connectivity that the mobile telephone promises to deliver represents a new and particularly potent means to establish one's identity and earn a meaningful place in the social hierarchy of family members and friends. A cross-cultural study done by Scott Campbell (2007) showed that people find that through mobile telephones, group connections are enhanced, conversations gain in intimacy, and opportunities for emancipatory praxis increase. The mobile telephone thus acts as an apparatus that 'liberates' expressive communication, largely because it makes opportunities for mediated dialogue and dissemination available to demographic groups which did not readily enjoy that privilege before the age of wireless communication devices, and because those people use mobile communication as a way to actively establish and manage their own social position in relation to others. In addition, compared to the fixed telephone, the mobile telephone offers far more direct and individualised links to other people, properties that have quickly turned the device into the primary locus where one's collection of social connections resides. Because mobile telephony is perceived as extending access to others to virtually infinite dimensions, the thought of being perpetually connected in the symbolically charged mobile network gives an increased existential significance to relational ties.

However, increased social connectedness comes with some unintended consequences that do not readily fit within idealized ideas of improved communication. The fact that mere connectivity has come to engulf present-day conceptions of communication has a compelling effect on our relational self, changing the perception of what it means to co-exist and communicate with others. The people we interact most with – those who reside in our more intimate social circles, like family members, friends, and colleagues – are now always only a phone call or text message away. As Kenneth Gergen has aptly diagnosed this social condition, we find ourselves continuously in a state of 'absent presence': physically absent, but electronically at hand (Gergen 2002). While the arrangement of absent presence offers a psychologically reassuring feeling of closeness, perpetual connectedness does not necessarily guarantee reaching a global coming together; Gergen notes that because communication with absent present others takes place via readily available channels, and therefore does not require a lot of effort or time in setting up, it tends to become simpler, shorter, and distributed among several fragmented micro-communities (Gergen 2003, 106-107). In addition, when people are inclined to enclose themselves in connections to their absent present social network, they exhibit a diminished care for those outside of their communicative bubble (ibid., 109).

What does markedly happen while the mobile network grows is that mediated communication is brought more out in the open, which presents us with new scenarios for experiencing being-with-others and strengthens the notion that anyone carrying a wireless communication device can, potentially, become part of anyone else's technology-mediated network. The drawback of the 'invasion' of the public by the private, however, is that mobile communication behavior in public spaces often invades and disturbs social events and face-to-face conversations with what is perceived as trivial and redundant chitchat or gossip. Now, gossip is the hard-wired social glue with which humans build and maintain social bonds, and mobile telephones are very apt at facilitating it anywhere and round-the-clock (see Fox 2001), but when experienced intrusively and only one-sided, it tends to aggravate companions, bystanders, and eavesdroppers, causing them to feel disempowered (Plant 2001, 31) or convinced that communication in the mobile age has become tawdry (Palen, Salzman and Youngs 2000, 207). This strained intermingling of public (outside) space with private (inside) space is what Kathleen Cumiskey (2005) calls the paradox of techno-intimacy: to ourselves, our mobile telephone is a highly convenient personal item and our own mobile communication behavior is perfectly acceptable, but we tend not to appreciate the same behavior and attitude towards the valuation of mobile communication in others. I would argue that techno-intimacy, the ambivalent relationship between the desire to be connected and know all on the one hand, and the need to stand apart from the multitude on the other, is itself a typical exponent of the paradox of idealized communication: an achieved complete togetherness will necessarily entail the loss of individuality, and mobile telephony will continue to stress this phenomenon.

Real-time relief of anxiety

If we are to see mobile telephones as personal apparatuses full of communicative potential that, through their capability to transgress space and time, can maintain and strengthen bonds with primary social group members and make coordination activities more ad-hoc and prominent, one of the following observations must be that the psychological fix attached to wireless communication relies heavily on the involvement of feelings of reassurance. For many, the emotional immediacy of the device has registered itself as an indispensable part of their everyday life, like the aura of a talisman worn for good luck and protection. And indeed, research has shown that a need for security, safety and reassurance is high on the list of initial reasons why people decide to buy wireless communication devices, either for themselves or for their children and other loved ones. In a 1999 qualitative survey of 36 focus groups in six European countries, Richard Ling reports,

> respondents were asked to what degree they agreed or disagreed with the statement 'The mobile telephone is useful in an emergency'. We found that approximately 82% of the respondents were in complete agreement. There was no other attitudinal indicator with regard to mobile telephony that had such an extreme score (Ling 2004, 37).

Similar results were obtained from studies in the United States and Australia (ibid., 38) and from cross-cultural field studies undertaken in Berlin, San Fransisco, Shanghai, and Tokyo (Chipchase 2005).

The human fear for calamities evidently provides a sound reason why feelings of security and safety play a significant role in the adoption of wireless communication technologies. The many folk-stories that tell of amazing rescue missions that involve the use of mobile telephones are adamant examples of how strong the desire is to stress that increased connectedness is a Good Thing. Idealized ideas of communication thrive on compelling anecdotes that 'prove' that progress has been made, and arguably nothing provides more conclusive evidence than accounts of lives saved or loved ones protected thanks to new communication technologies. So, we read in *The Guardian* that two British climbers caught in a blizzard on a Swiss mountain texted five friends, one of whom received the message in London at 5 am and immediately notified the rescue services in Geneva, who then finally rescued both climbers (Allison 2003). Similar stories tell of people being lost in a pass, shipwrecked on a boat off the coast of Indonesia, or stranded in the outback of Australia, who were all able to alert friends or family through their mobile telephones and consequently receive life-saving help (Turrettini 2004). Such stories readily feed myths of improved communication: without the new mobile communication devices, lives could have been severely impaired, or even lost.

However, increased security through networked wireless communication technologies can only be guaranteed if people are willing to sacrifice some or even all control over when they can and should be reached, and by whom. Forceful evidence of this highly charged problem created by the need to relieve anxiety can be found in one of the more common social relationships where reassurance plays an important role, namely that between parents and adolescents. On the one hand, the mobile telephone offers parents the ability to let their children discover the world on their own, with the added safety of knowing that the teenagers can always call in case of an emergency. But, on the other hand, notions of surveillance and accountability are sure to follow from a heightened absent presence of others. When one's whereabouts and activities are continuously under potential scrutiny, the mobile telephone becomes a mobile leash, exerting a strong influence over its carrier. Thus, in their adolescent quest for independence and in response to overly concerned parents, teenagers often develop 'parent management strategies' with which they regulate their reachability (Green 2002, 39).

While Green notes that the dominant association of terms like 'surveillance' and 'accountability' with state-controlled law enforcement does not do justice to the new ways in which individuals gather and share information, she holds that the proliferation of wireless communication technologies has 'normalized' the activity of checking up on others (ibid., 33). Through mobile devices, Green says, individuals 'engage in routine monitoring of themselves and each other (...), and assume that others are self-regulating and accountable for their use of devices in both co-present and tele-present contexts' (ibid., 43). Thus, everyday notions of what it means to feel reassured increasingly come to rely on knowing what others are up to, because the technological means to gain that knowledge are at one's disposal at all times. As a result, questions of privacy become more manifest. As sociologist James Rule asserts, compared to older, mass media systems, today's infrastructures of perpetual contact inherently generate more personalized information available to large institutions, corporations, and groups of individuals, making a future world of 'total surveillance' a conceivable reality (Rule 2002, 247). Although, like Green, Rule does not want to attach a specific value connotation to the term 'surveillance', he does point out that we should be cautious not to dismiss the dangers of this outlook too easily, or think that we can always escape observation by simply turning off our connections when we want to (ibid., 248). In the mobile age, perpetual contact becomes the norm, and participating without it difficult indeed.

These observations of ambivalence in mobile 'reassurance technologies' high-light the pitfall of the desire for pure communication: the more opportunities are created to connect and communicate, the more struggle there will be to hold on to established boundaries between the private and the public, between what can be known, should be known, and needs to be known. Wireless communication devices may be able to function as symbolic crowbars, breaking open social patterns of communicative behavior, but they can only do so at the expense of disclosing a lot more information than people might care to consider. What is more, there will always be the nagging uncertainty whether extra information is truly enough for one to be relieved of all anxiety. In fact, by seeking reassurance through radical connectedness, another type of anxiety is created, one that stems from simultaneously being connected to someone far away and knowing that that distance cannot be bridged physically. This spatial discrepancy may not be so problematic when a call is made for trivial reasons, but when related to an emergency, the state of being 'distant but present' can instil overwhelming feelings of isolation and powerlessness. A fickle balance between fear and relief manifests itself in the continuous search for reassurance; when Henrietta Thompson for instance states that mobile 'phones offer the best peace of mind it is possible to get', she does this in the context of Israel's continuous preparedness for terrorist attacks, where with 'the fear of [terrorism] always present, the need to communicate is paramount [and] people need to be able to check-up on their loved ones on short notice' (Thompson 2005, 55).

So, not only does the longing for perpetual contact create privacy issues, it also multiplies instances in which people are connected in extreme emotional circumstances while being physically apart. The torment of such 'intense immediacy', as James E. Katz (2006, 104) calls it, becomes adamantly clear in situations of life and death. Imagine, for instance, the conversation between the stranded mountaineer and his wife, whom he had called to say he was going to die (Cusk 2001). Or think of those other, highly profiled accounts of mobile calls in which Eros met Thanatos, made during and after the terrorist attacks in New York on September 11, 2001. People in the hijacked planes and those trapped inside the struck towers called family members to tell them that they loved them, sometimes right up to the moment when they died. After the towers had collapsed, rescue workers could hear people from under the wreckage use their mobile telephones to call for help, not seldom in vain. Most dreadful are the accounts of unanswered mobile telephones ringing in the rubble, or even in body bags.[2] All these cases vividly illustrate how feelings of reassurance and distress can come palpably close to merging into a single sentiment, how wireless communication technologies can augment both intimacy and isolation to such a degree that pure communication is indeed virtually reached, in all its real-time glory and ugliness.

Conclusion

As I aimed to show in the analyses of three of the most striking characteristics of mobile communication, a complex, ambivalent pattern can be distinguished in the ongoing process of mobilization. By increasing connectedness, transforming sociability, and opening up access to and the production of personal information, mobile communication devices fervently confront us with the paradoxes of pure communication, bringing us closer to the technological fulfilment of the desire for immediate togetherness, but at the same time letting us experience its ruthless blending of all actors involved. In all their ordinariness, mobile communication devices have showed and continue to show the potential to stealthily yet radically alter our perception of what it means to co-exist with others in a connected society.

This also means that our traditional understandings of concepts such as availability, privacy, accountability, safety, and security, which are all in particular ways dependent upon dominant modes of media deployment, will inevitably have to be rethought in order to reflect what it means to be in perpetual contact. In today's mobile communication condition, where the ability to 'just call' or 'just look up' is increasingly perceived as the primary solution to all kinds of problems, it becomes difficult – or even nonsensical – to think of people not being connected, or of information not being available. Not only will the social and political-economic pressure to join the growing interconnected communication network become more intense, the prevalent ideal of a fully transparent society will also force us to realize that everyone and everything is becoming subsumed within a single, all-encompassing communication regime, when it continues to be used as the fundamental guiding principle for new media developments. Unless we come to grips with the profound consequences inherent in the proliferation of mobile communication, we will fail to adequately address concerns of privacy, accountability, and safety in the connected society.

Notes

1. To illustrate this further, during the short-lived offer in 2000 by several mobile telephone operators to provide free calls in the evenings and on weekends, some people even chose to maintain a constant connection through their mobile telephones, and listen to each other sleeping (Licoppe 2003, 177).
2. Similar stories of 'ringing body bags' could be heard after the Madrid terrorist attacks in 2004 (BBC News 2004) and the Virginia Tech shootings in 2007 (King 2007).

References

Allison, Rebecca. 2003. Climbers on Alpine ridge rescued by text message. *The Guardian*. http://www.guardian.co.uk/uk_news/story/0,3604,1057271,00.html.

Arnold, Michael. 2003. On the phenomenology of technology: The 'Janus-faces' of mobile phones. *Information and Organization* 13 (4): 231–256.

BBC News. 2004. European press ask 'Why?'. *BBC News International*. http://news.bbc.co.uk/2/hi/europe/3504032.stm.

Campbell, Scott. 2007. A cross-cultural comparison of perceptions and uses of mobile telephony. *New Media & Society* 9 (2): 343-363.

Castells, Manuel. 1996. *The information age: Economy, society and culture, Volume 1: The rise of the network society*. Malden, MA: Blackwell.

Castells, Manuel, Mireia Fernandez-Ardevol, Jack Linchuan Qiu, and Araba Sey. 2007. *Mobile communication and society: A global perspective*. Cambridge, MA: MIT Press.

Chipchase, Jan. 2005. Why do people carry mobile phones? *Future perfect*. http://www.jan-chipchase.com/blog/archives/2005/11/mobile_essentia.html.

Cumiskey, Kathleen. 2005. 'Can you hear me now?': Paradoxes of techno-intimacy resulting from the public use of mobile communication technology. In *A sense of place: The global and the local in mobile communication*, ed. Kristóf Nyíri, 151-158. Vienna: Passagen.

Cusk, Rachel. 2001. Finding words. *The Guardian*. http://www.guardian.co.uk/world/2001/sep/14/september11.politicsphilosophyandsociety1.

Fox, Kate. 2001. Evolution, alienation and gossip: The role of mobile telecommunications in the 21st century. *Social Issues Research Centre*. http://www.sirc.org/publik/gossip.shtml.

Gergen, Kenneth. 2002. The challenge of absent presence. In *Perpetual contact: Mobile communication, private talk, public performance*, eds. James E. Katz and Mark Aakhus, 227-241. Cambridge: Cambridge University Press.

—. 2003. Self and community in the new floating worlds. In *Mobile democracy: Essays on society, self and politics*, ed. Kristóf Nyíri, 103-114. Vienna: Passagen.

Green, Nicola. 2002. Who's watching whom? Monitoring and accountability in mobile relations. In *Wireless world: Social and interactional aspects of the mobile age*, eds. Barry Brown, Nicola Green, and Richard Harper, 32-45. London: Springer.

—. 2003. Outwardly mobile: Young people and mobile technologies. In *Machines that become us: The social context of personal communication technology*, ed. James E. Katz, 201-217. New Brunswick, NJ: Transaction Publishers.

Ito, Mizuko, Daisuke Okabe, and Misa Matsuda. 2005. *Personal, portable, pedestrian: Mobile phones in Japanese life*. Cambridge, MA: MIT Press.

Johnsen, Truls Erik. 2003. The social context of the mobile phone use of Norwegian teens. In *Machines that become us: The social context of personal communication technology*, ed. James E. Katz, 161-169. New Brunswick, NJ: Transaction Publishers.

Katz, James, and Mark Aakhus, eds. 2002. *Perpetual contact: Mobile communication, private talk, public performance*. Cambridge: Cambridge University Press.

Katz, James. 2006. *Magic in the air: Mobile communication and the transformation of social life*. New Brunswick, NJ: Transaction Publishers.

King, John. 2007. Cell phones of dead still rang. *CNN.com – Anderson Cooper 360° Blog*. http://edition.cnn.com/CNN/Programs/anderson.cooper.360/blog/2007/04/volunteer-contributes-what-he-can-body.html.

Kopomaa, Timo. 2000. *The city in your pocket: Birth of the mobile information society*. Helsinki: Gaudeamus.

Licoppe, Christian. 2003. Two modes of maintaining interpersonal relations through tele-phone: From the domestic to the mobile phone. In *Machines that become us: The social context of personal communication technology*, ed. James E. Katz, 171-185. New Brunswick, NJ: Transaction Publishers.

Ling, Richard. 2004. *The mobile connection: The cell phone's impact on society*. San Francisco, CA: Morgan Kaufmann.

Ling, Richard, and Birgitte Yttri. 2002. Hyper-coordination via mobile phones in Norway. In *Perpetual contact: Mobile communication, private talk, public performance*, eds. James E. Katz and Mark Aakhus, 139-169. Cambridge: Cambridge University Press.

Myerson, George. 2001. *Heidegger, Habermas and the mobile phone*. London: Icon Books.

Palen, Leysia, Marilyn Salzman, and Ed Youngs. 2000. Going wireless: Behavior & practice of new mobile phone users. *Proceedings of the 2000 ACM conference on computer supported cooperative work*, 201-210.

Plant, Sadie. 2001. On the mobile: The effects of mobile telephones on social and individ-ual life. *Motorola*. http://www.motorola.com/mot/doc/0/234_MotDoc.pdf.

Rule, James. 2002. From mass society to perpetual contact: Models of communication technologies in social context. In *Perpetual contact: Mobile communication, private talk, public performance*, eds. James E. Katz and Mark Aakhus, 242-254. Cambridge: Cambridge University Press.

Sherry, John, and Tony Salvador. 2002. Running and grimacing: The struggle for balance in mobile work. In *Wireless world: Social and interactional aspects of the mobile age*, eds. Barry Brown, Nicola Green, and Richard Harper, 108-120. London: Springer.

Thompson, Henrietta. 2005. *Phone book: A handy guide to the world's favourite invention*. London: Thames & Hudson.

Townsend, Anthony. 2002. Mobile communications in the twenty-first century city. In *Wireless world: Social and interactional aspects of the mobile age*, eds. Barry Brown, Nicola Green, and Richard Harper, 62-77. London: Springer.

Turrettini, Emily. 2004. Lost hikers use text messaging to gain help. *Textually.org*. http://www.textually.org/textually/archives/2004/07/004683.htm.

—. 2007. Cell phones cause insomnia. *Textually.org*. http://www.textually.org/textually/archives/2007/08/016895.htm.

Vincent, Jane. 2003. Emotion and mobile phones. In *Mobile democracy: Essays on society, self and politics*, ed. Kristóf Nyíri, 215-224. Vienna: Passagen.

The work of art in the age of digital recombination

Jos de Mul

Artists, from the prehistoric painters who engraved and painted figures on cave walls to new media artists whose work depends on computer technologies, have always used media. Media, used here in the broad sense as 'means for presenting information'[1], are not innocent instruments. Ever since Kant's Copernican revolution, we know that experience is constituted and structured by the forms of sensibility and the categories of human understanding, and after the so-called linguistic and mediatic turns in philosophy, it is generally assumed that media play a crucial role in the configuration of the human mind and experience. Media are interfaces that mediate not only between us and our world (designation), but also between us and our fellow man (communication), and between us and ourselves (self-understanding). Aesthetic experience is no exception: artistic media are interfaces that not only structure the imagination of the artist, but the work of art and the aesthetic reception as well.[2]

In this paper I aim to contribute to this reflection by analyzing the way the computer interface constitutes and structures aesthetic experience. My point of departure will be Walter Benjamin's 'The work of art in the age of mechanical reproduction', first published in the *Zeitschrift für Sozialforschung* in 1936. In this epochal essay Benjamin investigates how mechanical reproduction transforms the work of art, claiming that in this ontological transformation the *cult value*, which once characterized the classical work of art, has been replaced by *exhibition value*. The thesis I will defend in this paper is, first, that in the age of digital recombination, the database constitutes the ontological model of the work of art and, secondly, that in this transformation the exhibition value is being replaced by what we might call *manipulation value*.

Before I turn to Benjamin's notions of cult value and exhibition value, I want to make a short remark concerning the scope of Benjamin's essay. Though the title of his work promises an analysis of art, the scope is actually much wider. It is also an essay on economics, politics and religion. And on a deeper level, connecting these and yet other domains, it deals with a fundamental ontological change, a transformation of human experience, closely connected to the mechanization of the reproduction of nature and culture. Likewise, the scope of my continuation of

Benjamin's analysis in the age of the digital recombination is broader than art or aesthetics. It deals with the digital manipulation of nature and culture that characterizes the present 'age of informatization' (De Mul 1999).

Cult value vs. exhibition value

Although Benjamin emphasizes at the beginning of his essay that the work of art in principle has always been reproducible, in principle he states that mechanical reproduction presents us with a new phenomenon. With the emergence of woodcut graphics, engraving and etching in the Middle Ages and lithography in the beginning of the 19th century, mechanical reproduction became a major artistic technique. However, it was only with the invention and the swift dissemination of photography and film that mechanical reproduction became the dominant cultural interface.

Before that time the work of art's dominant type was characterized by uniqueness (Einmaligkeit) and singularity (Einzigkeit) in time and space. The original work of art is here and now: 'Even the most perfect reproduction of a work of art is lacking in one element: its presence in time and space, its unique existence at the place where it happens to be' (Benjamin 1969). There is only one Mona Lisa, and when we want to see this painting, we have to go to the Louvre in Paris (Figure 1[3]).

According to Benjamin the unique existence of the work of art determines the history to which it is subject throughout the time of its existence. This includes, for example, the changes which it may have suffered in its physical condition over the years as well as the various changes in its ownership.

> The traces of the first can be revealed only by chemical or physical analyses which it is impossible to perform on a reproduction; changes of ownership are subject to a tradition which must be traced from the situation of the original. The presence of the original is the prerequisite to the concept of authenticity. (...) The authenticity of a thing is the essence of all that is transmissible from its beginning, ranging from its substantive duration to its testimony to the history which it has experienced.

Another word that Benjamin uses to designate the material and historical authenticity and authority of the unique work of art is 'aura'. Because of this aura, the unique work of art can easily become an object of a magical or religious cult.

> We know that the earliest art works originated in the service of a ritual – first the magical, then the religious kind. It is significant that the existence of the work of art with reference to its aura is never entirely separated from its ritual function. In other words, the unique value of the 'authentic' work of art has its

basis in ritual, the location of its original use value. This ritualistic basis, however remote, is still recognizable as secularized ritual even in the most profane forms of the cult of beauty.

In a footnote Benjamin introduces the concept of *cult value*, and he connects it with its aura. In this context he also gives an intriguing definition of the latter concept:

> The definition of the aura as a 'unique phenomenon of a distance however close it may be' represents nothing but the formulation of the cult value of the work of art in categories of space and time perception. Distance is the opposite of closeness. The essentially distant object is the unapproachable one. Unapproachability is indeed a major quality of the cult image. True to its nature, it remains 'distant, however close it may be.' The closeness which one may gain from its subject matter does not impair the distance which it retains in its appearance.

When we – anachronistically – apply a key concept of the new media studies to Benjamin's analysis, we might say that the auratic work of art acts as an interface between the sensible and the supersensible, that is: between the physical materiality of the work of art and its meaningful history. Although it may be close in its material presence – we could even touch the *Mona Lisa* if there were no glass separating it from its visitors in the Louvre – and as such it brings us in close contact with its history, at the same time we experience the historical tradition in which it is embedded and from which it derives its meaning as an unbridgeable distance.

It is important to notice that in the auratic work of art the sensible and the supersensible, the material signifier and the spiritual meaning, are inseparably linked with one another. As such, the auratic work of art, as Gadamer states in *The relevance of the beautiful* in connection with a short but illuminating discussion of Benjamin's essay, can be conceived of as a *symbol*.[4] The destruction of an auratic work destroys the distant presence of its history as well. For that reason the destruction of an auratic work of art is generally understood as an act of blasphemy – independent of whether it has a religious content or not.

It is also important to notice that for Benjamin the experience of aura is not restricted to historical objects such as works of art. Benjamin also applies the concept of aura to natural objects. When we watch a mountain range on the horizon or a branch casting its shadow over us, we also experience the aura – in this case: the natural history – of those mountains, of that branch. We could also think about the historical sensation we experience when we look at, or touch, a fossil, for instance the skeleton of a dinosaur.

One of the basic claims of Benjamin's 'The work of art' is that in the age of mechanical reproduction by means of print, photography and film, we experience a radical loss of aura:

> That which withers in the age of mechanical reproduction is the aura of the work of art. This is a symptomatic process whose significance points beyond the realm of art. One might generalize by saying: the technique of reproduction detaches the reproduced object from the domain of tradition. By making many reproductions it substitutes a plurality of copies for a unique existence. And in permitting the reproduction to meet the beholder or listener in his own particular situation, it reactivates the object reproduced.

One might say that mechanical reproduction of images brings things closer, spatially and temporally. In order to watch the Mona Lisa, I no longer have to travel to Paris, I can look up a reproduction in an art magazine or on my mobile phone with an Internet connection, immediately, here and now (Figure 2). Uniqueness and permanence of the auratic object are being replaced by transitoriness and reproducibility.

In a reproduction of the *Mona Lisa*, the reproduction still refers to the original work of art – something Andy Warhol smartly capitalizes on in his reproductions of Leonardo's famous painting (see Figure 3). Actually, in the media of mechanical reproduction the whole distinction between original and copy loses its meaning. No copy of a photo or a movie is more original than the others. Whereas traditionally things were first produced and then reproduced, in the age of mechanical reproduction things are being made directly with an eye to reproduction: 'To an ever greater degree the work of art reproduced becomes the work of art designed for reproducibility' (ibid).

According to Benjamin, together with the aura, the cult value of artworks will gradually vanish. For emotional or economical reasons one can, of course, try to conserve the cult value. For example by printing a photograph in a limited edition, having the photographer put his signature on it, or by promoting an actress as a unique movie star. Actually these 'cheats' only confirm the loss of the aura of the work itself. That does not mean, however, that the mechanical copy doesn't have value at all. Rather, in photography and film, the cult value gives way to *exhibition value*, which is precisely situated in the endless reproduction of the copies. This especially becomes clear in the case of celebrities like Paris Hilton, who do not have any unique talents but are just 'famous for being famous'. In the same vein, the success of politicians strongly depends on how mediagenic they are, that is: on their exhibition value. The fact that in the USA even a B-film actor like Reagan can become president is an ironic illustration of Benjamin's foresight.

Benjamin's essay has melancholic undertones. When he states that the aura emanates for the last time from the early photographs in the fleeting expression of a human face, he not only mourns the loss of the 'incomparable beauty' and 'melancholy' of these early photographs, but also the notion that we experience the human being itself as losing its aura. However, at the same time – and this shows the fundamental ambiguity of the essay – Benjamin also expresses his belief that the 'mechanical media' possess a fundamental democratic and even revolutionary potential. Not only do they enable 'access for all', they also enable the progressive artist to 'politicize the arts' and mobilize the masses against the fascist 'aesthetization of politics' (ibid.). By now we know that mass media can indeed mobilize masses, though more often in the direction of the shopping mall than in the direction of the government building.

The development of mechanical reproduction can neither simply be hailed as cultural progress nor simply doomed as cultural decline. Mechanical reproduction discloses the world in a new way, bringing along both new opportunities and new dangers. We should keep this fundamental ambiguity of the development of media in mind when we turn our attention to digital recombination.

Database ontology

No other text has been quoted so often in new media studies as Benjamin's 'The work of art' (Davis 1995; Harvey 1989; Thomson 1995; Gumbrecht and Marrinan 2003; Benjamin 2005). This is not surprising, as his prophetic vision only seems to have gained in relevance in the age of digital recombination. However, although the computer is still a mechanical machine, we should not simply equate digital reproduction with mechanical reproduction (and for that reason I prefer the phrase 'digital recombination'). Although the computer can simulate all kinds of classical mechanical machines and media, such as a typewriter, a sound recorder, or a device for the montage of images, it has some unique medium-specific characteristics that justify the claim that it represents a new stage in the development of media.

Understood as a medium, the computer is not one but many. Artists use computers in many different ways to produce, store, display and distribute so-called 'new media art'. As a means of production, for example, computers enable them to create digital images and sounds, to build interactive installations, to design multimedia websites, or to program self-evolving art forms. However, the thesis I want to defend is that on a fundamental level all media art works share some basic characteristics. Although concrete media art works may differ from each other in many different respects – and for that reason show a family resemblance rather than a single essence – on a fundamental level they all share the four basic operations of persistent storage, an integral part of almost all computer software. This ABCD of computing consists of the operations Add, Browse, Change, and

Destroy.[5] Together these four operations – which correspond to the structured query language (SQL) commands Insert, Select, Update, and Delete – constitute the dynamic elements of what we might call a *database ontology*.

In a basic sense the word 'database' can refer to any collection of items that is ordered in one way or another. In computing, a database can be defined as a structured collection of data records that is stored in a computer, so that a software program can consult it to answer queries. With the four basic operations all possible combinations of records can be retrieved in principle. Database ontology is dynamic, because the data elements can be constantly combined, decombined, and recombined.

In reality, not all databases are that flexible. The traditional 'flat' paper database, a phone book for example, is rather inflexible. The alphabetic order of the names is fixed, and to update the list you have to reprint the entire book. A card-index box, consisting of cards with a limited number of fields for the input of information (for example name, address, and phone number) would already be more flexible regarding updating. Reorganizing this database – for example to group the records per country for a mailing – is possible, but would consume a lot of time. Although an electronic version of a flat database – a spreadsheet – could speed up the sorting of the data, it remains inflexible with regard to the creation and exploration of structural relationships between the data.

From the 1950s on new types of electronic databases have been developed, the hierarchical model in the 1950s, the network model in the 1960s and the relational model in the 1970s. The last model, which is based on predicate logic and set theory (Codd 1970), contains multiple tables, each consisting of a 'flat' database of rows and columns. The relational database as a whole is multidimensional, and for that reason its complexity cannot be represented on a flat plane and often not even in a three-dimensional model. One of the strengths of the relational model is that, in principle, any value occurring in two different records (belonging to the same table or to different tables) implies a relationship between those two records. Relational databases are extremely flexible, because they enable the users to define queries that were not anticipated by the database designers.

The current development of database models shows a tendency to even more flexibility and a rapidly growing range of applications. Database applications nowadays span virtually the entire range of computer software, ranging from mainframe databases for administrative purposes and multimedia encyclopedias on cd-roms to search engines, wikis and other Web 2.0 applications on the Internet.

However, the impact of databases is not restricted to the world of computing. Databases often function as *material metaphors*. This happens when they evoke acts in the material world (Hayles 2002). Examples of these are biotechnological databases used for genetic engineering, or databases implemented in industrial robots, enabling mass customization. In addition, databases may create a surplus of meaning, on top of their instrumental function (cf. Van den Boomen, in preparation). In that case the database functions as a *conceptual metaphor* which structures our experience of ourselves and of the world.

The psychologist Maslov once noticed that for those who only have a hammer, everything appears to be a nail. In a world in which the computer has become the dominant technology – worldwide more than 50 billion processors are doing their job – everything is becoming a database. As Manovich states, databases have become the dominant cultural form of the computer age (Manovich 2002, 219).[6] They are 'onto-logical machines' that shape both our world and our world view. Benjamin argues in his essay that in the age of mechanical reproduction, everything becomes an object for mechanical reproduction. This has contributed to what is sometimes called a mechanization of the world view. In the age of digital databases, everything – nature and culture alike – becomes an object for recombination and manipulation.

Let us take genetic engineering as an example. The evolution of life on earth is no longer regarded as a natural history determined by the struggle for life and the survival of the fittest (as in classic Darwinism), but rather as one possible (contingent) trajectory through the gene pool. Actually, this biological database contains an infinite number of virtual organisms and life forms (trajectories), which in principle can be actualized. Although not yet as spectacular as in Spielberg's *Jurassic Park* or in science-fiction films such as *Robocop*, our world is increasingly being populated with life forms created with database technologies. Why not, for example, create a mouse with a human ear on its back or design a fluorescent rabbit to watch it (Figures 4 and 5)?

Unlike *Jurassic Park* and *Robocop*, these examples are not the products of mere digital imaging. The mouse with the engineered human ear implanted on its back is the result of a medical experiment, carried out by Charles Vacanti at the University of Massachusetts Medical Center in 1995, whereas the fluo rabbit was 'created' by the Brazilian artist Eduard Kac, who commissioned the 'transgenic' bunny from a French lab, where scientists injected green fluorescent protein (GFP) of a Pacific jellyfish into the ovum of an Albino rabbit (Vesna 2007).

Both Vacanti's and Kac's experiments have lead to heated ethical debates. In the case of Kac's fluo rabbit, the question was also raised whether this 'work' can be called a work of art. In this sense the rabbit provokes similar questions as did, about ninety years ago, Duchamp's ready-mades, such as L.H.O.O.Q., a cheap postcard-sized reproduction of the *Mona Lisa*, upon which Duchamp drew a mustache and a goatee (Figure 6). Both Duchamp's L.H.O.O.Q. and Kac's fluo rabbit raise the question of whether they are a work of art since they both employ a new, seemingly non-artistic medium of production as a means for artistic expression, questioning the very distinction between artistic and non-artistic objects. While this may elucidate the reason for posing this aesthetical question, it does not provide an answer to it. As Benjamin's essay suggests an answer, we will return to it once more.

Database aesthetics and politics

In 'The work of art' Benjamin remarks that there is no timeless answer to the question of whether a particular object should be regarded as a work of art. An object that was once an instrument of magic could later come to be recognized as a work of art. In the same way, Benjamin suggests, 'by the absolute emphasis on its exhibition value the work of art becomes a creation with entirely new functions, among which the one we are conscious of, the artistic function, later may be recognized as incidental' (Benjamin 1969).

Whereas in the age of mechanical reproduction it was already becoming difficult to distinguish between the artistic and non-artistic functions of the reproduction – hence, for example, the aesthetization of politics and the politization of art which plays such an important role in Benjamin's essay – in the age of digital recombination, the distinction seems to get blurred altogether. Let me illustrate this by discussing a recent database work of the Dutch computer artist and video jockey Geert Mul. Commissioned by the Dutch Photo Museum in Rotterdam, he built the interactive installation W4 (WHO, WHAT, WHEN, WHERE).[7] This installation consists of a database containing 80,000 photographs from the digital archive of the museum and four posts that function as a filter (Figure 7). With the help of the functions who, what, when and where, the user can explore the entire digitalized collection. For example, one can investigate all photographs of flowers made in Germany in 1936. Or all pictures of the Mona Lisa made between 1900 and 1920. The installation can be regarded as an interface designed to enable the visitors to display the collection. Every visitor of the museum becomes a curator, able to create her own exhibitions. At the same time it is a powerful interactive artwork which transforms the visitors into VJs who create rhythmic compositions of photographs.

What makes this installation both a brilliant example of human-computer interface design and an autonomous work of art is its *manipulation value*. In the age of digital recombination, the value of an object depends on the extent of its openness for manipulation.[8] For a contemporary scholar, a 'databased' version of the collected works of a philosopher is of much greater value than a traditional paper edition, because it enables her to execute all kinds of sophisticated searches, to investigate implicit relationships between the texts, and to make new recombinations of existing texts (De Mul, 2008). The aesthetic quality of a work strongly depends on the elegance of the structure of the database and its user interface.[9] As soon as the database play becomes a goal in itself, the database becomes an autonomous work of art. As W4 shows, a database can be both an instance of applied user interface design and an autonomous work of art.

As the number of recombinations of a database is almost infinite, the work of art in the age of digital recombination brings about a return of the aura. Especially in those cases where the user is enabled to change the contents of the database and to insert new elements in the database, each query becomes a unique recombination. And as a consequence, the digitally recombined work of art regains something of its ritual dimension. It becomes an interface between the sensible and the supersensible again, now no longer located in the history of the work, but in its *virtuality*, that is: the intangible totality of possible recombinations. In the domain of culture we could think, for example, of websites such as *Mega Mona Lisa*, where vistors are being invited to create and discuss their unique own version of Leonardo's *Mona Lisa* (Figure 8). In these versions we witness 'the return of the aura'. However, it is a return with a twist: what we experience is a series of 'original, auratic copies' (Davis 1995). The return is also twisted because digitally manipulated objects are even more transient than mechanical reproductions. Because of their manipulability, digital objects seem to be inherently unstable, like the performing arts process rather than product (cf. Bolle 1992).

As already noted, database ontology is not restricted to the domain of culture, but applies to nature as well. In both domains database ontology shows a posthistorical character. In the age of digital recombination, dinosaurs are no longer exclusively extinct species, they have become a future possibility as well.[10] Again, the result will be a series of 'auratic copies'. After all, as they will appear in a drastically changed environment, they will unavoidably be a different species.

Like Benjamin we may ask how such digitally recombined works can function as political works of art. Digital recombination as a means of production is no less political than mechanical reproduction. Power, political power included, is becoming increasingly dependent on the ability to manipulate information. One of the most prophetic claims in Benjamin's essay is that in the age of mechanical reproduction, the success of political leaders became increasingly dependent on their exhibition value. However, in the western world Ronald Reagan was probably the last president who could still mainly rely on his exhibition value. In the age of digital manipulation, politicians are becoming more and more dependent on their manipulation value. We could think of Bush's intended manipulation of computer-mediated elections, or the rhetorically motivated recombination of images in Geert Wilders's propaganda movie *Fitna*, but also of the non-criminal everyday recombination of data in order to create, control and evaluate financial, economical and social policies.

Yet for a work of art to be political, it is not enough to be digitally recombined. Digitally recombined works of art differ from other digitally recombined objects because they have a reflective quality as well. A work of art challenges its recipients by directing their attention to the medium itself. Works of art are not political because they manipulate politics, but because they reflect (on) the politics of manipulation. Only insofar as the fluo rabbit makes us reflect on such media politics can it be called political art.[11]

A work that invites the spectator to political reflection is Geert Mul's *Match of the day* (2006), part of an art works database series, entitled *Split Representations*. In the case of *Match of the day*, 'a computer collects images from about thirty international satellite television channels at random intervals. During the night, image-recognition software analyzes the recorded images. It compares television news with television commercials. The software compares every image with every other single image stored in the computer, checking 5000 specified characteristics in each image. After 1,000,000,000 comparisons, the computer generates a list. Images that share the most characteristics appear in pairs at the top of this list. The artist then selects a few pairs of images out of the hundreds of pairs of images, which according to the computer make a good visual match. In a daily e-mail-series subscribers receive this selection: the match of the day' (Figure 9, Mul 2006).

By combining television news with television commercials, the matches of the day represent the current socio-economic situation of the western world. On this level it is a representation and manipulation of politics. However, the recipient also gradually becomes aware of the politics of representation and manipulation. 'The computer does not "understand" the images, it just applies pixel statistics. For the human eye visual similarity is something else than pixel statistics. Because of our inability to "see" without interpretation we attach "meaning" to everything we see. This becomes especially evident when similar images appear to have a different or even contrary meaning. The "matches" found by the computer and selected by the artist, trigger sensations of poetry, humor, beauty or disgust' (Mul 2006).

Gradually, we become aware of the inapproachability of the workings of a technology that we have invented. And we might even start to reflect on the non-human and maybe even inhuman character of this new medium. Or on the possibility that it will gradually outstrip our skills to add, browse, change and destroy. And that we might become the ultimate object of digital manipulation. In 'The work of art' Benjamin worries about the fact that mechanical reproduction alienates human beings. Realizing the possibility that we might be the first species that creates its own successors in the evolution of life and by doing so makes *itself* redundant, Benjamin's worries may soon become an object for nostalgia.

Notes

1. We should realize that the concept 'media' covers many different categories by which we define media and differentiate them from other media. Even when we restrict ourselves to so-called 'new media', the word 'media' might refer to a variety of different things, such as material carriers, production technologies or distribution apparatus.

2. This view does not imply media determinism. 'Technology does not determine society: it embodies it. But neither does society determine technological innovation: it uses it' (Castells 1996, 5). In other words: media develop in a constant dialectical interplay with other cultural domains, such as science, economy and politics, and cannot be abstracted from human action and decisions.
3. The illustrations are available online: http://www2.eur.nl/fw/hyper/illustrations.htm.
4. 'I propose that the symbolic in general, and especially the symbolic in art, rests upon an intricate interplay of showing and concealing. In its irreplaceability, the work of art is no mere bearer of meaning – as if the meaning could be transferred to another bearer. Rather the meaning of the work of art lies in the fact that it is there' (Gadamer 1986, 33).
5. These four basic operations are also referred to with the acronyms CRUD (Create, Read, Update, Delete) and ACID (Add, Change, Inquire, Delete).
6. Manovich defines the database as 'an *unstructured* collection of images, texts, and other data records' and claims that 'the database in its most purest form' is 'a set of elements *not ordered* in any way' (Manovich 2002, 219, 238, italics JdM) and for that reason opposes the database to the cultural form of the narrative, which 'creates a cause-and-effect trajectory of seemingly unordered items' (ibid, 225). I would argue, rather, that narrative and database structure our often chaotic world in a different way. Whereas a narrative is linear and structures the world through linking events (predominantly past) by narrative causality, the non-linear tabular structure of the database enables the user to manipulate future events. The narrative is not so much an antagonist of the database, but rather one particular trajectory through a database, as Manovich himself acknowledges: 'The "user" of a narrative is traversing a database, following links between its records as established by the database's creator. An interactive narrative (which can be also called a hypernarrative in an analogy with hypertext) can then be understood as the sum of multiple trajectories through a database' (ibid., 227, cf. De Mul 2005).
7. See http://www.geertmul.nl/Geert_Mul/NederlandsFotomuseum.html.
8. A similar point has been made by William J. Mitchell: 'If mechanical image reproduction substituted exhibition value for cult value as Benjamin claimed, digital imaging further substitutes a new kind of use value – *input* value, the capacity to be manipulated by computer – for exhibition value' (Mitchell 1994, 52).
9. Cf. Daniel 2000: 'A "conception" of the "beauty" of a database is not located in the viewer's interpretation of a static form but in the dynamics of how a user inflects the database through interaction with its field or frame. A database incorporates contradiction; it is simultaneously recombinant and indexical, precise and scaleable, immersive and emergent, homogeneous and heterogeneous. It is a field of coherence and contradiction. The aesthetic dimensions of the database arise when the user traverses this field of unresolved contradictions. (...) Continuously emergent ontological states resolve as new subfields from each interaction and are integrated into the field – changing and transforming the content and structure of that field and constituting the "art object" as a continuously evolving and fluid system. These are the conditions of possibility of a "database aesthetics"' (Daniel 2000).
10. In this sense the database ontology combines *virtual reality* (understood as the infinite number of possible recombinations) with *real virtuality* (the recombinations that are actually being realized).
11. Although the intention of the artist is not decisive, in the case of Kac the aim without doubt is political: 'My work doesn't visualize science, it is not meant to duplicate the information that circulates from science to media to the public. It is meant to intervene, to change, to criticize, point out, reflect and modify' (quoted in Allmendinger 2001).

References

Allmendinger, Ulli. 2001. One small hop for Alba, one large hop for mankind. *NY Arts Magazine* 6 (6).

Benjamin, Andrew E. 2005. *Walter Benjamin and art.* London/New York: Continuum.

Benjamin, Walter. 1969. The work of art in the age of mechanical reproduction. In *Illuminations.* New York: Schocken Books.

Bolle, E., ed. 1992. *Book for the unstable media.* Den Bosch: V2.

Boomen, Marianne van den. In preparation. *Transcoding the Internet: How metaphors matter in digital praxis.* PhD thesis, Department of Media and Culture Studies Utrecht University, Utrecht.

Castells, Manuel. 1996. *The rise of the network society.* Oxford: Blackwell Publishers.

Codd, E.F. 1970. A relational model of data for large shared data banks. *Communications of the ACM* 13 (6):377-387.

Daniel, Sharon. 2000. Collaborative systems: Evolving databases and the 'conditions of possibility': Artificial life models of agency in on-line interactive art. *AI & Society: The Journal of Human-Centered and Machine Intelligence* 14: 196-213.

Davis, Douglas. 1995. The work of art in the age of digital reproduction: An evolving thesis. *Leonardo* 28 (5):381-386.

Gadamer, Hans Georg. 1986. *The relevance of the beautiful and other essays.* Cambridge: Cambridge University Press.

Gumbrecht, Hans Ulrich, and Michael Marrinan, eds. 2003. *Mapping Benjamin: The work of art in the digital age.* Stanford: Stanford University Press.

Harvey, David. 1989. The work of art in the age of electronic reproduction and image banks. In *The condition of postmodernity.* Oxford: Basic Blackwell.

Hayles, N. Katherine. 2002. *Writing machines.* Cambridge, MA: MIT Press.

Manovich, Lev. 2001. *The language of new media.* Cambridge, MA: MIT Press.

Mitchell, William J. 1994. *The reconfigured eye: Visual truth in the post-photographic era.* Cambridge: MIT Press.

Mul, Geert. 2006. Match of the day. http://www.geertmul.nl/Geert_Mul/MATCH-OF-THE-DAY.html.

Mul, Jos de. 1999. The informatization of the worldview. *Information, Communication & Society* 2 (1):604-629.

—. 2005. The game of life: Narrative and ludic identity formation in computer games. In *Handbook of computer games studies,* eds. J. Goldstein and J. Raessens. Cambridge: MIT Press.

—. 2005. Résonances de la mort de Dieu, après les fins de l'art. *Figures de l'Art. Revue d'Études Esthétiques* No X: 265-277.

—. 2008. Wittgenstein 2.0: Philosophical reading and writing after the mediatic turn. In *Wittgenstein and information theory,* eds. A. Pichler and H. Hrachovec. Wien: AWLS.

Thomson, Douglass H. 1995. The work of art in the age of electronic (re)production. http://www.erudit.org/revue/ron/1998/v/n10/005805ar.html.

Vesna, Victoria, ed. 2007. *Database aesthetics: Art in the age of information overflow.* Minneapolis: University of Minnesota Press.

The design of world citizenship

A historical comparison between world exhibitions and the web

Berteke Waaldijk

In this article I propose to compare the web, and especially Web 2.0, with world exhibitions organised in the second half of the 19th century.[1] Such a historical and intermedia comparison may raise new questions that analyse processes of inclusion and exclusion and the role of the medium in these processes, especially regarding the way in which political and commercial aims are purposefully combined in both instances.

The Internet and world exhibitions both provide assemblages of information, entertainment, commerce, social cohesion and possibilities for political participation. At the world exhibitions, political objectives (popularisation of imperialism, educating inhabitants into national citizens), commercial goals (profits by selling food, drinks, and entertainment), and educational aims (informing citizens of new developments in technology, promoting knowledge of the world) complemented each other (Rydell 1984; Greenhalgh 1989; Grever and Waaldijk 2004). The historical comparison helps me to ask new questions about the citizenship that is created in the context of digitally mediated environments.

World exhibitions constituted a new medium in the 19th century. Exhibitions were fenced-off spaces wherein experiments in new forms of representation took place. It is therefore possible to study the connections between external exclusion and the hierarchies produced within the gates of the exhibition. It is this interconnection that I want to compare to the ways by which digital information and communication technology exclude and include people, set them free, entertain and mobilise them.

Historical comparisons

Historical comparisons have quite a tradition in new media research. Reaching back to historical predecessors and forerunners is a significant narrative structure in understanding the digital revolution. John Barlow (1996), who dismisses all forms of governmental interference in the 'new world' of digital communication, wrapped this message in a rewriting of the United States Declaration of Independence for cyberspace. Hakim Bey (1991) compared autonomous internet communities in the 1990s to 18th-century pirate zones. Several studies have shown that such comparisons carry undertheorized assumptions regarding class, gender and ethnicity. Richard Barbrook and Andy Cameron (2001) pointed out that the digital freedom claimed by the 'Founding Fathers' from Silicon Valley was modeled on a system of slavery with economic inequality. Laura Miller (1995) showed how the image of cyberspace as the Wild West irrefutably leads to representations of women and children as weak creatures who need protection. Lisa Nakamura (2002) argued that, contrary to the idea of 'leaving our bodies behind' in this supposedly unmarked new country, racial stereotypes are hardwired into online interactions.

Historical comparisons have also been employed to research specific aspects of the introduction of new media. Comparisons between form and extent of governmental support for the introduction of radio allowed Robert McChesney (1999) to describe the interactions between public space and commercial objectives in digital media. Lisa Gitelman (2006) described how recorded sound and digitally networked text each emerged as local anomalies embedded within the logic of public life and public memory. Liesbet van Zoonen (2000) pointed to the introduction of the telephone to indicate the gender specificity of a new medium. Lev Manovich (2002) compared the rise of digital media to early cinema, and through literary studies, Marie-Laure Ryan (2006) compared the ways immersion and interactivity are created in classic literary texts and in computer games.

Historical comparisons may allow us to see elements in new (and old) media and forms of representation that were not (yet) explicit. In order to play that role, historical research should go beyond producing either timeless similarities between all forms of representation or teleological stories of progress or decline. This article is meant as a push for more historical comparative research in order to understand better the possibilities and limitations of new media in processes of inclusion and exclusion.

Utopia or nightmare?

The boom of the Internet in the 1990s has given rise to heated debates with diametrically opposed perspectives. Those adhering to the emancipatory and democratic potential of the new medium hailed the coming of a 'cyberutopia' with unlimited participation and opportunities to speak one's mind (Lanham 1993; Barlow 1996; Landow 1997). These optimists foresaw the democratisation of all communication, as well as the erosion of traditional authorities and power relations. Alternately, pessimists saw heightened exclusion. According to them, the development of the Internet enforces white men's power and their financial interests, and strengthens the renewed exclusion of groups that were already marginalised on the basis of gender, skin colour, poverty or sexual preference (Luke 2000; Barbrook and Cameron 2001).

Hence, on the one hand, digital culture and communication were praised as the cradle of total democratisation; on the other hand, they were condemned as the newest form of social division. The current debates about Web 2.0 are also marked by these opposites. Web 2.0 is praised as 'the architecture of participation' (O'Reilly 2005; Jenkins 2006) and as final democracy in the form of 'wisdom of the crowds' (Surowiecki 2004; Leadbetter 2008). Others warn that Web 2.0 sites like Hyves, MySpace, YouTube and Flickr constitute just another way to commercially exploit interhuman communication, now by extracting data and free labor from users (Terranova 2004; Lovink 2008).

It can be observed that cyberoptimists focus primarily on the internal functions of the medium, whereas cyberpessimists are predominantly tainted by external structures, such as unequal access in the 1990s or business models in the era of Web 2.0. Optimism is easier when the authors limit themselves to the inside of the medium: non-hierarchical forms of communication are visible within the confined spaces of virtual communities, and unequal access can easily be forgotten. Conversely, pessimistic views tend to neglect the fact that digital communication has also resulted in the creation of counter publics. The anti/alter-globalization movement, many grassroots movements, but also the survival of the alternative music scene have profited from digital connectivity (Sassen 1999; Franklin 2001). The enthusiasm about the increase in the percentage of women who have access to computers and the Internet alternates with apocalyptic visions of child pornography and trafficking in women mediated by the Internet (Miller 1995; Green and Adam 2001). The connections between external and internal aspects, however, are hardly ever explored in the same context. A historical comparison with world exhibitions may begin to address this problem.

In this chapter I focus on three fields of similarities between the web and world exhibitions. Firstly, I discuss what I call the 'immersion' that is created when images, texts, and sounds are assembled together. Secondly, I focus on the fact that both media are non-linear: the millions of visitors have the relative freedom to choose which sites they visit and in which sequence. Lastly, visitors of both types of representation are part of the spectacle viewed: they listen and are listened to; they see and are being seen; they follow digital tracks and leave their marks. As a pamphlet from the world exhibition in St. Louis in 1901 warned the visitors: 'Please remember: the moment you enter the gates, you are part of the show' (Bennett 1995, 68-69).

Immersion

Digital-optimists as well as digital-pessimists describe how the anonymity of surfing the web is crucial to the experience of cyberspace (Trend 2001; Weinberger

2002). Seducing visitors in this anonymous mass is crucial: attractive design, well-chosen images, catchy texts and interactivity are supposed to create 'sticky websites' to which visitors keep returning. By constantly introducing new combinations, the boundaries between communication, entertainment, commerce, and information fade: advertisements on informative sites, information on game sites, and games on informative pages.

Davenport and Bradley (1997) compare the web to an amusement park. The visitor to the latter is surrounded by attractions, temporarily allowing her to forget the limiting daily reality of embodiment and social relations. On the roller coaster she forgets gravity; in gambling halls the necessity to work for money; and magical parks allow her to believe that fairies exist. The visitor constantly shifts roles.

The same observation can be made for Internet users. Online games perfect the sensation of navigating in another world, but also the 'regular' web search for information or entertainment entails opening yet another window, and entering into a different world. According to some, this experience leads to new forms of self-awareness and identity. The Internet-using subject is not unitary, coherent and stable, but can be seen as fluctuating, fluid and rhizomatic (Plant 1998; Braidotti 2002). For feminist critics, aware of the dangers of essentialist notions of gender and ethnicity, this aspect of the Internet looks promising. The digital revolution may end previous forms of cultural exclusion, enabling people to enact new identities (Turkle 1997; Landow 1997). However, critics describe how what appears to be free entertainment, efficient gathering of information, or easy buying is in fact commercial profiling; corporations have found yet another aspect of human existence to exploit (Luke 2000; Terranova 2004; Lovink 2008).

However, no matter whether the end of univocal identity is welcomed as a desired transformation or disqualified as a way to create superficial consumers, the question remains of whether this process is a direct result of the creation of digital worlds. At this point, a comparison with the experiences of world-exhibition visitors in the second half of the 19th century may be useful. In such spaces visitors could lose themselves in many different worlds by traveling into virtual spaces. Just like the surfer clicking from website to website, performing different roles – as customer, information searcher, or participant in a political discussion – the world exhibition visitor's role altered when moving from pavilion to pavilion. Sometimes she was a student being taught about the world, other times a customer at a mischievous show, sometimes a colonial ruler imagining herself in imperialist power structures. Just like the web, world exhibitions constructed all-encompassing experiences, where visitors could lose themselves in images, sounds, and information.

The first world exhibition took place in London in 1851. Millions of visitors flocked to the glass palace where the glory and the power of the British Empire were celebrated (Hobsbawm 1975). France, having a long tradition of national industry exhibitions, soon followed (Paris 1855, 1867, 1889, 1900), alternating with the United States (1876, 1893) and other European cities. The last decades of the 19th century beheld an immense array of international and colonial exhibitions (Rydell 1984; Gudehus 1992). The First World War implied a decrease in frequency but not in scope.

Soon, a fixed design for world exhibitions was established. In the central section of the venues several countries exhibited, and systematic attention was paid to raw materials, industry, crafts, art, and social relations. The intention was to enlarge international prestige and status. The organising countries constructed large building projects and infrastructure. The Eiffel Tower is the most famous example, but also in Chicago, Barcelona and Vienna the remains of the buildings and terrain of the world exhibitions are still to be found. The enterprises were often joint ventures of national authorities and corporations. The Krupp firm displayed their newest cannons; Edison revealed the possibilities of electricity; and the new medium of film was introduced to the larger public (Grever and Waaldijk 2004).

Millions of people visited these events, paying a substantial entrance fee, but the exhibitions did not derive their success from just national and company propaganda. The entertainment industry that emerged in the margins soon became the economic core through which exhibitions remained afloat. The operation of restaurants, cafes and a wide range of attractions such as dance and theatre shows (the Wild West Shows by Buffalo Bill, the shows by Barnum and Bailey), and fairground attractions (the roller coaster, the Ferris wheel) yielded the organisers a vast sum of money (De Cauter 1993; Kasson 2000). To the visitors, these attractions often constituted the core of the exhibition experience (Greenhalgh 1989). The accompanying attractions provided a range of sensorial experiences that heightened the sensation of entering new worlds: the visitor smelled, felt, tasted, and heard strange things. The visitor was immersed in another world; one needed to travel to get there and had to cross the turnstile to enter.

Visiting the world exhibition was also a virtual visit to a different part of the world. Timothy Mitchell (1989) described the effort made by designers to entice visitors to feel as though they were in Egypt while being in Paris. Even the paint on the Egyptian houses was artificially made to flake off. Annie Coombes (1987) showed how the feeling of being lost in an unknown jungle was often used to sell the imperialist idea of the 'white man's burden' to British working class visitors.

Such observations reveal that the visitors' experiences were carefully orchestrated. The displays and attractions that constituted the world exhibition were purposefully designed. This was clear to the visitors; they saw the backside of the decor and read the accompanying pamphlets. In that sense, the difference between the representation and the represented was affirmed. In his analysis of colonial exhibitions, Mitchell asserts that even though the representations yield to full immersion, simultaneously a strict division was created between exhibition and visitor: 'the more the exhibit drew in and encircled the visitor, the more the gaze was set apart from it, as mind (in our Cartesian imagery) is said to be apart from the material world' (Mitchell 2000, 301). According to Mitchell, Western visitors were trained to view the world from a colonial perspective. They learnt to look at the world as a collection of representations from which they could distance themselves.

Mitchell stresses the confusing multitude of impressions imposed on the visitor, but he also showed how this paradoxically contributed to a heightened feeling of distancing and control. Especially the visitors' capacity to know exactly what was real and what make-believe affirmed their 'Cartesian judgement' and the omnipotent fantasy of Western imperialism. At exhibitions they learnt to look at the entire world as a representation, and to imagine themselves as superior, more capable than others of understanding what was represented. Visitors of world exhibitions were thus not completely engrossed in the representation; their immersion was bound up with Cartesian distance.

Applying Mitchell's thesis to the digital domain begs the question of how Internet users experience immersion. Do they immerse completely in a transparent medium, or is their immersion connected to the capability to switch from one role or window to the next, thus producing a sense of distanced control? In this context I wish to refer to the comparison with 'forgetting oneself' that occurs according to literary theorist Ryan (2001) when reading literary texts. She argues that a reader may lose herself in a text even when aware of the literary techniques. A detective novel may be especially thrilling when the reader is conscious of the author's textual techniques to hide clues. Modernist authors like Brecht and Woolf experimented with ways to make readers conscious of the literary means employed, and postmodern novels often use these techniques as the core of the construction.

From that observation one can compare the experiences of exhibition visitors and surfers. A lot points to the fact that exhibition visitors were both impressed by what was represented and by the technical ingenuity involved. As they had at their disposal visual reconstructions (villages, real cannons, live performances) as well as printed meta-information, visitors switched between immersion and distancing. In the colonial sections, partly serious and partly amusing, this double focus was strikingly apparent. Visitors were invited to lose themselves in watching exotic performances and could later feel themselves colonial officials who superiorly overlooked the colony.

This phenomenon resembles the results of game studies research which claim that computer gaming is marked by a double consciousness. In the game the player is immersed as a hero, discoverer, or town planner aiming for victory or success, but she is simultaneously aware of the rules of play and the developers' strategies (Copier 2007). In short, gamers too oscillate between immersion and distancing.

It seems plausible that the combination of immersion and distancing is present in other computer and Internet practices as well. Several new media scholars (Turkle 1997; Bolter and Grusin 2000; Manovich 2002) stress the importance of the metaphor of the plurality of windows, enabling a less defined subject position: the user can see and relate to several things simultaneously, alternating between immediacy and hypermediacy, between transparency and opacity, between immersion and distance.

The historical comparison between the web and world exhibitions enables a deepening of the understanding of the relation between power and immersion. Just like world exhibition visitors, web visitors do not languidly succumb to the commercial goals of entrepreneurs – immersion and distance go hand in hand. Users (viewers, readers) do not indiscriminately swallow what is offered; they construct a useful meaning while being aware of the rules of the genre. Access to the web not only requires hardware and a connection, but also knowledge of the medium, such as skills in browsing, searching and selecting, and acquaintance with end user license agreements. In that sense the web visitors' set of capital, knowledge and skills is comparable to the entry tickets and pamphlets of the exhibition that reminded the visitors time and time again of the technical ingeniousness of the designers. I argue that in both cases the entrance conditions guide the visitors in their experiences of both power and immersion.

The end of linearity

The next question is what this temporary immersion implies for the visitor's self-image. Characteristic of both modes is that the visitors participate in an experience in which different behavioural aspects alternate. On the Internet another genre is always within reach, subsequently and simultaneously, by opening another window. A teenager may visit gamezone.com while chatting on MSN, simultaneously downloading music, and casually searching for the latest episode of her favourite TV show.

The combination of 'seriousness' and 'entertainment' at world exhibitions meant that political goals, whether to popularise British imperialism or to celebrate women's emancipation, always took place in the context of the touristic and consumptive pleasure of a trip. World exhibitions were one of the first occurrences of modern mass tourism (Hobsbawm 1975, 47). Visitors could choose in which sequence and order of priority to indulge in the various aspects of the world exhibition. A visit to the exhibition was not a linear experience like listening to a speech, reading an essay, or visiting a museum.

For the first generation of cyberoptimists such as Lanham (1993) and Landow (1997), the non-linear structure of digital texts was one of the most promising aspects of the digital revolution. Landow mentions the convergence of post-structuralist deconstruction and digital technology, whereas Lanham argues that hypertext echoes Barthes's view on text as the result of the interplay between reader and author. According to these writers, the disciplining power of print dissolves in digital hypertext: the power that forces the reader to start at the beginning of a sentence and follow the author to the full stop, thus abiding by the author's authority. Non-linear texts were supposed to create responsible and independent readers, and even turn them into writers themselves since their reading strategies produce a new text. Weinberger (2002) describes the technology of hyperlinks as a revolution comparable to the transition of oral to written culture. This liberatory aspect of hyperlinking is celebrated even more by Web 2.0 advocates, who claim that a collective intelligence is emerging through non-linear patterns of tagging and linking (Leadbetter 2008; Shirky 2008).

However new this may seem, modes of representation which do not force the viewer or reader into a linear tunnel have existed for a long time. I consider world exhibitions an important example of this. Though directed and carefully scripted, often by a national committee, the focus of such control was limited. Organizers could not contribute more than marginal suggestions. The exhibition terrain was characterised by far-reaching freedom, thus markedly different from its contemporary museums, which directed sequence, hierarchy and meaning for its visitors (Coombes 1987; Greenhalgh 1989).

Visitors to exhibitions used such liberties extensively. Documented accounts suggest that visitors enjoyed the knowledge they gained about the structure of the exhibition. They advised others about attractive routes and not-to-be-missed exhibits.

From financial reports we know that the success of the exhibitions was largely due to visits to the entertainment sections, though official reports remarkably lack these accounts; the organisers were especially proud of their educational successes. They described how groups of laborers (often at their employers' expense) learnt about industry and the colonies (Grever and Waaldijk 2004). The fact that most visitors fondly remembered the entertainment rather than the official aims of the exhibition was not mentioned in the official reports. These were strongly biased by the hierarchical distinction between education (raising good citizens) and entertainment (selling to consumers).

The visitors' experience of freedom to choose sequence and priority is crucial to understanding the success of world exhibitions. This freedom resembled the freedom of customers in a market or a department store: they watched, tested, and weighed. The comparison between world exhibitions and department stores was taken up by both Walter Benjamin (see Buck-Morris 1999) and Mitchell (1989). In department stores customers could 'vote with their feet'. They went to sections that interested them the most and stopped in front of shop windows that attracted their attention. Mitchell points out that the glass of the shop window transformed merchandise into objects. Through the distance and the glass that separated viewer from object, the consumer article changed into an object, and the visitor into viewer. Anne McClintock (1995) further extends this comparison and describes how advertising techniques and the popularisation of imperialism strengthened each other. World exhibitions place the world in a shop window, turning Western visitors into window shoppers, and thereby altering their world view. World citizenship came to include the consumers' freedom to choose.

Historians' focus on the consumption and amusement side of exhibitions can be useful for a nuanced insight into the identities constructed by such freedom. By showing how the combination of being a citizen and a consumer was an indispensable element of visiting exhibitions, it urges us to take consumerism seriously. This also holds true for the Internet. Websites are deeply marked by advertising. Yet, focusing on commerce as the sole dimension of the web is insufficient. Just like world exhibitions, Internet meeting places combine commercial entertainment with serious instruction, with education, and with propaganda. It is precisely this combination which enables visitors to constantly oscillate between identities: one moment citizen, the other consumer.

The political effects of this switching mechanism are profound and need to be analysed in terms of gender, class and ethnicity. The world exhibitions turned imperialism into nationally supported projects. Inhabitants who had never set foot in a colony suddenly felt connected with overseas officials and entrepreneurs by buying products and enjoying colonial arts and crafts (Legêne and Waaldijk 2001). This meant a rearrangement of gender and colonial citizenship. Since women in the colonial metropolis were supposed to be experts in the field of food and clothing, they could relate to and identify themselves with colonial projects of the mother country (Grever and Waaldijk 2004).

The exhibitions also offered possibilities for opposing political identities. Sections dealing with the position of women were often featured, and advanced the international infrastructure of the women's movement (Waaldijk 1999; Grever 2000). At the world exhibition in Chicago in 1893, Fredrick Douglas and Ida B. Wells protested against the discrimination of black Americans in the US (Douglas 1893; Carby 1987). The socialist Second International was established during the world exhibition in Paris in 1889. These examples raise the question of interaction between consumption-based entertainment and emancipation movements: how did these political minority movements succeed in foregrounding their goals, while being surrounded by fairground attractions? Lauren Rabinovitz (1998) provides a new perspective on this issue as she points out that world exhibitions, together with department stores, were the first public spaces in which women could look and inspect. According to Rabinovitz, the new role of women as consumers of the entertainment industry was a crucial moment in the history of the emancipation movement. Research into how Internet users combine political participation with consumption and entertainment may profit from analyses of such spectacular events as world exhibitions.

Being part of the show

Many cyberpessimists stress the unprecedented possibilities of digital communication for surveillance and control. The almost unlimited potential of the state and business to gather details of people's lives and the subsequent loss of privacy is regarded as too high a price for the convenience of the Internet. Conversely, many forms of digital activism show that digital control can be reversed or otherwise subverted. Again, it is illustrative to establish the comparison with exhibition visitors' resistance and critique.

Men and women from the colonies and other non-western regions were present at the world and national exhibitions, as human showcases. The visitors were invited to look at them, but of course the empire looked back. Fascinating moments occur when the gaze is reversed. The initial logic of representation was interrupted when the people on display gazed back. Fredrick Douglas's protest exemplifies this. Other examples are the strikes by Dutch carpet weavers and Javanese dancers at the Dutch National Exhibition of Women's Labour in The Hague (Grever and Waaldijk 2004).

Because world exhibitions reached for the sky in representing the world, large parts of the world were indeed present at the exhibition. The people who were there to ensure that the represented countries looked 'real' did actually originate from those countries. They were the ones who performed shows and presentations. Time and time again they resisted confinement in a virtual world. They bridged the gap between the actual space of the exhibition and the representation of other spaces. They approached visitors, asked for money, and voiced their opinions (Rony 1998). The perfection of the life experience of visiting an unknown culture or foreign country reaches a limit when viewers and the viewed realise that the one who looks can also be looked at.

Though the power differentials between viewers and viewed were unsymmetrical, they did allow for this relation to be subverted. Cracks in the image appeared: visitors felt exposed, ill at ease in their roles, wondered what the exhibited people thought of them, and established contact in some instances (Grever and Waaldijk 2004). Fatimah Rony (1996) described how exhibited people at ethnological exhibitions in the beginning of the 20th century could escape their imposed role of exotic 'other'. They returned the gaze, approached visitors, tried to collect money, established sexual contacts, and became involved in conflicts taking place across the fence.

Moreover, visitors ogled not only the exhibited people but also each other. The slight feeling of unease that people felt when facing the exhibited 'other' caused them to realise they were part of the show. Rabinovitz (1998, 50) analysed the intersecting gazes on the exhibition terrain. In a meticulous analysis of images and drawings of the world exhibition in Chicago, 1893, she showed that visitors of exhibitions were always watched. Gender and ethnicity play a crucial part in these processes. White women looked at other visitors and at exhibited (mostly non-Western) men and women. In turn, these white women were looked at by men. Such analyses show that the traditional gender inequality between looking men and to-be-looked-at women may in some ways become subverted at exhibitions.

How do the insights into the directions of gazes at world exhibitions contribute to insight in the uses of Internet and Web 2.0? The visitor of websites is in a way invisibly visible by digital traces. Studies into these issues are generally conducted in the light of concerns about state surveillance and privacy (Lyon 1994). But the surfer is not only the object of political monitoring by governments and investigation services, but also of marketing strategies and market surveillance. Website visits dissolve the boundary between consuming, gathering information, and political participation. Presumably not every Internet user knows about IP numbers, a unique identification number assigned to every device connected to the Internet, or cookies, small packets of user data stored on the user's computer, allowing websites to track surfers' exact behaviour and choices. Combined with the data of other users, this results in personally targeted advertisements: 'People who ordered this book were also interested in...' Most Web 2.0 services are based on collecting and reassembling such user-generated data, and derive their business models on these principles of 'harnessing collective intelligence' (O'Reilly 2005). Those whose information is gathered may demand goods or services in return; in fact, you pay with your privacy. This 'customer-card model' turns surfers into consumers, and their protests into consumer strikes, even when the service seems to be free of charge. The sense of being free to see anything on the web has its counterpart in being viewed. In some ways this requires knowledge – just as exhibition visitors had to be warned that they themselves were part of the show, web surfers should be educated about the risks of their visibility.

The historical and intermedia comparison I have conducted in this article helps me to formulate new questions about the citizenship that is being created in web-based environments. As in world exhibitions, a visitor in a web context is not just 'losing herself' in immersion but also exercising the power of a navigator who knows the rules of the genre. To a certain degree both kinds of visitors can create their own trajectories, swapping the identity of a citizen for the identity of a consumer and back again. If we want to understand the participation and citizenship that results from these alternating roles, it is crucial to see how this implies a close link between political participation and consumerist 'picking and choosing'. When citizenship and consumer experiences become so deeply intertwined, the crucial question is what happens to those who do not share in the power of consumption? Will political participation be the privilege of those who know how to consume?

Finally, the comparison of contemporary web environments with world exhibitions of a century before allows us to explore the implications of the connection between seeing and being seen. The fact that visitors know themselves to be the object of the gaze of others is not just a price to be paid for entertainment, it becomes part of a sense of power and authority. Again, this shows how the division between the political and the commercial cannot be maintained, either at world exhibitions or in web environments. Choosing a YouTube video is a social, commercial, and political act. These cannot be understood within the limits of sociological, economic or political analyses. Citizenship in multimedia contexts consists of civil, political, economic and cultural elements, and understanding citizenship requires studying the interactions between these elements. Without such an approach, it seems impossible to understand how external access and internal freedom interact.

Note

1. This article is an updated version of 'Wereldtentoonstellingen en het World Wide Web: Een historische vergelijking', published in Dutch in *Tijdschrift voor Genderstudies* 6 (1) (2003). I want to thank Marianne van den Boomen for her generous and perceptive advice about references to the critical debate on Web 2.0. I profited from discussions about citizenship in several contexts. Special thanks are due to the working group Teaching Empires of the ATHENA3/Socrates Network, and the colleagues and students in the Utrecht University Graduate Gender Programme.

References

Barbrook, R. and A. Cameron. 2001. The Californian ideology. In *Crypto anarchy, cyberstates, and pirate utopias*, ed. P. Ludlow, 363-87. Cambridge, MA: MIT press.

Barlow, J.P. 1996. *A declaration of the independence of cyberspace*. http://www.eff.org/~barlow/Declaration-Final.html.

Bennett, T. 1995. The exhibitionary complex. In *The birth of the museum*, ed. T. Bennett, 59-88. London: Routledge.

Bey, H. 1991. *The temporary autonomous zone*. http://www.to.or.at/hakimbey/taz/taz.html.

Bolter, J.D., and R. Grusin. 2000. *Remediation: Understanding new media*. Cambridge, MA: MIT Press.

Braidotti, R. 2002. *Metamorphoses: Towards a materialist theory of becoming*. Cambridge, UK: Polity Press.

Buck-Morris, S. 1999 (1991). *Walter Benjamin and the arcade project*. Cambridge, MA: MIT Press.

Carby, H. 1987. *Reconstructing womanhood: The emergence of the Afro-American woman novelist*. New York: Oxford University Press.

Cauter, L. de. 1993. The panoramic ecstasy: On world exhibitions and the disintegration of experience. In *De panoramische droom: Antwerpen en de wereldtentoonstellingen 1885, 1894,*

1930 / *The panoramic dream: Antwerpen and the world exhibitions of 1885, 1894, 1930*, eds. M. Nauwelaerts, 46-50. Antwerpen: Antwerpen 93 VZW.

Coombes, A. 1987. The Franco-British exhibition: Packaging empire in Edwardian England. In *The Edwardian era*, eds. J. Cherry Becket and D. Cherry Becket, 152-66. Oxford: Phaidon Press.

Copier, M. 2007. *Beyond the magic circle: A network perspective on role-play in online games.* PhD thesis, Universiteit Utrecht.

Davenport, G. and B. Bradley. 1997. The care and feeding of users. *IEEE MultiMedia* 4 (1): 8-11.

Douglas, Fredrick. 1893. Lecture on Haïti: The Haitian pavilion dedication ceremonies delivered at the world's fair, in Jackson Park, Chicago, Jan. 2d, 1893 *African American Perspectives: Pamphlets from the Daniel A.P. Murray Collection, 1818-1907.*

Franklin, M. 2001. Inside out: Postcolonial subjectivities and everyday life online. *International Feminist Journal of Politics* 3 (3): 387-422.

Gitelman, L. 2006. *Always already new: Media, history, and the data of culture.* Cambridge, MA: MIT Press.

Green, E. and A. Adam, eds. 2001. *Virtual gender: Technology, consumption and identity.* London: Routledge.

Greenhalgh, P. 1989. Education, entertainment and politics. In *The new museology*, ed. P. Vergo. London: Reaktion Books.

Grever, M. 2000. Reconstructing the fatherland: Comparative perspectives on women and 19th century exhibitions. In *A fatherland for women*, eds. M. Grever and F. Dieteren, 13-29. Amsterdam: IISG-beheer.

Grever, M. and B. Waaldijk. 2004. *Transforming the public sphere: The Dutch National Exhibition of Women's Labor in 1898.* With an Introduction by Antoinette Burton. Durham & London: Duke University Press.

Gudehus, B.S. and A. Rasmussen. 1992. *Les fastes du progrès: Le guide des expositions universelles 1851-1992.* Paris: Flammarion.

Hobsbawm, E. 1975. *The age of capital, 1848-1975.* London: Abacus.

Jenkins, H. 2006. *Convergence culture.* New York: New York University Press.

Kasson, J. S. 2000. *Buffalo Bill's Wild West: Celebrity, memory, and popular history.* New York: Hill and Wang.

Landow, G. 1997. *Hypertext 2.0: The convergence of contemporary critical theory and technology.* Baltimore: Johns Hopkins University.

Lanham, R. 1993. *The electronic word: Democracy, technology, and the arts.* Chicago: University of Chicago Press.

Leadbetter, C. 2008. *We-think: The power of mass creativity.* London: Profile Books Ltd.

Legêne, S. and B. Waaldijk. 2001. Reverse images – patterns of absence: Batik and the representation of colonialism in the Netherlands. In *Batik drawn in wax*, ed. I. van Hout, 35-69. Amsterdam: KIT-publisher.

Lovink, G. 2008. *Zero comments: Blogging and critical internet culture.* New York: Routledge.

Luke, T. 2000. Dealing with the digital divide: The rough realities of cyberspace. *Telos*, Winter 2000.

Lyon, D. 1994. *The electronic eye: The rise of surveillance society.* Cambridge: Polity Press.

Manovich, L. 2001. *The language of new media.* Cambridge, MA: MIT Press.

McChesney, R.W. 1999. *Rich media, poor democracy: Communication politics in dubious times.* Urbana: University of Illinois Press.

McClintock, A. 1995. *Imperial leather: Race, gender and sexuality in the colonial contest.* New York: Routledge.

Miller, L. 1995. Women and children first: Gender and the settling of the electronic frontier. In *Resisting the virtual life: The culture and politics of information*, eds. J. Rook and I.A. Boal, 49-59. San Francisco: City Lights.

Mitchell, T. 1989. The world as exhibition. *Comparative Studies in Society and History* (31): 217-36.

Mitchell, T. 1998. Nationalism, imperialism, economism: A comment on Habermas. *Public culture: Bulletin of the Society for Transnational Cultural Studies* 10 (2): 417-24.

Nakamura, L. 2002. *Cybertypes: Race, ethnicity and identity on the Internet.* New York: Routledge.

O'Reilly, Tim. 2005. What is Web 2.0: Design patterns and business models for the next generation of software. O'Reilly Net. http://www.oreillynet.com/pub/a/oreilly/tim/news/2005/09/30/what-is-web-20.html.

Plant, S. 1998. *Zeros and ones: Digital women and the new technoculture.* London: Fourth Estate.

Rabinovitz, L. 1998. *For the love of pleasure: Women, movies, and culture in turn-of-the-century Chicago.* New Brunswick: Rutgers University Press.

Rony, F.T. 1996. *The third eye: Race, cinema, and ethnographic spectacle.* Durham, NC: Duke University Press.

Ryan, M.L. 2001. *Narrative as virtual reality: Immersion and interactivity in literature and electronic media.* Baltimore: Johns Hopkins University Press.

Ryan, M.L. 2006. *Avatars of story: Narrative modes in old and new media.* Minneapolis: University of Minnesota Press.

Rydell, R. 1984. *All the world's a fair: Visions of empire at American international expositions, 1876-1916.* Chicago: University of Chicago Press.

Sassen, S. 1999. Digital networks and power. In *Spaces of culture, city, nation, world*, eds. M. Featherstone and S. Lash, 49-62. London: Sage.

Shirky, Clay. 2008. *Here comes everybody: The power of organizing without organizations.* London: Allen Lane.

Surowiecki, J. 2004. *The wisdom of crowds: Why the many are smarter than the few and how collective wisdom shapes business, economies, societies and nations.* New York: Doubleday.

Terranova, T. 2004. *Network culture: Politics for the information age.* London: Pluto Press.

Trend, D. 2001. *Welcome to cyberschool: Education at the crossroads in the information age.* Lanham, ML: Rowman & Littlefield.

Turkle, S. 1997. *Life on the screen: Identity in the age of the Internet.* London: Phoenix.

Waaldijk, B. 1999. Colonial constructions of a Dutch women's movement: 1998. In *Differenzen in der Geschlechterdifferenz – Differences within genderstudies: Aktuelle Perspektiven der Geschlechterforschung*, eds. K. Röttger and H. Paul, 286-299. Hamburg: Erich Schmidt Verlag.

Weinberger, D. 2002. *Small pieces loosely joined: A unified theory of the web.* Cambridge, MA: Perseus Publishing.

Zoonen, L. van. 2000. *Virtuele vrouwen: Constructies van gender online.* Oratie Universiteit Maastricht: Centrum voor Gender en Diversiteit.

'And machine created music'

Cybergothic music and the phantom voices of the technological uncanny

Isabella van Elferen

> *And God saw everything that he had made and behold: it was good*
> *And God created man*
> *And man created Machine*
> *And Machine created music*
> *And Machine saw everything it had created and said—behold*

As many of the chapters in this book show, technology and culture cannot be separated from one another in early 21st-century daily life. New media technologies shape the way we perceive and interact with the world around us: since they guide our perception and have acquired their own agency, they are also actors in the networked structure of our day-to-day activities. Digital music is an interesting example of these two aspects of technological mediation: not only do we hear this music through the digital media of keyboards, samplers and MIDI – and we might download it in mp3 format via P2P networks – we also interact with it with the help of digital agents such as iPods, Internet radio and club turntables. The lyrics to Apoptygma Berzerk's 'Kathy's Song (Come Lie Next to Me)' quoted above ponder the possibility that technology has even acquired its own *creative* agency: it is Machine, not God or man, that created music, and Machine that observes the human perception of and interaction with it.

The possibility of autonomous technological agency has given rise to utopian as well as doom scenarios in literature, film and music since Mary Shelley's *Frankenstein* (1818). With the rise of digital technology and artificial intelligence, the number of such scenarios has increased. Characters such as *Star Wars'* Darth Vader, Agent Smith in *The Matrix* trilogy and even the dreaded 'millennium bug' all signify that although the seemingly limitless possibilities of technology open fascinating new perspectives, they could simultaneously threaten some of the borders of humanity and even morality that we always thought were stable. In a similar vein, the autonomous agency of music technology has evoked enthusiasm as well as resistance among music lovers. If electronic and digital genres such as house, trance, industrial and minimal explore the possibilities of computer-generated noise to its utmost borders, other genres such as rock, indie and singer-songwriting explicitly prefer human voices over digital ones. The infamous public rejection of Bob Dylan's electric guitar was followed by the distrust of synthesizers and drum computers in the early 1980s, and of digitally produced house and electro in the 1990s and 2000s. Theorists such as Kodwo Eshun and Richard Middleton have asked the question of whether what we hear in digital music is the voice of the cyborg, and how this cyborg music challenges the borders of 'natural' music as we know it (cf. Eshun 2000; Middleton 2006).

In this chapter I address these aspects of digital music through the lens of Gothic criticism. I shall study the contemporary Gothic phenomenon of cybergoth music, arguing that bands like Apoptygma Berzerk and Tanzwut mingle the technological agency of digital music with the human agency of the voice and let the resulting cyborg sound interrogate the fluid borders between these mixed agencies. This is networked music, originating from a close collaboration between humans and nonhumans – it is the tune sung by the golem come to life and enjoying its technocultural origin. From the point of view of Gothic theory, moreover, cybergothic music has adopted an aesthetic that is thoroughly liminal, that is, located in a borderland: it dwells in between anthropomorphic and Frankensteinian sensibilities and confronts the uncanniness that such emphatically de-humanised mediation brings along. The Gothic approach to these themes allows for digital music and nonhuman musical agency to be studied from new angles: what does the borderland between human and nonhuman music look like? Can we distinguish the ghosts that its mediation might evoke and identify the uncanny sides of the 'digital material' of cybergothic music?

The Gothic dimensions of technoculture: the uncanny, ghosts, mediation

The Gothic is a form of cultural criticism that foregrounds the shadow side of self and the margins of culture. By doing so, the Gothic interrogates and often personifies the uncannily present subcurrents which may render a person or culture irrational, unpredictable, possibly dangerous. From the 18th-century Gothic novel to contemporary Goth subcultures,[1] it has served as a signifier of cultural crises and negotiated the anxieties that accompany them through an active confrontation with feelings of unease (cf. Punter and Byron 2004, 39). The critical stance of the Gothic highlights the fragmentation, distortion and hidden dimensions of selfhood and reality. It works like a rearview mirror, unveiling the absent presence of the past, of the Other, of the imaginary, of fear within the here and now. Thereby, it forces the one who looks into that mirror to discern such spectres roaming the spaces in between existing dichotomies. The spectres visible in the Gothic mirror are the forces that, according to Freud, give us the uneasy feeling that our home – that is, the domestic sphere, our perception of identity, of consciousness or culture – has become unhomely, *unheimlich*, uncanny. The uncanny may remain a paranoid feeling that we try to suppress, it may take the shape of the barely perceivable spectre of the unconscious haunting consciousness, and it may also appear in a ghost story that makes us contemplate the stability of our respective homes and discover to our dismay that perhaps it is not so stable and safe after all (cf. Smith 2007). While moving to and fro between opposites, the Gothic reaches for the uncanny borderland beyond dialectic. The Gothic is located in an eternal in-between; simultaneously dialectic and motionless, it signals and negotiates cultural crises through a radical incorporation of ambivalence.

This ambivalence takes on many shapes, starting with the presence of past and future in the present that is endorsed by the Gothic's rewriting gesture. The simultaneously nostalgic and transgressive rewriting of past situations and attitudes furnishes one of the consistent links between the various historical appearances of the Gothic. While 18th-century Gothic novels focused on the unspoken presence of medieval and spiritual pasts in enlightened Europe, the Goth genre in contemporary popular music and subculture has rewritten texts and themes from earlier (Gothic) times ever since Bauhaus's 1979 single 'Bela Lugosi's Dead', which is often considered the first Gothic rock song (Hodkinson 2002, 36). In spite of the constant recontextualisations that cause slight alterations in its outward appearance, it is the nostalgic and transgressive gesture of the Gothic that gives it a transhistorical quality (Van Elferen 2007, 2ff). A specific type of rewriting takes place in the remediation of a story from one medium into another; Bram Stoker's novel *Dracula*, for instance, has been recast in paintings, films, songs, and computer games, each not only narrating the story, but also adding new layers of interpretation through the medial agencies of the (moving) image and sound themselves. Gothic rewriting can also take the practical guise of re-enactment. In re-enactment, the nostalgic and transgressive rewriting of the Gothic is directly embodied. Dressing up as Dracula or dancing to Bauhaus, the remediation of Stoker's protagonist through the body enables the modern Goth to act out her own interpretation – and that in turn engenders wholly new meanings in her social surroundings. Gothic rewriting, then, always endorses a chronological overlap between various historical times, and this uncanny act of (re)mediation excavates the ghosts that lie buried under the surface of the culture it originates in.

Present-day techno- and cybergothic currents look into the rearview mirror of technoculture and confront the spectres that roam it. As Gothic stories from Frankenstein to the 'millennium bug' testify, the possibility of nonhuman agency and virtual worlds has given rise to feelings of destabilisation regarding notions of humanity and reality. Although nature-technology and information-material dichotomies are arguably obsolete in the current academic debate (Schäfer and Rieder 2008), the remains of them still seem to be alive in early 21st-century culture. Even if ambient, wireless and on-demand technology have become indispensible partners for our everyday activities, the (un)thinkable limits of technological autonomy still cause individuals and societies to worry. Many theorists have argued that we therefore live in an age of technocultural crisis in which the presence of nonhuman agents has rendered our familiar world uncanny. Building on Kittlerean media theory, Fred Botting has demonstrated how the Gothic genre offers a means to reflect upon the possibly uncanny sides of technology. The agency of technology confronts the media user with the 'spectres, monsters and undead' that are conjured up by magic lanterns, cinematography, digital realities and artificial intelligence alike (Botting 2005, 24). These are spectres that originate in a world in which technology and culture are no longer distinct, but still those ghosts frighten us – might our own desire for clear demarcations between the two be undead?

In Gothic fiction, the uncanny borderlands beyond taxonomy are often symbolised by deserted houses, landscapes or cityscapes, or labyrinths. These desolate spaces are invariably haunted, as they house repressed or tabooed desires and anxieties that are otherwise safely tucked away in categorised truths. Gothic ghosts like Darth Vader, the Borg in *Star Trek* and the Terminator represent the concrete (and anthropomorphical) manifestation of such ambivalences regarding cyberculture. They signify the fear of posthuman agency, technologically produced doppelganger, and moral vacuum, respectively; and these feelings occur simultaneously with the unbridled fascination for cyberculture that is symbolised by the characters in Gibson's book *Neuromancer*, Cronenburg's film *eXistenZ*, and Faithless's hymn 'God is a DJ'. When examined through a Gothic lens, technoculture – and cyberspace in particular – thus appears as a new deserted and uncanny place, simultaneously inhabited by the ghosts of enthusiasm and fright for the potencies of technology.

But it is not only within the Gothic *narrative* that a liminal borderland comes into being. Julian Wolfreys has demonstrated that telling a story can open up a Gothic space (Wolfreys 2001, 3). The act of narration, he argues, is a kind of phantasmagoria that is not necessarily pleasant: it allows the past to enter the present, and alternative realities to overlie the known. The uncanny accompanies storytelling; it is the unrepresented lurking behind presentation, the unknown saliently present in the known. While an omniscient narrator seems to possess hidden knowledge simply because he represents the literary medium, a reader knows more than a book character because she holds the medium itself in her hand and can flip through to the end. And this holds true for more than just literary narration. Indeed, every act of mediation, be it textual, visual or auditory, can evoke a Gothic conflation of overlapping temporalities and realities, and can foreground the hiatus between fantasy and fantasist through the effects of hypermediacy (Bolter and Grusin 2000) or – with Botting – between medium and spectator (cf. Law 2006). A medium itself can function as a 'third place' between the mediated phenomenon and its audience: the mobile phone may appear as a phan-tom voice, music technology may allow ghosts from the past to sing their song, digital avatars may be perceived as disembodied spectres. Gothic narratives are thus encapsulated by the Gothic *narratology* of mediation and rewriting, which gives technoculture a second layer of uncanniness: not only does technology chal-lenge old taxonomies of what is real/human and what is not through its creation of third order simulacra, new media also destabilise the narratological basis of those very simulacra. Technogothic ghosts roam the borderland beyond the na-ture-technology distinction, but they simultaneously haunt the media themselves that facilitate that borderland's existence. The protagonist Trinity in *The Matrix*, for instance, lives both in a computer simulation ('the matrix') and in what is left of the pre-technological world ('the real world'), but she also haunts Neo as a text-based avatar on his PC during his hacking activities. The ghost is in the ma-chine as well as in the new reality that the machine creates.

Uncanny music technology and the cybergothic

If every act of mediation can evoke a Gothic conflation of temporalities and reali-ties, this holds especially true for musical mediation. The medium of music itself functions as a performative 'memory machine' that involuntarily stirs past emo-tions and experiences (Benschop 2007), even in the case of hearing music one has never heard, for even the smallest entities of music – the timbre of a violin, the melody of a bass riff, the rhythm of a techno beat – will stir the memory of a similar musical experience, transport the listener into that past experience and reinscribe it with present connotations (Van Elferen and De Vries forthcoming). Gilles Deleuze and Félix Guattari argue that music is 'on the side of the nomadic' because the moment it is activated, it challenges spatial and temporal constella-tions (Deleuze and Guattari 1986, 88). These qualities render music vectral as well as spectral: music's memory machine activates vectors into the realm of memory, emotion, and imagination, and in this capacity, like other media, it invites alter-native realities to shroud the listener's known reality. And these musical qualities cannot but be activated. 'The indefensible ear' (Schwartz 2003) *must* hear music, the listener *must* embark on its lines of flight towards the spaces in between past and present, *must* rewrite her own history. Music can function as a Gothic med-ium *par excellence*: not only does it endorse an overlap of past and present, it simul-taneously foregrounds itself as the mediator of that overlap ('This music reminds me of...'). For these reasons music's vectors are an excellent vehicle for Gothic transgression: they provide gateways to liminal borderlands beyond the here and now.

The advent of music technology has intensified the vectral and spectral facul-ties of music. Douglas Rushkoff has described how music technology engenders a timespace of its own whose effect is Dionysian: it creates a suspension of the boundaries of everyday time and space that is nearly orgiastic in character (Rushkoff 1994, 217-18). Digital production and performance, moreover, have removed human agency from musical narration. Music recording is dehumanised rewriting: it is phenomenologically determined through the mechanical replaying of bits of past time in the present time, allowing past experiences to interact with present ones (Evens 2005, 53). The uncanny aspect of mediation is thereby enlarged to uneasy proportions: recording technology, sampling and digitalization, not only generates musical echoes from the past, but also doubles, transforms and distorts them. Musical mediation forces the listener to perceive the disembodied 'voices of the dead' (Sterne 2003) and even phantom 'voices from the void' (Sconce 2000): echoes from a hollow space, presences without origin whose sole agent seems to be the technology generating their sound. Digitally produced music rubs the spectral narrative principle of the ghost story in our face, and cybergothic musical styles thrive on exactly that starting point.

The Goth scene appropriated technological developments from an early stage. Shelley's *Frankenstein* has been followed by numerous technogothic books and films, the Net.Goth communities of the early 1990s have evolved into countless Gothic web communities (Whittaker 2007), and since the mid-1990s cybergoths have incorporated technology in music, lyrics and clothing. One difference between the historical Gothic and Goth subcultures is that the latter embody the Gothic spectres of their age. Dressed up like cyborgs, cybergoths enact the ghosts that haunt technoculture, and as such perform the uncanniness that pervades our evaluation of technology. Just like those ghosts, they signify ambivalence; neither rejecting nor embracing technology, neither judgmental nor ecstatic about it, they are a living emblem testifying that in our encounter with cyberreality, fascination goes hand in hand with fear – they enact the utopian and the shadow sides of technoculture at once. This Gothic stance is expressed in various ways in cybergoth subculture, most notably through the uncanny sound of cybergothic music.

A distinct portion of Gothic music is heavily imbued with technology, with regards to instrumentation, compositional processes, and lyrics. In the 1980s, the Belgian band Front 242 created Electronic Body Music (EBM). Front 242 mixed Depeche Mode's synthpop, The Cure's new wave, and Kraftwerk's industrial noise, and garnished the resulting mechanical drones with dark lyrics celebrating undeath and science-fiction utopias/dystopias. EBM's orchestra is the synthesizer, one of the instruments described by Richard Middleton as creators of musical doubles, non-sounds and 'siren bodies' (Middleton 2006). It works according to the principle of schizophonia, the separation of a sound from its origin (Schafer 1977, 273), that gives birth to second- or even third-order simulacrum sounds. The synth's phantom voices operate as musical symbols of the themes in EBM lyrics. EBM was very influential in Goth and industrial musical scenes of the late 1980s and early 1990s; from the early 1990s onwards, bands such as Feindflug in

Germany and VNV Nation in England started to combine EBM with the ultimately machine-made musical style, techno, into cybergothic music. This musical style typically has a high bpm (beat per minute) count, and its harmonic structure is built on the rhythmical basses of techno and trance; synthesizer chords, industrial and digital sounds function as characteristic fillers of the musical texture. Cybergoth replaces the lyrical melodies laid out over mainstream techno with (mostly male) low-pitched vocals, grunts, or echoed voice distortion. Musical form in cybergothic is often remarkably traditional in the sense that it consists of an intro, two or three verses, a refrain, a bridge, and an outro.

The lyrics of cybergothic music show that its appropriation of technology is by no means uncritical, but rather ambivalent; in this sense, cybergoth bands give a more differentiated (if somewhat cynical) reaction to the musical cyberutopianism of artists such as Justin Timberlake and Missy Elliott (cf. McCutcheon 2007). As an example follow the intro to and very last line of 'Kathy's Song (Come Lie Next To Me)' by Norwegian band Apoptygma Berzerk (from *Welcome to the Earth*, Metropolis Records 2000), in which Machine is the next deity of the Genesis, who creates music like God creates man:

In the beginning God created the heaven and the earth
And the earth was without form and void
And darkness was upon the face of the dead
And God said: let there be light
And there was light
And God saw the light, that it was good
And God divided the light from the darkness
And God called the light day and the darkness he called night
And God saw everything that he had made and behold: it was good
And God created man
And man created Machine
And Machine created music
And Machine saw everything it had created and said—behold

[beat sets in]

[verses and refrain describing ill-fated love]

And on the seventh day, Machine pressed stop.
[music stops abruptly]

'Kathy's Song' reflects the musical heritage of cybergothic music and EBM, evoking associations of Depeche Mode 'gone digital' (and as such in fact does not sound unlike Depeche Mode's 2005 album *Playing the Angel*). In line with the intro text, a drum computer, a synthesizer and digitally manipulated voices are the main determiners of the song's timbre. These compositional choices foreground the autonomous agency of music technology: this cybercultural narrative is not only facilitated but also underlined by its own mediation, and what we perceive are voices from the borderland between biological and technocultural musical realities. The love story in the song's core text is balanced by Machine's powers in intro and outro, which once again stresses the cooperation of human and non-human actors in the creation of Apoptygma Berzerk's musical universe.

There are several videos available for 'Kathy's Song.' The 'official' MTV version consists only of digitally visualised soundwaves that are entirely consistent with the band's version of Genesis; the more popular 'Ferry Corsten remix' video shows a pan view of New York City interspersed with digital manipulations of growing plants in empty spaces like deserts and jungles filmed from warped camera angles. These videos visualise the blurred boundaries between God's and Machine's creation that are thematized in the song's music and lyrics. From a cyber-gothic perspective, the one grows from the other, and both the urban labyrinth and the vastness of the desert may at once appear a safe haven and an alienating wasteland. And just like the musical narrative, the video narrative uncannily foregrounds its own mediation through the pervasive 'absent presence' of camera and editing.

Though quite different in thematic scope, a similar instance of the uncanny echoes in cybergoth musical culture can be found in 'Tanzwut' ('Dance Rage') by the German band Tanzwut (from *Labyrinth der Sinne*, EMI Music 2000). Tanzwut's members are also in the pagan Goth band Corvus Corax.[2] Both parallel projects use medieval instruments such as bagpipes and medieval – or medieval connotated – percussion, and take either originally medieval or self-concocted Latin and German texts as the starting point for their lyrics. Whereas Corvus Corax, however, usually refrains from digital production in favour of a more traditional metal sound that is complemented by medieval bagpipes and percussion, Tanzwut's music is heavily imbued with technology and explores the convergence of pagan Goth, industrial techno and *Neue Deutsche Härte*.[3] The band members usually perform half-naked, wearing only long leather or fur skirts and pagan attributes. The lyrics of their signature song 'Tanzwut' speak of the transgressive forces of music and dance:

Inter Deum et Diabolum
Semper musica est
Durch Feuer und Glut
Ein Heulen, Jammern,
Kreischen
Klägliche Reue
Satans Werk der Tanz

Verwirren
Verdammen
Verführen

[Between God and Devil
There is always music
Through fire and glow
A howling, whining,
Screeching
Piteous mourning
Satan's work of the dance

Confusion
Doom
Seduction]

If sounding music creates lines of flight towards liminal spaces of history and reality, Tanzwut's lyrics moreover stress that music's transgressive qualities may even lead to a space beyond morality, 'inter Deum et Diabolum'. The pagan element in this song is represented by the bagpipe bourdon (an open fifth interval) in the refrain and basic onbeat rhythms, while distorted guitars playing power chords lay out the metal sound wall, and distorted drum computer and bass establish a firm techno beat. The vocals in 'Tanzwut' consist of grunts and vocoder-morphed sounds. Like Apoptygma Berzerk's 'Kathy's Song', 'Tanzwut' is thus musically characterised by a convergence of biological and phantom voices, human and nonhuman actors. Both songs in this way create uncanny echoes of technocultural futures – but the latter allows the 'medieval' and metal past to reverberate into such futures as well.

As noted above, the nostalgic rewriting of the past has long been identified as one of the main characteristics of the Gothic. Botting describes Gothic nostalgia as the yearning for a romanticised past: 'Gothic novels seem to sustain a nostalgic relish for a lost era of romance and adventure, for a world that, if barbaric, was (…) also ordered' (Botting 2007, 5). However, such nostalgic rewriting often also results in transgressions of the past. Discussing the nature of nostalgia, Linda Hutcheon has argued that the nostalgic drive does not so much signify the desire to literally *go back* to the past, but rather reflects the *will to yearn* for something which is essentially irrecoverable (Hutcheon 2000). As a result of this subjective sentimental drive, she asserts, 'nostalgia "sanitizes" the past': by nostalgically remembering, we conjure up a past we desire to long for, and thus paradoxically transgress history itself by way of memory.[4] It is precisely in this liminal space between history and memory that the Gothic roams – and the cybergothic shows that the future, too, is nostalgically and uncannily appropriated by Gothic fiction.

Anne Williams states in her evaluation of Gothic literature that it 'offers its readers an imaginative space that both insists on "reality", on historicity, on materiality, and at the same time liberates the reader from the constrictions of that history' (Williams 1997, 122). Embracing both the freedom and the uncanniness resulting from this entrance into the borderland between the real and the virtual – the same borderland that is inhabited by cybergoths – the Gothic actively appropriates and acts out the symbiosis of futuristic nostalgia and transgression. And it does so in the superlative: it underlines the transgressive force of nostalgia by deliberately perverting the orderly texture of the yearned-for past or future. If nostalgia is characterised by the retrospective or prospective creation of an idealised homeland, the Gothic renders this very homeland uncanny by perverting its idyllic quality.

Medieval or pagan Goth music is characterised by precisely this Gothic gesture of transgressing the borders between past, present and future. Rebekah Ahrendt has interrogated the remediation of the Middle Ages by Gothic bands Helium Vola and Qntal, arguing that the sentimentalised nostalgia of its sounds does not reflect a leap back into history, but rather invokes a timeless memory space, allowing Goths to enact their desire for an idealized past whilst dancing away in the 'fantastic vision' of the medieval Gothic (Ahrendt 2007). Tanzwut even goes one step further, as it adopts the future as well as the past into this fantastic vision by blending pagan Goth, metal and trance into a musical amalgamate depicting quite literally how music moves beyond chronology. The video of 'Tanzwut' shows a computer-game interface with figures playing medieval instruments in the background, in which the display functions blink rhythmically. The message here is the medium: music allows for an escape from chronological and moral taxonomies and may take the listener on a trip between the medieval past and the technological future as well as 'between God and Devil'.

The digital material of cybergothic music

In digital music, technology is both an agent and a medium. Technology creates music, it mediates music, and it allows us to interact with music. I contend that in cybergothic music by bands like Apoptygma Berzerk and Tanzwut, the agency of music technology is uncannily pushed to the foreground and into the footlight. This music thus explores the Gothic dimensions of digital music culture. It engenders Gothic dialectics through the musical interplay between biological and technological realities on the one hand, and the past, present and future on the other – an interplay which must remain without a winner: it is the motionless dialectic in between such categories that is the issue. As the transgressions in the song lyrics are increased by the fact that they are musically (as well as visually) mediated by the phantom voices of digital technology, these songs demonstrate that digital music can operationalise the Gothic ghost story principle and create a medial space of its own. The hypermediacy of this music evokes reflections upon the very theme it represents: the blurring of boundaries between human and non-human musical agencies. Cybergothic music has escaped the dichotomies of human versus nonhuman sounds, information versus materiality: it is the musical 'digital material' originating from the convergence of music technology and music culture. But it is, moreover, *uncanny* digital material, as it dwells in the borderlands beyond those dichotomies of musical experience and self-consciously mediates their in-betweenness. As the phantom voices of the cybergothic sing their uncanny song, the listener is confronted with the undead spectres they conjure up: the simultaneous enthusiasm and skepticism for music technology's autonomous creative agency. Those spectres are embodied by cybergoths, who dance their cyborg bodies to this music – but that is the subject matter of another ghost story.

Notes

1. The term 'Goth' is used here to distinguish present-day Goth subculture from the trans-historical Gothic genre evolving from the 18th-century Gothic novel.
2. 'Pagan' and 'medieval' Gothic musical genres are very much alike both in instrumentation, melodic and rhythmic outline, and performance. Although they are not synonymous, Tanzwut could be categorised in both genres.
3. *Neue Deutsche Härte* is a metal/industrial genre that originated in the reunited Germany in the 1990s and that is characterised by distorted metal guitars, industrial and electronic noise, upbeat tempo, and German lyrics. The internationally most famous representative of NDH is Rammstein.
4. Pierre Nora has made the important differentiation between factual *history* on the one hand and desired and sentimentalised *memory* on the other (Nora 1996: 626ff).

References

Ahrendt, Rebekah. 2007. Celts, crusaders, and clerics: The 'medieval' in gothic music. In *Nostalgia or perversion? Gothic rewriting from the eighteenth century until the present day*, ed. Isabella van Elferen, 96-112, Newcastle: Cambridge Scholars Press.

Benschop, Ruth. 2007. Memory machines or musical instruments? Soundscapes, recording technologies and reference. *International Journal of Cultural Studies* 10 (4): 485-502.

Bolter, Jay and Richard Grusin. 2000. *Remediation: Understanding new media*. Cambridge, MA: MIT Press.

Botting, Fred. 2005. Reading machines. In *Gothic technologies: Visuality in the romantic era*, ed. Robert Miles. Romantic Circles. http://www.litgothic.com/LitGothic/general.html.

Botting, Fred. 2007. *Gothic*. London: Routledge.

Deleuze, Gilles and Félix Guattari. 1986. *Nomadology: The war machine*. New York: Semiotext (e).

Elferen, Isabella van. 2007. Introduction. In *Nostalgia or perversion? Gothic rewriting from the eighteenth century until the present day*, ed. Isabella van Elferen, 1-10. Newcastle: Cambridge Scholars Press.

Elferen, Isabella van, and Imar de Vries. Forthcoming. The musical *Madeleine*: Communication, performance and identity in musical ringtones. In *Popular Music and Society* 33 (2).

Eshun, Kodwo, 2000. Visions of rhythm in the kynematic pneumacosm of Hype Williams. *Machine times*, ed. J. Brouwer, 116-133, Rotterdam: Nai Publisher / V2.

Evens, Aden. 2005. *Sound ideas: Music, machines, and experience*. Minneapolis: University of Minnesota Press.

Hodkinson, Paul. 2002. *Goth: Identity, style and subculture*. Oxford/New York: Berg.

Hutcheon, Linda. 2000. Irony, nostalgia, and the postmodern. *Studies in Comparative Literature* 30: 189-207.

Law, Jules David. 2006. Being there: Gothic violence and virtuality in Frankenstein, Dracula, and Strange Days. ELH 73 (4): 975-996.

McCutcheon, Mark A. 2007. Techno, Frankenstein and copyright. *Popular Music* 26: 259-280.

Middleton, Richard. 2006. Last night a dj saved my life: Avians, cyborgs and siren bodies in the era of phonographic technology. *Radical Musicology* 1. http://www.radical-musicology.org.uk/2006/Middleton.htm.

Nora, Pierre. 1996. The era of commemoration. In *Realms of memory: The construction of the French past, Vol. III: Symbols*, ed. Pierre Nora. New York: Columbia University Press.

Punter, David and Glennis Byron. 2004. *The gothic*. Malden: Blackwell.

Rushkoff, Douglas. 1994. *Cyberia: Life in the trenches of cyberspace*. London: Flamingo.

Sconce, Jeffrey. 2000. *Haunted media: Electronic presence from telegraphy to television*. Durham: Duke University Press.

Schafer, R. Murray. 1977. *The tuning of the world: Toward a theory of soundscape design*. New York: Random House.

Schäfer, Mirko Tobias and Bernhard Rieder. 2008. Beyond engineering: Software design as bridge over the culture/technology dichotomy. In *Philosophy and design: From engineering to architecture*, eds. Pieter E. Vermaas, Peter Kroes, Andrew Light, and Steven A. Moore, 152-164, Dordrecht: Springer.

Schwartz, Hillel. 2003. The indefensible ear: A history. In *The auditory culture reader*, eds. Michael Bull and Les Back, 487-501, Oxford/NY: Berg.

Smith, Andrew. 2007. Hauntings. In *The routledge companion to gothic*, eds. Catherine Spooner and Emma McEvoy, 147-154, London: Routledge.

Sterne, Jonathan. 2003. *The audible past: Cultural origins of sound reproduction*. Durham: Duke University Press.

Whittaker, Jason. 2007. Gothic and new media. In *The Routledge companion to gothic*, eds. Catherine Spooner and Emma McEvoy, 270-279, London/New York: Routledge.

Williams, Anne. 1997. Edifying narratives: The gothic novel, 1764-1997. In *Gothic: Transmutations of horror in late twentieth century art*, ed. Christoph Grunenberg, Boston: The Institute of Contemporary Art & Cambridge, MA: MIT.

Wolfreys, Julian. 2001. *Victorian hauntings: Spectrality, gothic, the uncanny and literature*. London: Palgrave Macmillan.

Network

Moving beyond the artefact

Lessons from participatory culture

William Uricchio

I can't seem to shake a *déjà vu* feeling when considering the current moment of media change as if, knowing what I do now, I was present during cinema's first decade. How, I often wonder, did that new medium's contemporaries fail to preserve films, key texts, and audience experiences? But when I consider the lax and, with a few notable exceptions, unsystematic efforts that are being made to preserve our latest 'new' media, it should come as no surprise. In the pages that follow, I will speak as a cultural historian who makes extensive use of archives and has an abiding interest in heritage and access. But I also speak as one whose personal and working life is increasingly bound up in new media and particularly social media. These two positions are hardly incompatible; on the contrary, they seem to me to offer not only real advantages thanks to the computerized archive, but real opportunities for historians to reflect upon the birth and development of the latest 'new' medium. And they bring with them the responsibility of learning from the past and preparing for the future, and urging the thoughtful and systematic archiving of this latest chapter in our cultural history. What follows will therefore of necessity have a polemical edge. The stakes for our culture and our ability to understand are both immediate and profound.

Posing the problem

The 'digital turn' has enabled the transformation of such familiar media as photography, film, recorded sound and the printed word, introducing new platforms, standards and applications. As Hollywood's growing dependence on digital production techniques and DVD sales shows, and the press's routine embrace of computer-based information flow attests, the media industry has quickly accommodated these transformations. There are of course some concerns about putting low-cost professional digital production equipment in the hands of ordinary citizens, but the media industry is quickly learning to turn a profit on the results. The revolution provoked by digital distribution seems more of a problem, and although 'piracy' is the term most often asserted by the industry, its own failure to develop adequate digital distribution models is a far more serious liability. But these problems largely reside in the domain of business strategy, and while many in the business and political community fret about the implications of digitalization for the bottom line, few have bothered to ask whether digitalization has fundamentally altered the nature of the media with which they are concerned.

The archival world has, by contrast, shown deep concern with what might best be termed 'media ontology' and the implications of the differences between, for example, the grain and pixels that constitute a film image. Although digital technologies have demonstrated their advantages for helping with the task of image and sound restoration and preservation, a significant cohort of archivists has argued that a shift in mediality, from analog to digital, fundamentally undercuts their mission. They argue that preserving film is not the same as storing compressed digital data.[1] Yet while profound in its implication, even this shift leaves the basic parameters of the traditional archive largely intact. Whether digital or analog, pixel or grain, the archive remains concerned with the restoration and preservation of cultural artefacts that are still called films, books, audio recordings and photos. True, a fundamental debate regarding media ontology remains unresolved and the indiscriminate use of nomenclature such as 'film' and 'photography' is problematic, but collections still adhere to the basic selection and cataloguing parameters of the analog past.

Of far greater concern to our culture's memory institutes should be new categories of digital culture that have been enabled particularly by networked computers – categories that are growing exponentially. Consider the case of e-mail – computerized versions of the physical letter (of course with a fabric of stylistic and formal differences) that generally speaking enjoy no systematic archiving or even technical standard. Future historians of the 'information age' will, ironically, face a gap in key evidentiary domains when attempting to make sense of their topic since most business archives are designed to account for paper records, but not electronic. And e-mails are a best-case scenario.... Social media such as blogs (web logs), wikis, massively multiplayer role-playing games, and various on-line social spaces that lack any homologies to traditional archival objects face a far more difficult situation. In the case of social media, there are neither pre-existing archival categories nor memory institutes charged with collection, selection, restoration, preservation and access.

Indeed, there seems to be a very real debate about how to even think about these emerging media forms. They do not adhere to the familiar 'mass' distribution of the traditional media (although their reach can be greater than many traditional media), nor are they as atomized as telephone calls and individual correspondence (although they can be uniquely person to person), nor is their textual identity necessarily stable and fixed in the way that we think of photographs or films or books (although they can inhabit a range of positions from dynamic, like games, to stable, like e-books). They fall outside of the familiar limits of our cultural habits and expectations, and since memory institutions are largely involved in the business of creating and maintaining tradition, it's easy to see why these new forms are so awkward.

The challenges to those concerned with preserving cultural heritage are enormous. Not only must we move beyond familiar objects and homologies in our choice of what to save, we must also attend to the larger cultural shift towards participation and collaboration. Blogs and wikis are not only highly dynamic as texts; they are examples of networked and collaborative cultural production. They depart from the strictures (and legal definitions) of authorship familiar from the book or film, and are instead accretive, multiply voiced, collective, and ongoing. Although we have some historical precedents for this type of authorship (examples ranging from the Old and New Testaments to quilts come to mind), they have tended either to acquire an institutionally imposed stability (the Bible) or been repositioned from media text to artistic artefact (quilts).[2] Yet, this collaborative dynamism is a core defining aspect of today's new social media. Without familiar criteria such as authorship or the text as an authoritative and fixed entity, or the many institutions that help us to construct hierarchies of importance, how will we know what to save? What evaluative criteria should we deploy? And even if we could answer these questions, what would be an appropriate point to 'freeze' and hold these dynamic artefacts in the archive? Where do we draw the line between the cultural and the social, between the artefact and the means of its production? And even if we accept the social and acknowledge that patterns of interaction are as important as the text, how do we go about documenting them in meaningful ways? The answers are not clear, but there might at least be productive new ways of posing the questions.

The stakes of facing such questions go beyond the need to document a significant change in how our cultures represent themselves and their experiences and how they circulate those representations. These are, of course, vital issues particularly at moments of transition, where new constituencies are empowered to represent and circulate, or where people develop new technological affordances and new ways of using them. Such broad concepts as knowledge and the public are redefined and empowered at such moments. And while of great interest to cultural historians such as myself, these concepts also help to define the fabric of our daily lives.

Consider our changing relationship to the news. Once vetted and produced by trained journalists and centralized institutions with carefully cultivated ideological profiles and professional reputations, news has slipped onto the Internet where it is often neither vetted nor contextualized and where it circulates at the speed of light. When there were well-established filters and a clear line of responsibility, one could agree or disagree, but the status of the information was known. Having 'seen it on the Internet' does little to pin down critical parameters or accurate sources of information. Yet, perhaps even more than rumor, such information can take on a life of its own, confusing public discourse. As we now know about so-called misinformation campaigns, digitally altered photographs, and re-worked press releases, even the highest levels of some national governments have made use of the new media to manipulate the record and with it public perception and knowledge. The policy implications both for day-to-day politics and for the historical record couldn't be more profound. Here, too, is an area where systematic archiving of social media – dynamic texts as well as circulation patterns – could greatly assist the functioning of our political lives by allowing us to go back to the record and check instances of manipulation.[3]

Such an intervention, it needs to be said, can only serve the present to the extent that the public is educated in the critical assessment and use of these new media. Our cultural knowledge and assumptions are grounded in the traditional centralized media. The press and book publishers, film and music companies, broadcasting authorities, and the rest have long exercised a near paternalistic control over media production and circulation. More importantly, at least in the West, interpretive systems grounded in 2,000+ years of biblical exegesis, legal precedent working out the meanings of terms, and dictionaries and lexicons pin-ning down the precise functioning of language have all worked hand in glove with centralized media systems to circumscribe meanings and enforce responsi-bility. Audio and visual culture challenged the precision of the word, but even here rather strict protocols developed in order to minimize charges of libel and maximize impressions of consistency and professionalism. But the digital turn and the steady emergence of bottom-up and collaborative media require new ways of encountering texts and new skill sets on the part of media users. This new literacy can no longer take the news at face value, but rather must consider it as partial, as a construction, and as data that must be critically assessed and com-bined with other sources in order to yield some sense of the truth. But I digress....

Web 2.0: social media

In a world where people increasingly manage, direct and redefine when and where they experience media, how they share it, and what it means to produce and consume, we need to think about cultural processes in dramatically new ways. The shifts from analog to digital, from centralized to dispersed, from mass media to social media, from information transmission to collective intelligence, from old statistical extrapolations to new data feeds, all point to media use that is social by design, not social by default. The descriptors used by Tim O'Reilly and others for Web 2.0 are revealing: 'an architecture of participation,' 'harnessing collective intelligence,' 'exchanging,' 'pooling,' and 'collaboration'. Whether we look to social media communities such as Technorati (http://technorati.com) or social networking sites such as Friendster (www.friendster.com) and MySpace (www.myspace.com) or media fashion communities such as Digg (http://digg.

com), we see new logics that have to be understood if we are to make use of them. I'd like to borrow a term from the worlds of biology, neurology, and computer science that speaks to these new conditions: *high connectivity*. High connectivity in these various domains refers to dynamic networks, high magnitudes of contact among many nodes, and both interactive and iterative behavior.

Before looking a bit more closely at what these developments portend for culture and, in consequence, our memory institutions, first a few words about the technologies that have been drawn upon. The World Wide Web was largely made possible thanks to the introduction of web browser Mosaic and the Pentium chip a little over ten years ago (ca 1995). Making far more effective use of networked computers, these developments were also aided by significant increases in cable carrying capacity (broadband), compression algorithms, and cheap memory. These developments have continued, and two parameters in particular have a bearing on the archive: memory and transmission speed. Memory capacity is growing ever vaster and cheaper, as a look at the retail electronics sector will demonstrate. As production capacities grow, so too does our ability to hold the massive amounts of data that are being produced. Transmission speeds have also improved significantly: in 2007, Alcatel-Lucent announced that it had broken the 25.6 terabyte optical data transmission speed, or the equivalent of sending the information on 600 DVDs in one second. Together, massive increases in memory and the new transmission speeds combine with a near geometrical progression of wired households in some national contexts to suggest that the developments we have seen since the introduction of Mosaic are but the tip of the iceberg. We have a sense of what is looming in the distance, but its magnitude is not yet visible or even imaginable. Yet we also know that these changes are touching most parts of our lives, from banking and buying train tickets, to entertainment and leisure, to driving and working. But the most interesting developments – and the developments that we need to think about archiving – remain submerged and out of sight.

As suggested at the outset, the implications of the digital turn for media *production* have gotten most of the press coverage. Armed with a modestly priced computer and video camera, a skilled teen can produce films or music that achieve industry technical standards. And while this is a big advance on the 8mm or 16mm home movies of two or more decades ago, the real advantage of digital culture has been in transforming 'home' movies into 'world' movies. New logics of *distribution* have enabled grassroots producers to sidestep the control long exercised by media corporations and governments, and reach a global audience. The rapid circulation of digital texts has also stimulated the growth of cultural hunters and gatherers who cut and mix, collect and reassemble, borrow and re-purpose, and who do so as collectives. These practices are not so distant from those evident in pre-industrial and agrarian cultures (or said another way, in the era of pre-commodified culture) – again, consider the work of quilters, folk singers and storytellers that might be characterized in precisely the same terms. And just as notions of ownership were blurred in folk cultures, so they are unclear with many of today's new media practitioners. The contemporary blurring of intellectual property can be attributed in part to the new logics of digital culture, and in part to the increasingly draconian control over our cultural heritage asserted by corporate copyright and trademark holders. As intellectual property protection steadily expands at the behest of corporate interests, the public is increasingly deprived of anything other than paid access to their own popular culture. And as corporate profits invariably decline in traditional sectors such as music and film, the pressure to expand control over intellectual property only grows, even though the decline correlates to the increasing market share of cell phones, computer games, and exponentially increasing involvement with social media.[4]

The challenges posed to the old order by the collaborative logics of Web 2.0 can be seen in many sectors. Collaborative news networks such as Slashdot ('News for Nerds, Stuff that Matters', www.slashdot.org) and Kuro5hin ('Technology and Culture from the Trenches', www.kuro5hin.org) have blurred the distinctions among editors, readers and writers, with their participants fulfilling all roles. They draw on correspondents and commentaries from around the world, complicating, contradicting, and compositing various bits of information so that the reader must actively consider multiple points of view and sources before making a determination about the news. In a similar way, open source software initiatives such as Linux draw upon a community of collaborators, and by keeping the source code open, they direct their energies towards improving functionality rather than building encryption systems. Moreover, with ample networked input and development, they have the advantage that their software mutates and improves more quickly than proprietary models. Add low costs into the mix, and it is little wonder that Linux is steadily winning terrain from centralized companies such as Microsoft.

Decentralized, networked, collaborative, accretive, ephemeral and dynamic... these developments and others like them bear a closer resemblance to oral cultures than to the more stable regimes of print (writing and the printing press) and the trace (photography, film, recorded sound). Time-bound and contingent, they are at odds with the durability of the printed word and photographed image. Spread from person to person, with the always present possibility of manipulation and mutability, they differ in the main from the relative stability and uniformity of the traditional fixed media.[5] And like oral cultures, they seem to evade the preservation frameworks that we have put in place in our institutions of memory, built as they are around tangible media. And yet, despite these conditions, these collaborative efforts also enjoy embodiment as digital text, image and sound, and as such differ from oral culture. They can be apprehended, but the question is, at what point? What constitutes a sufficient 'capture' in a dynamic and fast-evolving distributed network where any of the nodes is capable of change.

If we take an instance of social media such as Wikipedia, we can see the benefits of collaboration and mutability. A reader-edited and written encyclopedia, its entries change over time to reflect new developments, complications in and regional inflections of meaning, and the lively debates among its contributors. Its entries evolve, and as such are responsive to the latest undulations of scholarship. Yet, for all of the Wikipedia's value as a documentary history of changing cultural conceptions and definitions, it confronts the archivist with a problem: what point is the right point to fix and hold for posterity? Social networks such as Friendster and Flickr will offer future researchers invaluable information about the construction and functioning of our society. Not only are they as textually dynamic as Wikipedia, but the fabric of thematic tags (the elements that permit associations on the basis of location, interest, or background) and the patterns of links (as users form elaborate networks) are themselves valuable data. Indeed, the textual data only acquires meaning thanks to these other parameters. Again, what is the archivist to do? It is as if we expected librarians not only to keep books but to track their circulation as well. Yet with social media, circulation is a crucial and defining measure of meaning and import. A third complicating parameter is introduced by on-line games, for example MMORPGs (massively multiplayer on-line role-playing games) in which the texts are extraordinarily dynamic, the social networks are crucial to the substance of the game, and the interactions of players with one another are actually constitutive of the gaming experience. Pity the archivist! Yet these games occupy a significant amount of cultural space, have social implications, and provide voice to their users on a variety of topics. The game *America's Army* (www.americasarmy.com) not only offers an interesting text against which to read US involvement in Iraq, but it includes remarkable debates among its users over issues that range from the political to the tactical and offer informed readings from voices that researchers rarely have access to.[6] In some cultural settings, South Korea for example, the penetration of virtual worlds is enormous and growing (South Korea Telecom's Cyworld includes nearly half of the population). Is this something that we can afford to ignore, fixating instead on the extension of traditional 19th- and 20th-century cultural forms in our digital and networked present?

Signs of success

Social media differ fundamentally from the media around which our archival policies have been constructed. Their rootedness in community and collaborative interactions and their responsiveness to an ever-shifting present give them an unique quality as *Zeitdokumenten*, finely grained embodiments of culture. Of all the differences from traditional media discussed above, perhaps the two most difficult ones for memory institutes are 1) that these media are dynamic and always in progress rather than having a final, completed state; and 2) that these media are networked, and that the web of connections bears heavily on the meaning of any one site. These two parameters are not only unfamiliar, but somewhat daunting in terms of their potential storage requirements. Fortunately, as mentioned at the outset, memory is getting cheaper by the day, and transmission speeds are improving significantly. But just as importantly, the very distributed logic that enables social media and peer-to-peer (P2P) applications holds a potential solution to the storage problem. Consider music file exchanges such as Napster or Grokster and the like. They managed something well beyond the physical (let alone financial) capacities of the traditional music industry by digitalizing a vast amount of music, storing it, and distributing it on demand to millions of users. They did this by networking millions of personal computers in homes across the world, distributing the tasks of digitalization, storage and access in such a way that the cost was negligible and the labor involved was freely given. Millions of modestly sized memory chips and processors, when properly linked, emerge as a formidable and robust computing force far beyond the potentials of any one centralized system. This network, the basis after all of social media, could also potentially be put to use as a decentralized memory institute, complete with the redundancies, checks, and quality controls currently evident in many existing applications. And the best part is that there are working examples of this principle!

One of America's founding fathers, Thomas Jefferson, summarized the principle upon which a new distributed archive would operate:

> let us save what remains: not by vaults and locks which fence them from the public eye and use in consigning them to the waste of time, but by such a multiplication of copies, as shall place them beyond the reach of accident (1791, n.p).

Jefferson was speaking of ways to assure the preservation of America's founding documents, but a clearer and more succinct summary of the differences between the traditional and the new archive is difficult to imagine. In this spirit, LOCKSS ('Lots of Copies Keep Stuff Safe', www.lockss.org) offers a splendid working example. In their own words, 'LOCKSS is open source software that provides librarians with an easy and inexpensive way to collect, store, preserve, and provide access to their own, local copy of authorized content they purchase. Running on standard desktop hardware and requiring almost no technical administration, LOCKSS converts a personal computer into a digital preservation appliance, creating low-cost, persistent, accessible copies of e-journal content as it is published. Since pages in these appliances are never flushed, the local community's access to that content is safeguarded. Accuracy and completeness of LOCKSS appliances is assured through a robust and secure, peer-to-peer polling and reputation system.'

Just as LOCKSS is exemplary of a solution that makes use of distributed computing, other examples have tackled the problem of capturing the dynamic and extensive character of the web. Nearly synonymously with the appearance of the World Wide Web, Brewster Kahle initiated his remarkable Internet archive known as the Wayback Machine (www.archive.org). With over 50 billion web pages archived since its inception in 1996, the archive is composed of 'snapshots' of websites taken at regular intervals, allowing the interested researcher to go back in time and track changes. The previously mentioned 'discrepancy' in the White House Press Secretary's rewriting of a press release or attempts to rewrite the CVs of Enron officials after their company's collapse came to light thanks to this archive. But for the cultural historian, having access to the first decade of the World Wide Web's existence and with it the ability to track the emergence of social protocols, home page formats, early games, etc. is an invaluable resource. And the best part is that Mr. Kahle managed to capture the dynamic character of the web with a modest infrastructure and limited budget. With a mirror site in Alexandria, Egypt, the archive's discursive claim is loud, clear and, I think, not at all overstated. With a more fulsome budget, the archive could expand its operations and the frequency of its 'snapshots', but for the moment, its beauty is that it works efficiently and outside the entanglements of national governments and funding agencies. For once in our media history, someone has managed to both think ahead and act accordingly.

LOCKSS and the Wayback Machine offer two splendid examples of what is possible, one growing out of the efforts of progressive librarians and the other from an insightful and resourceful individual. Together, they have solved several of the problems unique to the digital domain. The issue of mapping links and social-networking patterns has been taken on in the aggregate (social-network mapping and analysis is a developed field, and can take on the face-to-face as easily as the digitally networked). The difficulty here turns on issues of privacy and the potentials for misuse, just as the problems potentially facing Internet archives turn on issues of intellectual property. Social problems rather than conceptual or technological difficulties seem to be the order of the day, which is where an organization like UNESCO can be of great help.

Conclusions

Digital media have blurred relations between the once clearly demarcated realms of producers and consumers. As these digital technologies have become networked and entered a state of high connectivity, a process that is roughly a decade old, we have seen the fast emergence of new social media forms. Social media have enabled new forms of collaboration, and they provide what Pierre Lévy describes as a collective intelligence. In so doing, they have rapidly intensified the erosion of traditional and highly centralized organizations through a process of redefinition. Collaborative news networks compete with established journalism, in the process redefining the news from an institutional assertion of facticity to an act of critical engagement and a struggle for meaning. Music file exchanges such as KaZaa compete with the established recording industry, in the process transforming music from a commodity to be bought and sold into communities of taste built upon distributed sharing. And open source software developers compete with the Microsofts of the world, in the process redefining software from a commodity to a collaborative language and community tool.

So, too, the world of the archive. The traditional archive has served as a social agent active in the reproduction of culture. By serving as a repository of what key institutions deem valuable, archives preserve cultural values and sustain hierarchies of social and cultural power. Given the very real limits of space and resources, difficult decisions have been made regarding whose letters to keep, which newspapers to store, and which sort of artefactual ephemera to hold. Not surprisingly, these decisions reflect an institutional sense of importance and relevance, which in turn largely maps onto the vision of the dominant classes. Little wonder that researchers seeking traces of immigrant life in the US at the turn of the century, or marginal political and social movements of the present, have such difficulty in finding relevant archival sources. But new archival practices that attempt to account for social media forms such as blogs, wikis, chat spaces, games, etc., enabled through distributed logic, enhanced storage capacity and accelerated transmission speeds, can redefine the archive from social agent to social practice. By embracing bottom-up dynamics, they will better reflect a wide range of social values, not just the ruling elite. By addressing cultural production that takes place outside of confines of corporate media, they will assume a much wider range of social granularity. And by taking advantage of the new affordances of digitally networked culture, they will encourage widespread participation.

Archives reflect the environments in which they are situated, and new environments require new policies. As I have attempted to argue, networked digital technologies and 'participatory culture' offer new challenges to both cultural producers and archives, generating new producers and users, new content and collaborators. But they also offer solutions that might be used to rethink the capacities and logics of the archive (storage, distribution, dynamic capture). The examples of the Wayback Machine and LOCKSS show what is possible and provide provocations to more traditional archives to consider these new possibilities. Challenges, of course, remain. We need to think carefully about issues of privacy (for the archiving of network maps) and intellectual property (long overdue for an overhaul in the age of cut and paste). We must make careful distinctions in the weights of various cultural artefacts between say, diplomatic documents and Coke bottle collections, and develop different strategies for safeguarding and making both available. But above all, we must build upon the pioneering efforts of the few visionaries who have ventured into this new world, archiving the fast development of this dynamic cultural sector, and guarding against their selective and strategic use/misuse by those in positions of power, and making information accessible to all in accordance with the cultural logic of the age.

This article is an updated version of 'Moving beyond the artifact: Lessons from participatory culture' in *Preserving the digital heritage: Principles and policies*, eds. Yola De Lusenet and Vincent Wintermans, 15-25. Amsterdam: Netherlands National Commission for Unesco, 2007.

Notes

1. For a detailed examination of this issue from the perspectives of both film theory and archival practice, see Giovanna Fossati's *From grain to pixel: The archival life of film transition* (PhD dissertation, Utrecht University 2009).
2. In fact, most of our cultural texts are profoundly intertextual, relying upon layer upon layer of precedent, commentary and reference. Particularly since the Romantic Era, we have tended to suppress this unruly aspect of authorship, a practice today enforced by the strictures of intellectual property. The digital turn has forced the question upon us, and as we think through the implications for new media forms, we might reconsider the questions put forward by the likes of Michel Foucault and Roland Barthes and reflect upon what we have long forgotten about the reign of authorship.
3. But one example involves President Bush's 2003 'mission accomplished' declaration in regard to Iraq on the USS Abraham Lincoln. If we set aside for a moment the staging of the press conference (the background contained a banner reading 'mission accomplished' and photographers were forbidden to take any shots that would show that the ship was in fact not at sea, but instead docked in San Diego harbor), the White House took an additional step to control information that amounted to rewriting history. The office of the Press Secretary initially issued a statement on its website on May, 1 2003, entitled 'President Bush announces combat operations in Iraq have ended'. Later, after it was clear that combat had not ended, the headline was modified to read 'Major Operations'. The press release, a matter of record, was reworked to accord with White House spin, but backdated to May 1, and attempts were made to prohibit access to the earlier and now telltale version. Thanks to regular archiving of the website, the White House was found out, and future historians will understand that the criticism generated by the first version was based on real events, not the fantasies and misinterpretations alleged by the White House after its revision of the historical record.
4. The market success of Japanese *manga* and *anime* in the US (where *manga* outsells domestic comic books by a factor of four to one) is due in large part to the work of fans who imported, translated and circulated these cultural products without copyright clearance. They effectively created a commercial market, tested it, and their translations in many cases remain superior to commercial alternatives. The industry understands the value of these 'pirates', and both sides have worked out a harmonious co-existence.
5. Although in truth, written texts such as Shakespeare's plays have undergone hundreds of small (and sometimes major) transformations, and films routinely change as they pass through the hands of censors and countless projectionists. Nevertheless, they are relatively stable compared to the dynamic state of wikis, blogs, and other social media.
6. For an extensive discussion of *America's Army*, see the chapter by David Nieborg in this book.

References

Jefferson, Thomas. 1984 (orig.1791) Thomas Jefferson to Ebenezer Hazard, Philadelphia, February 18, 1791. In Thomas Jefferson: *Writings: Autobiography, notes on the state of Virginia, public and private papers, addresses, letters*, ed. Merrill D. Peterson. New York: Library of America. Cited on the homepage of LOCKSS.

DIGITAL MATERIAL

Participation inside?

User activities between design and appropriation

Mirko Tobias Schäfer

In the summer of 1999, a little cat awakened the monolithic music industry that was sleeping its way into the digital age. The cat wore headphones and was the logo of a small application called Napster crawling over the Internet. Millions of people used the application to search for music files and download them on their computer. Developed by a 19-year-old university student, the Napster software did nothing more than index music files stored on a user's computer and share this information with other users in the network.

Napster changed the logic for the distribution of digitized artefacts for good as peer-to-peer (P2P) file-sharing technologies enabled the global distribution of digital information at negligibly low costs. But first and foremost Napster is remarkable because it represents an effective concept of global distribution of artefacts neither developed nor controlled by those industries that have built their business models and economical power on the control of distribution. Napster and its successors tell a well-known tale of computer technology and the Internet, a story of media use as a battle between consumers and producers. Distribution through peer-to-peer systems was soon recognized as subverting the established cultural industries. It also fostered the legend of enthusiast amateurs producing artefacts of a quality that can meet or even beat industrial products.

Due to these and other developments, new media have gained the imago of being enabling technologies that could turn the former consumer of corporate media content from dupe into hero, mastering the new means of production and actively participating in the creation and distribution of – mostly digital – artefacts. And indeed, the new technologies have led to an emerging media practice where users participate significantly in the production and distribution of the cultural industry's goods (Bruns 2008; Jenkins 2002, 2006a, 2006b; Jenkins et al. 2006; Jenkins and Thoburn 2003; Schäfer 2005, 2006). Recently, popular discourse is embracing the phenomenon of producing users, labeling them *Generation C* (c for content), [1] anticipating a revolution of *pro-ams*, professional amateurs (Leadbeater, Miller 2004), and describing their production logic as *Wikinomics* (Tapscott, Williams 2006). With reference to Pierre Lévy, the aspect of a plurality of users collectively producing content and creating artefacts online has been understood as 'collective intelligence' (Jenkins 2001). Metaphors such as the *wisdom of crowds* (Surowiecki 2005) or the *wealth of networks* (Benkler 2006) show collective interactions to be an 'invisible hand' in creating prosperity. To Henry Jenkins, the emerging media practice constitutes a *converging* of different participants and old and new media practices into a field where the distinctions between user and producer are increasingly blurred (Jenkins 2006). Axel Bruns has coined the term *produsage* for the newly emerging practices, and labels participants in production communities as both users and producers (Bruns 2008).

The second coming of the World Wide Web – Web 2.0 – thrives on the immanent promise of user participation in social interactions, and the collective generation and sharing of content. In 2006, *Time* magazine put a face to this promise when it nominated the generic computer user ('YOU') Person of the Year.[2] By claiming that YOU, the user, has risen to become the hero of the Information Age, the perception of consumers as dupes seems to have been abandoned for good, and we seem to have finally become a *participatory culture* (Jenkins 2006a).

However, as the examples above have indicated, this take on new media culture often leads to simplified and rather romanticized interpretations, in popular culture as well as media theory. Only a critical analysis of the term and its connotations can help to understand the underlying mechanisms and the intertwined dynamic of the various participants.

According to Jenkins, the criteria defining participatory culture are 'low barriers to artistic expression and civic engagement', 'strong support for creating and sharing one's creations with others', and 'informal mentorship whereby what is known by the most experienced is passed along to novices', as well as the belief 'that their contributions matter' and that 'members feel some degree of social connection with one another' (Jenkins et al. 2006; Benkler 2006). Participation is here formulated as a community-based activity determined by a high degree of social interaction and mutual understanding among its participants.

In cultural studies the term *participation* describes audiences engaging in culture by receiving, interpreting, and deconstructing media texts, and most recently through acts of appropriation and creation. This perception is highly influenced by ideological connotations (Jenkins et al. 2006; Benkler 2006) that identify participation as a process of explicit and conscious, often intrinsically motivated activities of users claiming their cultural freedom from the culture industries.[3] Along with the explicit participation described by Jenkins and others, the emergence of the so-called Web 2.0 shows an *implicit* participation where user activities are channeled and directed through software design. Recent research has demonstrated how media industries have implemented those activities in their business models, questioning the romanticized understanding of participation (Van Dijck and Nieborg 2008; Scholz 2008; Zimmer 2008).

The mechanisms shaping explicit and implicit participation are far more complex, however, and a thorough analysis of the dynamic interaction between users, corporate companies, artefacts, and socio-technical ecosystems is lacking. Another aspect that deserves more attention is the dynamic interplay constituting aspects of collectivism and collaboration. Bruns has recently pointed out that the community and the collective are misleading metaphors in describing the social interaction on the Internet (Bruns 2008:327). This chapter tries to design a new concept that appropriately describes and analyzes the phenomenon of massive user interactions.

Mapping user activities

In general, participatory culture unfolds in three domains described hereafter as *accumulation*, *archiving*, and *construction*. These three domains are not mutually exclusive and overlap to a certain extent. The logic of electronic distribution and copying of files applies to all three of them. As will be described later, recent software design for information management systems channels these user activities and proposes interfaces and functions that stimulate and regulate them.

Accumulation describes all activities evolving around texts originally produced within the established media industries. This content is collected, altered, further developed or remixed by users and dedicated fans. Examples include the large *Star Wars* fan community producing their own Star Wars movies on websites such as *TheForce.net* or the so-called slash fiction communities Jenkins has described (1991). These communities alter traditional media texts, for example by developing homosexual narratives involving popular media characters like Harry Potter.

Archiving refers to the organization, maintenance and distribution of digital artefacts. This ranges from providing public-domain books in digital formats, such as Project Gutenberg does, to hosting the productions of specific cultural niches like demos or music files from the demoscene – a subculture developing animated realtime graphics – or the independent music production and free distribution of the so-called netlabel scene.

The Internet Archive (Archive.org) is probably the most well-known example for storing and preserving data online. This important resource archives material provided by common users as well as established institutions and professionals and is maintained by a foundation. Although archiving tends to be more institutionalized than accumulating, both areas overlap, for instance in fan archives and the often sophisticated strategies users employ to allocate and share licensed content like movies, audio files, and computer games. In general, the sector of archiving describes all means of indexing, storing, and structuring data for access and easy information retrieval.

Construction describes forms of production that take place outside the established production and distribution channels. Prime examples are open-source software, the demo scene, and the netlabel scene. The domain of construction overlaps with accumulation insofar as users alter software-based products and build new applications for devices initially programmed by commercial vendors. It shows overlaps with archiving in all areas where infrastructures for storing, organizing, and maintaining information are built and knowledge systems are created, such as online software repositories (e.g. Sourceforge.net), and collectively created open-access encyclopedias such as Wikipedia.

The three domains of user activities extend the established culture industries and form a new and complex set of relations between producers and consumers (see Figure 1). Instead of replacing them, these new modes complement older modes of production, distribution, and consumption, and can therefore be described as establishing an *extended culture industry*. The extended culture industries are characterized by the dynamic interaction of all participating parties. Production processes are not only extended into the domain of users – where the (old) culture industry's media texts and products are appropriated – but also happen completely independent of established production and distribution channels. In conclusion, we can state that this present culture is constituted by new design and appropriation of existing content, unfolding along the lines of accumulation, construction, and archiving from the culture industries to its fringes and beyond.

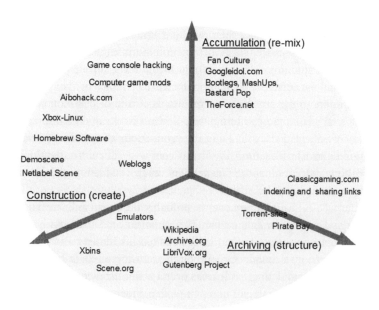

Figure 1: User activities extend the culture industries

Material aspects of design and appropriation

The agency of technology in enabling or averting certain media practices has only recently been acknowledged in media theoretical analysis (Rieder and Schäfer 2008; Schäfer 2006; Hughes and Lang 2006). Due to their technological make-up, some digital artefacts can be reused, modified, and developed more easily than others. Hughes and Lang describe this quality as *transmutability* (2006). In general, all software-based artefacts are transmutable because computer components and software are open to modification. There is a relatively superficial level, like enthusiast fans who photoshop their favorite TV characters or remix their personal hit songs, but in fact every commercial software-based product or digitized artefact can enter a second stage of development, and rigorous transmutations yield surprising results. A Microsoft *Xbox* becomes a Linux computer, Nintendo's *Gameboy* is turned into a musical instrument, Sony's robot dog *Aibo* learns how to dance, and the robotic vacuum cleaner *Roomba* attracts skilled programmers who use the affordable device for experiments in artificial intelligence and robotics.[4] The modifications of these products are rooted in the basic affordances of computer technology, software, and the Internet. Affordances are specific qualities of material and artefacts, and they affect design and use to a great degree (Norman 1998, 9). To be more precise, the affordance of electronic computers to copy files without loss is crucial to an application like Napster and the new logic of distribution. This logic is inherent to electronic computers; for the execution of any given task, they need to copy files from memory to a central processing unit. As such, computers can be described as universal machines that can execute basically every task formulated in a language the machine understands. Software constitutes the many different applications that can be executed by any computer (Turing 1948). Despite the fact that software is bound to a material data carrier, it shows parallels with language in its structure, while in its effect it is similar to machinery (Rieder and Schäfer 2008, 163). Software is a means of production organized and structured as (programming) language. Like language, it is also modular, and parts of one software application can be used for a completely different activity. Such pre-programmed modules are available with a framework for software development. Programming software therefore implies the reuse of previously written software. Taken together, all available software constitutes a reservoir, a cultural resource, that programmers use and to which they contribute at the same time. Software as a cultural resource is distributed and made available through the Internet that forms a global infrastructure and connects all users. It is due to this hybrid constellation of technological qualities that the Internet has become today's primary medium for collaboration and communication, and a universal archive for all kinds of information.

An application like Napster is profoundly related to the affordances of computer technology, software and the Internet, and the way users deal with these tech-

nologies. While Napster is nothing more than a bricolage of a file-transport protocol combined with a chat program and a graphical user interface for convenient
use, it satisfied the technological requirements of the digital age: Napster's design perfectly fitted the qualities of the Internet. While the music industry was
unaware of the looming digital revolution, the logic of distributing media texts
electronically through computer networks developed through the appropriation
of a set of existing technologies, such as the file transfer protocol (FTP), the
MPEG format for compressed audio and movie files (e.g. mp3 and DivX), music
player applications as WinAmp, and programs for automated indexing, retrieval
and distribution of files.

The history of Napster teaches us that the availability of technologies plus the
knowledge of how to generate, use, and recombine them create potentiality. William Gibson's well-known line 'the street finds its own uses for things' (2003,
199) obviously applies to the virtual landscape of the Internet and its users. Napster also demonstrates that participation and collective collaboration can take
place on a very basic level and that the user-collective can improve the infrastructure for retrieving files and information. It worked like this: after downloading
the Napster application, the user contributed to the overall file-sharing network
by allowing a part of her hard drive to function as a server for file exchange, by
uploading files to the network. The Napster application indexed the files a user
shared and made those data available for search requests. P2P file-sharing clients
such as Napster have revealed that file sharing has much less to do with explicit
participation and community-driven objectives than enthusiast commentators anticipated. Actually – and by technological design – participation became an automated process, completely unrelated to community values, social interaction or
communication in general. Although those aspects are optional in many software
applications, they are far from necessary for sharing files.
    In an attempt to limit the damage caused by digital distribution through P2P
networks, the music industry started appropriating the technology itself by setting
up networks of fake users, so-called bot networks, that flooded the file-sharing
systems with corrupted song files. Old business models and new media practice
collided at the level of popular discourse, where fans promoted piracy as an appropriate activity in view of the music and movie industries' tight control over
how music is consumed, a debate also reflected by the design of P2P networks
and the attempts of the industry to protect their products through copy-protection
systems and Digital Rights Management (DRM). Triggering a reciprocal competition, the protective move of the established industries stimulated the improvement of file-sharing protocols like *eDonkey* and *BitTorrent*, as each new copy-protection system was countered by a more advanced cracking technology.[5] This
combat not only charged technology emotionally. The harsh reaction of the media giants and their representative associations also revealed another aspect of

technologies' social use: due to its affordances, its development is very much driven by users' appropriation and its resulting formalization in new design solutions.

The interplay of technological design and appropriation analyzed here using the example of Napster, sheds a different light on participation. Participation cannot be assigned only to users who get involved with media and 'oppose' a dominant vendor. The original producer and other commercial units – who are either actively involved in the process of modifying the original design or benefit from its outcome – are also part of participatory culture. Implementing user labor in the development of design by commercial vendors is a usually neglected aspect in enthusiasts' descriptive texts on participatory culture (e.g. Jenkins 2006b; Benkler 2006). The most recent Microsoft game console, for example, features many aspects developed by the so-called *homebrew scene*. As unlicensed users of the Microsoft *Xbox Development Kit* (XDK), these hackers designed many useful applications for the Xbox. Their work was distributed within user networks and, due to its unlicensed status, not commercially exploitable. Microsoft however learned from this experience and integrated many features into the next *Xbox 360*, also providing an *Integrated Development Kit* (IDK) that can be used to create software and distribute it through the Xbox network. Microsoft achieved technological closure by consequently implementing user activities and appropriation into the design and legal regulation of the successive Xbox model.

It is claimed that user activities revolve around explicit participation, which thrives on intrinsic motivation and often takes place in teams or ad-hoc and team-like collectives (e.g. Bruns 2008 on Wikipedia; Jenkins 2006 on fans of the television program *Survivor*; Raessens 2005 on game modifications; Schäfer 2005 on the modification of the Xbox). However, there is also implicit participation. Implicit participation can be part of the software design as the sharing of a part of the user's hard drive in P2P file-sharing. It is automated and delegated to an information system, not requiring any intrinsic motivation, community feeling or collaborative effort. Implementing participation into software design entails formalizing and channeling user activities. It is no coincidence that Tim O'Reilly has dubbed this design step an *architecture of participation*. In his programmatic text 'What is Web 2.0', he describes basic configurations of channeling user participation for commercial ends (2005). User activities are thus employed for the improvement of information systems and the generation of content, which either extends the content of the commercial provider or constitutes its main potential.

The explicit participation of user communities in developing technology is implemented into new design decisions, but Web 2.0 applications show that next to explicit participation, implicit participation can be employed to improve existing information systems and to build new business models of cultural production.

Participation as design or the return of the audience

Culture industries are witnessing a shift from creating content to providing platforms for user-driven activities. On these platforms the users create content or alter existing content from the proprietary resources of the cultural industries according to their regulations. The *Star Wars MashUp* editor, for example, aims at fans who accumulate media texts relating to their favorite subject and alter them or create new ones. The fansite *TheForce.net* has become a popular platform for creating, promoting, and hosting fan movies. Featuring tutorials on how to make fan movies or create computer-generated imagery for space ships and special effects, it has earned a reputation as the best Star Wars website out there. The copyright holder Lucasfilm acknowledged the need for fans to play with the media texts but controls this play through a corporate web platform. The *Star Wars Mash-Up* editor offers fans the opportunity to exercise their creativity and equips them with the means to do so. It does so, however, with strict restrictions, trapping the fans on the Death Star so to speak, as they are bound to the corporation's design and legal regulations. The *MashUp* editor prevents downloads of any content to users' hard drives, and editing of content is possible only in the web-based editor Lucasfilm provides. Using other editing programs is prohibited as well, as are certain forms of representation. Nudity for instance is recognized and filtered through the Eyespot editing software, avoiding displays of naked persons in user-created remixes.[6] Furthermore, fans' creations may be published by the corporate platform only, and any distribution through YouTube or other services is forbidden. Finally, Lucasfilm requires that users grant to Lucasfilm, 'its licensees, successors and affiliates a perpetual and irrevocable, exclusive, royalty free, worldwide license in all rights, titles and interests of every kind and nature' to their self-created content.[7] This practice of extending the value of a proprietary resource through fans while at the same time denying these fans any form of authorial compensation and even freedom of creativity is highly questionable (Lessig 2007).

Increasingly, user creations are subject to the software design and legal administration of corporate platforms that explicitly integrate user activities into their services. The so-called Web 2.0 applications O'Reilly refers to take participation to another level by implementing it into software design for the purpose of channeling user activities implicitly. On the photo platform Flickr users might not even notice how publishing their personal photos, adding a title to them, or even placing them on a map is extending the Flickr information system. By simply uploading a photo, users contribute data on the camera model, date and time of picture, camera settings, etc. These so-called Exchangeable Image File (EXIF) data are metadata generally attached to pictures taken by standard digital cameras. By adding *tags*, keywords, to the pictures, users compensate the information systems' lack of semantic information retrieval. The machine cannot read a picture, but it can read the meta-information provided either by the camera through the EFIX data or by users who add title, location, and certain keywords. By using it, users extend the overall information system and contribute to an improved information management. By providing valuable meta-information in tags of up-loaded photos, users improve the information retrieval of Yahoo's search engine, Flickr's owner. Thanks to Flickr's tagging system, Yahoo is able to compensate the inability of search engines to recognize a picture's content. User-generated meta-information teaches the machine to answer complex search requests.

Contrary to earlier accounts of participation, I have shown that systems that thrive on the implementation of user activities are not dependent on or encouraging community activities. There are Flickr groups, which might be considered communities because they share objectives, rules, regular communication, and recurring patterns of social interaction as well as offline gatherings. But these activities are an optional function in the system's design and not a precondition for the cultural production it generates. Despite the fact that users are participating in the creation of an information system and collectively building a resource of stored data and metadata for efficient information retrieval, they do not necessarily share a common goal or social interaction. Adding photos to Flickr can involve different uses and gratifications and therefore is not limited to explicit participation as commonly understood. The idealizing connotations of participation as a critical, communal and social activity has to be revisited in the light of software design that channels user activities as implicit participation.

The affordances of networked media, which enable large groups of users to actively participate in cultural production, and the high amount of user-generated content in different domains of cultural production have led to the assumption that the promise of participation has been fulfilled. But software design employing these user activities as implicit participation calls for critically revisiting the way technology is designed, used, and appropriated. Large user numbers providing valuable personal data through the interfaces of platforms such as social network sites (e.g. *Facebook*, *MySpace*, *Orkut*, *Hyves*, and *LinkedIn*), giving ratings through media sites such as YouTube, and affecting search results in Yahoo through the provision of metadata to Flickr once again posits the audience as a source for market research and target for advertising. This clearly contrasts the utopian ideal of a user-controlled participatory culture. Figure 2 shows a number of applications that successfully employ user activities from the domains of accumulation, archiving, and construction, and implement them into corporate-controlled platforms.

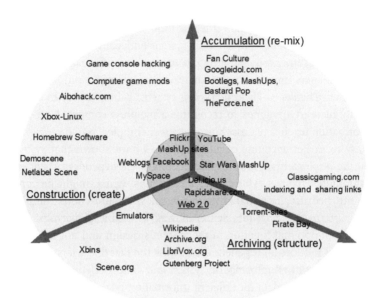

Figure 2: Implementation of user activities into commercial applications

The interaction of large numbers of users, user activities-channeling interfaces, and intelligent information systems show participatory culture to be a hybrid, a socio-technical ecosystem. The many possible motivations for using these systems, as well as the plurality of social interaction, reflects heterogeneous participation that can hardly be grasped with the ideological connotations of earlier enthusiast accounts. It will be necessary instead to critically analyze how software design affects user behavior and how power structures are re-established through implementing participation in information systems.

Notes

1. Generation C. In *Trendwatching.com*, March 2004. www.trendwatching.com/trends/GEN-ERATION_C.htm (accessed June 2008).
2. *Time*, December 25/January 1, 2007.
3. For a further analysis and critique of the utopian perception of participation, see Eggo Müller in this volume.
4. The Xbox-Linux Project is hosted at: www.xbox-linux.org (accessed June 2008). There are a number of musicians using the software Little Sound DJ, Nanoloop or Pocketnoise to produce music on the Game Boy; see Game Boy Music Club Vienna http://www.gameboymusicclub.org/ (accessed June 2008). The hacker Aibopet offers a large number of programs on his website www.aibohack.com. The program DiskoAibo, which

makes Aibo dance, is available there as well. The Roomba modders meet at Roomba Community, http://www.roombacommunity.com/ (Acessed June 2008).

5. Companies like Overpeer flooded P2P networks with corrupted files on behalf of music companies and industry associations. In order to do so, they set up fake networks of virtual file sharers distributing the corrupted files. As Thomas Mennecke (2005) argues, these efforts consequently lead to the development of safer and less corruptible file-sharing protocols such as BitTorrent and eDonkey. Due to its inefficiency, Overpeer was discontinued in 2005 after three years of anti-P2P activity.

6. Ideological and sociopolitical issues can be channeled through software design. Developing hermeneutics and methods of analysis is an important task for media studies to accordingly interpret and criticize 'back-end politics' inscribed into design decisions.

7. Section C and E of the Lucasfilm's *Star Wars MashUps* Terms of Service. http://starwars.com/welcome/about/mashup-copyright (accessed August 2007).

Acknowledgements

I am indebted to Bernhard Rieder, Tanja Sihvonen and Kim de Vries for their comments and helpful remarks.

References

Benkler, Yochai. 2006. *The wealth of networks: How social production transforms markets and freedoms.* New Haven, London: Yale University Press.

Bruns, Axel. 2008. *Blogs, Wikipedia, Second Life, and beyond: From production to produsage.* New York: Peter Lang.

Dijck, José van, and David Nieborg. 2008. De opmars van de cybernauten: Drie nieuwe studies geven hun visie op de digitale participatiecultuur. *Academische Boekengids* 65, November 2007, 7-10.

Gibson, William. [1982] 2003. Burning chrome. In *Burning chrome*, William Gibson, 179-204. New York: Eos.

Gillmor, Dan. 2006. *We the media: Grassroots by the people, for the people.* Sebastopol: O'Reilly Media.

Hughes, Lang. 2006. Transmutability: Digital decontextualization, manipulation, and recontextualization as a new source of value in the production and consumption of culture products. *Proceedings of the 39th Hawaii International Conference on System Sciences.* http://doi.ieeecomputersociety.org/10.1109/HICSS.2006.511.

Jenkins, Henry. 2002. Interactive audiences? The collective intelligence of media fans. In *The new media book*, ed. Dan Harries. London: BFI.

—. 2006a. *Fans, bloggers, and gamers: Exploring participatory culture.* New York: New York University Press.

—. 2006b. *Convergence culture: Where old and new media collide.* New York: New York University Press.

Jenkins, Henry, Katie Clinton, Ravi Purushotma, Alice J. Robison, and Margaret Weigel. 2006. Confronting the challenges of participatory culture: Media education for the 21st century. *MacArthur Foundation.* http://www.digitallearning.macfound.org/atf/cf/%7B7E45C7E0-A3E0-4B89-AC9C-E807E1B0AE4E%7D/JENKINS_WHITE_PAPER.PDF.

Jenkins, Henry, and David Thoburn. 2003. *Democracy and new media*. Cambridge, MA: MIT Press.

Lessig, Lawrence. 2007. Lucasfilm's Phantom Menace. *The Washington Post*, July 12 2007. http://www.washingtonpost.com/wp-dyn/content/article/2007/07/11/AR2007071101996_pf.html.

Leadbeater, Charles, and Paul Miller. 2004. *The pro-am revolution*. London: Demos.

Lévy, Pierre. 1999. *Collective intelligence: Mankind's emerging world in cyberspace*. Cambridge, MA: Perseus Books.

Mennecke, Thomas. 2005. End of the road for Overpeer. *Slyck News*, December 10 2005. http://www.slyck.com/story1019.html.

Norman, Donald. 1998. *The design of everyday things*. Cambridge, MA: MIT Press.

O'Reilly, Tim. 2005. What is Web 2.0. http://www.oreillynet.com/pub/a/oreilly/tim/news/2005/09/30/what-is-web-20.html.

Rieder, Bernhard, and Mirko Tobias Schäfer. 2008. Beyond engineering: Software design as bridge over the culture/technology dichotomy. In *Philosophy and design: From engineering to architecture*, eds. Pieter E. Vermaas, Peter Kroes, Andrew Light, and Steven A. Moore, 152-164. Dordrecht: Springer.

Schäfer, Mirko Tobias. 2005. Homework: The extension of the culture industry. In *Data browser 01: Economising culture*, eds. Geoff Cox, Joasia Krysa, and Anya Lewin, 191-199. Brooklyn: Autonomedia.

Schäfer, Mirko Tobias. 2006. Partizipation als Output des Konsums softwarebasierter Produkte. In *Das Spiel mit dem Medium: Partizipation – Immersion – Interaktion*, eds. Britta Neitzel and Rolf Nohr, 296-310. Marburg: Schüren.

Scholz, Trebor. 2008. Market ideology and the myths of Web 2.0. *First Monday* 13 (3). http://www.uic.edu/htbin/cgiwrap/bin/ojs/index.php/fm/article/view/2138/1945.

Surowiecki, James. 2005. *The wisdom of crowds: Why the many are smarter than the few and how collective wisdom shapes business, economies, societies and nations*. New York: Random House.

Tapscott, Don, and Anthony D. Williams. 2006. *Wikinomics: How mass collaboration changes everything*. New York: Portfolio.

Turing, Alan M. 1948. Intelligent machinery. *National Physical Laboratory Report*. http://www.alanturing.net/turing_archive/archive/l/l32/L32-001.html.

Uricchio, William. 2004. Cultural citizenship in the age of P2P networks. In *European culture and the media*, eds. Ib Bondebjerg and Peter Golding. Bristol: Intellect Books.

Zimmer, Michael. 2008. The externalities of Search 2.0: The emerging privacy threats when the drive for the perfect search engine meets Web 2.0. *First Monday*, 13 (3) 2008. http://www.uic.edu/htbin/cgiwrap/bin/ojs/index.php/fm/article/view/2136/1944.

Challenging the magic circle

How online role-playing games are negotiated by everyday life

Marinka Copier

'Darn,' I cursed at myself as I walked up to my desk to turn on my computer. It was mid-September 2006, I looked at my watch, it was already 7:15 pm and I wanted to be logged onto the online game World of Warcraft around 7:30 pm. Considering that it was a Sunday evening, there would probably be a queue of a few hundred players who wanted to connect to the Argent Dawn role-play server, just like me. This meant it would be impossible to get logged on before 8:00 pm. I tried to remember what Eiswein wrote in his post on the official server forum. The caravan of the Argent Archives would leave for Thelsamar from outside the gates of the Alliance city of Ironforge at 8:30 pm. The dwarven Archivar Eiswein, a character played by Jørgen (24, Norwegian), head of the Argent Archives role-play guild and organizer of the event, had asked player-characters to arrive early so he could hand out assignments and missions. While Windows loaded, I made a quick to-do list: 1) As we would be traveling through the virtual winter landscape of Dun Morogh I had to dress my gnome character Speckles Snapwiggle in proper clothes – gloves and furry-looking boots would be essential for a wintry feel, 2) I had to move Speckles from the Alliance capital city of Stormwind to Ironforge – the Deeprun Tram that runs between the two cities would probably be the fastest, 3) I wanted to answer some letters sent through the in-game postal system. Most of them were job offers for Speckles, who together with her twin sister Freckles formed a photographers duo called the Snap Sisters. This means they take on jobs that involve photographing characters and role-play events such as weddings, sporting events, trials, beauty pageants, markets, and, in this case, the Archives caravan. I (29, Dutch) picked up my mobile phone and rang my friend Zoe (28, Dutch), who played the role of the character Freckles. 'Are you already in?' I asked, 'Is there a queue?' It turned out that she had been playing the whole day, and yes, she heard there was quite a queue. There were 260 players in front of me in the queue – I mumbled. Zoe laughed: 'Be happy if you make it by eight.' 'I'll get something to eat first, then,' I replied.

The ambiguity of play

In massively multiplayer online role-playing games (MMORPGs) such as *World of Warcraft* (WoW, Blizzard Entertainment 2004), large numbers of players come to-gether in a complex online environment not only to defeat monsters and each other in return for virtual gold and armour, but also to turn their avatars into colourful characters by roleplaying them. The above is an excerpt of my auto-ethnographic account of the gnome warrior and photographer Speckles Snapwig-gle, one of the characters I played during my two-year participatory ethnographic study of role play in WoW (Copier 2007).

According to the game studies concept of the 'magic circle', games proceed within their own boundaries of time and space, absorbing players utterly into a separate world set off from ordinary life (Salen and Zimmerman 2004). In this chapter I challenge the concept and metaphor of the magic circle. As T.L. Taylor argued in *Play between worlds*, an ethnographic study of the MMORPG *Everquest* (Sony Online Entertainment 1999), the notion that we can or should (re)constitute game boundaries 'thereby solving the deeper social and regulatory issues that can nag us' is very problematic (Taylor 2006, 151).

Although at first glance the above thick description of logging onto WoW might seem to illustrate a process of entering into a magic circle, I argue that the magic circle, which resonates references to 'walled off' magic rites and places, supernatural powers, illusions and experiences, blinds us to the ambiguous qua-lities of games and game play. The thick description also shows that game play is not only shaped by experiences *within* the online gaming environment but – often simultaneously – by (mediated) experiences outside, both online and offline. Not only before and after logging onto the game, but also while being logged on, I find myself *negotiating* the spatial, temporal and social dimensions of the game play experience. It is precisely this process of negotiating rules and boundaries that shape not only role play in MMORPGs, but games and game play in general. As the emergence of Fantasy[1] gaming culture from the 1970s onwards, of which WoW is merely the latest incarnation, ties in with the development of what Man-uel Castells termed the 'network society' (Castells 1996), I introduce the network perspective as an alternative to the magic circle. The network perspective makes it possible to understand the ambiguous qualities of online role-playing games.

Role-playing games and the network society

More than 30 years ago, in January 1974, in a garage in the city of Lake Geneva near Minneapolis, Gary Gygax and Dave Anderson hand-assembled the booklets that made up (what is generally considered to be) the first Fantasy role-playing game called *Dungeons and Dragons* (D&D). Back then it must have been unthinkable that this blend between war-gaming, educational role play, and Fantasy would have such an impact on the development of computer games (King and Borland 2003). Since the release of D&D, the Fantasy gaming world has developed from what pioneer researcher Gary Alan Fine in 1983 called a 'rather small, perhaps trivial, social world' (Fine 1983, 1), mostly consisting of white, middle-class boys and men, to a 'rather big, important, social world in which females now also make up a significant part' (Fine 1983, Yee 2005). Between 1999 and 2008, the number of people playing online role-playing games increased from one to fourteen million. Approximately ten million people play *World of Warcraft*; which equals the population of Belgium.

The current Fantasy gaming world not only includes online games, but also tabletop role-playing games, live-action roleplaying, wargaming, board games, and collectible card games. The Dutch *Elf Fantasy Fair*, the largest Fantasy convention in Europe that attracts around 20,000 visitors each year, shows how Fantasy gaming often blends in with a love for Fantasy books, films, television series, clothing and jewelry, folk music, historical re-enactment, and (neo)pagan spirituality. A three-year study that I initiated of the visitors to the Fair, in which I inquired into their interests ranging from gaming to clothing and from music to spirituality, showed the heterogeneity of the public. Not only in age (ranging from children to 70-year-olds), but also in gender (an average of 60 per cent female and 40 per cent male) and interests: participants create their own mix of Fantasy culture in which games often take up a central role (Copier 2005; Copier and Ramstedt 2006). In the last three decades, the heterogeneous Fantasy gaming world has grown exponentially; it has also changed dramatically. While it is still mostly boys and men playing war games, card games, and tabletop role-playing games, women and girls are very active in live-action roleplaying and MMORPGs.

In his trilogy *The information age: Economy, society and culture* (1996, 1997, and 1998), Castells used rich empirical case studies to map how, from the late 1960s onwards, we are witnessing a shift from hierarchies to networks in all sectors of society. According to Castells, this shift is due to three interdependent processes: the information technology revolution, the economic crisis of both capitalism and statism, and the blooming of cultural social movements, such as libertarianism, human rights, feminism, and environmentalism. Whereas Castells focused on an analysis of the socio-political forms of social interaction, such as business networks in Asia and the Mexican Zapatista movement led by Subcomandante Marcos, online networks of play are also important global and distributed forms of sociability. Castells's work is part of a growing body of network theory in which our society, including science itself, is understood as a complex system shaped by flows within and between actor networks that are often powered by information and communication technologies. In order to study the interactions that are going on between the human and nonhuman actors in these networks, I conducted an ethnographic study of role play in WoW from the perspective of the actor-network theory (ANT), a theory and methodology that is part of the network discourse. ANT, was first developed in Science and Technology Studies (STS) in the mid-1980s (Callon 1986; Law 1987; Latour 1987, 2005). This method not only allows us to research collaborative play, it also uncovers how MMORPG researchers and their work are tied in with the networks of play and design that they study.

When Callon, Law, and Latour originally formulated ANT in 1980s, they argued that to understand the process of knowledge production in science and technology, we should map the networked interactions between both human and nonhuman actors. In his latest work, Latour reformulated ANT as a new form of social science that consists of a 'tracing of associations', thus offering insight into complexity, instead of mapping a material domain or providing a singular social explanation (Latour 2005). In order to understand how actor networks are formed, stay together, or fall apart, Latour proposed ethnographic research of actual processes. In turn, these experiences should be reassociated and reassembled into a 'thick description'. In a thick description, behavior is described in its context, in such a way that it becomes meaningful to the reader (Geertz 1973). Latour insists on calling ANT a travel guide instead of a methodology. This way, he argued, we cannot confuse ANT with a frame that is imposed on its object of research. Like a travel guide, ANT offers suggestions for tracing associations and for traveling through webs of interrelations. 'Tracing associations' allows us to understand the constant morphing process of the social in and around MMORPGs. Using a slogan from ANT, you have to 'follow the actors themselves': 'it is no longer enough to limit actors to the role of informers offering cases of well-known types. You have to grant them back the ability to make up their own theories of what the social is made of. Your task is no longer to impose some order, to limit the range of acceptable entities, to teach actors what they are, or to add some reflexivity to their blind practice' (Latour 2005, 12).

In what follows I first introduce my ethnographic study of role play in WoW, after which I will discuss the historical and theoretical background of the concept and metaphor of the magic circle. Going back to *Homo ludens* (1938), the book in which the Dutch historian Johan Huizinga first introduced the term magic circle in relation to games and play, I argue that his work is often misinterpreted by modern game scholars. The network perspective allows us to work from Huizinga's main premise: understanding the play element *of* culture.

Role play in online role-playing games

In order to 'follow the actors' I became a WoW player, on 11 February 2005, the day that WoW was released in Europe, along with thousands of others. I had already been playing tabletop and live-action role-playing games for a few years and was an active participant in the Dutch Fantasy game culture as a designer, researcher, and organizer. Ethnography involves studying a natural research setting over a substantial period of time, thus collecting rich data in order to develop an empathic understanding of the behaviour and meaning-making of persons in that setting. In traditional ethnography, three levels are distinguished in which the researcher can integrate into the culture: observer, participant-observer, or participant. In an ethnographic study of play in MMORPGs, the researcher does not have this choice, he or she has to become a participant in order to play; thus, there is no observer position possible. The participant position makes the MMORPG researcher into an active actor, both in play and in research networks.

As a player-researcher I chose to focus on the role-play (RP) game mode which is remarkably absent from MMORPG research. The name 'Massively Multiplayer Online Role-Playing Game' suggests that all its players role play. Paradoxically, *World of Warcraft* is coded for instrumental play. As the word 'warcraft' in the title emphasizes, playing the game is about battling monsters and other players. In order to participate in instrumental play, it is not necessary to perform your avatar. The result of this is that most players use their avatar as a pawn. Psychologist Nick Yee even feels that the 'RP' in MMORPG is ironic, as 'most MMORPGs have had to deliberately set aside designated role-playing servers, and these have always been in the minority' (Yee 2006). In WoW, these role-play servers are technically no different from PvE (Player versus Environment) or PvP (Player versus Player) servers, which means that role play is not written into the code of the game; rather, it consists of a set of meta-game rules. In order to encourage players to enact their characters, the developer, Blizzard Entertainment, added special guidelines, known as 'role-play policies': 'Players who choose to play in an RP realm should abide by the Role-Playing realm policies and remain in-character at all times. Role-Playing realms give players the chance to develop characters with a backstory who do not go blindly from quest to quest, but instead assist or hamper the efforts of others for reasons of their own' (Realm types, WoW website 2004). Most scholars focus on the 'instrumental' play that the PvE and PvP modes offer. The role-play cultures that develop on designated RP servers, complete with their own rules and etiquette, are not a representative sample of online play and culture. However, Taylor suggests, by telling 'border stories', in other words, looking at areas of gaming that are normally neglected, we can learn more about both the games themselves and about the broader culture in which they are embedded (Taylor 2006, 10).

Let us return to the caravan of the Argent Archives, a role-play guild that Eiswein had started as an imaginary subdivision of the Ironforge Library. The narrative of the game holds minimal information on this library in the city of Ironforge, which enabled Eiswein to make up his own story, without breaking the rules of Warcraft's lore as represented throughout the different games that Blizzard Entertainment published in this setting.

Upon returning with tea and a cheese sandwich, the queue was down to 145. The good thing was that the queue gave me some time to clean off the stacks of research papers and teaching materials from my desk. While eating my sandwich, I turned on MSN and started chatting with Zoe while I simultaneously went through my e-mail. As Freckles was recovering from a previous role-play adventure (in which we were stranded on a deserted island), Zoe would use one of her other characters to travel with the caravan. It was 7:50 pm when I was finally able to log on.

As she should, Speckles appeared where I had logged out the last time – in a tavern in the Dwarven district of Stormwind. The top view angle of the camera made my gnomish character look unpleasantly small, as if I was a giant looking down on her. Using my mouse I quickly turned and lowered the camera and as I zoomed in, I smiled at the combination of her funny-looking three red ponytails and the determined expression on the character's face.

After arriving in Ironforge I spotted Archivar Eiswein standing in front of a table that was positioned underneath a simple tent. In order to have a better look I scrolled the mouse wheel forward to turn the camera into first-person perspective. The older dwarf had a long white beard and was wearing a gray robe combined with a silver-gray tabard that displayed a compass, and green gloves kept his hands warm. Player-characters had lined up to talk to him, and he was using a combination of chat and emotes to hand out assignments and missions. 'Oh, hello, Miss Snapwiggle,' Eiswein said. 'Yes, hullo,' I replied. 'Here I am.' While I waited for my turn to talk to the Archivar, the group of player-characters wanting to join the caravan grew fast, and as a result it became almost impossible to follow all the conversations taking place in the vicinity. I pulled the camera back to third person so I could focus on the chat of the player-characters nearby, which showed up in the text bubbles above their heads. 'Now, I will need you to take as many photographs of those that are with us here,' Eiswein told Speckles. 'Do not fear the price of the film you use. The Archives will pay.'

Eiswein asked Speckles to document the trip in snapshots 'so that nothing be- comes lost or forgotten'. This not only meant that I would perform the role of photographer but also that I would take screenshots during the event. Later Eis- wein used the screenshots taken by both himself and others to make what he calls a photoreel, a report of the caravan to be posted on the role-play community website ArgentArchives.org. Here, players document their characters, guild and role-play experiences in stories, drawings, and screenshots. If we consider the above auto-ethnographic fragment in terms of the magic circle, is ArgentArc- hives.org part of World of Warcraft?

Challenging the magic circle

The magic circle became a popular game studies concept due to the work of game designers and researchers Katie Salen and Eric Zimmerman. In their book on game design fundamentals, Rules of Play (2004), Salen and Zimmerman adopted the term 'magic circle' as one of the core concepts to define the game experience. In a chapter that opens with an image of a chalk circle they argue: 'To play a game means entering into a magic circle, or perhaps creating one as a game begins. (...) The term magic circle is appropriate because there is in fact something genuinely magical that happens when a game begins (...) Within the magic circle, special meanings accrue and cluster around objects and behaviors. In effect, a new reality is created, defined by the rules of the game and inhabited by its players' (Salen and Zimmerman 2004, 95-96).

Salen and Zimmerman borrowed the term 'magic circle' from Huizinga, who in *Homo ludens* defined play as an activity that 'proceeds within its own proper boundaries of time and space according to fixed rules and in an orderly manner' (Huizinga 1938, ed. 1955, 13). Huizinga did not label this bounded activity as taking place within a magic circle, however. He refers to the magic circle, or 'toovercirkel' in Dutch, when he compares the playground to similar arenas: 'the card-table, the magic circle, the temple, the stage, the screen, the tennis court, the court of justice, etc., are all in form and function playgrounds, i.e., forbidden spots, isolated, hedged round, hallowed, within which special rules obtain' (Huizinga 1938, ed. 1955, 10). Salen and Zimmerman seem to have picked the appealing term 'magic circle' from Huizinga's list and matched it with both Huizinga's and their own definition of games. The term magic circle thus became a powerful concept and metaphor, leading to a perception of games as safe havens of imagination and experimentation that are separated from 'real' or 'ordinary' life. The game space is understood as a 'special space', a 'fun space', because players enter into it voluntarily and are temporarily freed of work. Even though the metaphor of the magic circle might seem to be especially fitting for research into Fantasy role-playing games, some researchers, including myself, have expressed their concern about the magic circle (Castronova 2005; Consalvo 2005; Copier 2005, 2007; Lammes 2006; Montola 2005; Nieuwdorp 2005; Roderiquez 2006; Taylor 2006; Pargman and Jakobsson 2006).[2]

In trying to find a way around the 'magic' and the 'strong boundaries' of the metaphor of the magic circle in order to express how they can both be open and closed, a few game researchers reformulated the magic circle. In discussing pervasive games, Eva Nieuwdorp (2005) chose to adapt Erving Goffman's metaphor of the screen: 'the screen not only selects but also transforms what is passed through it' (Goffman 1961, 33). In his economic analysis of MMORPGs, Edward Castronova opted for the term 'porous membrane': 'people are crossing it all the time in both directions, carrying their behavioral assumptions and attitudes with them. As a result, the valuation of things in cyberspace becomes enmeshed in the valuation of things outside cyberspace' (Castronova 2005, 150). In her ethnography of *Everquest*, Taylor defined MMORPG play as 'play between worlds': 'Playing EQ is about playing between worlds – playing back, and forth, across the boundaries of the game and the game world, and the "real" or nonliteral game space' (Taylor 2006, 17). Building on these modifications of the magic circle, Daniel Pargman and Peter Jakobsson proposed a 'weak-boundary hypothesis' (Pargman and Jakobsson 2006). In order to adopt a more flexible idea of the boundaries of play, they (re)introduced Erving Goffman's concept of 'frames' and Fine's idea of 'frames-within-frames', which suggests that inside the primary framework (which is the basis for everything we do), we establish roles and subframes that redefine the situation. Pargman and Jakobsson argued that gaming creates a specific set of roles or subframes. Thus, they replaced the magic circle with the porous or weak boundaries of the game framework, which holds the conventions of the game. In line with the work of Goffman and Fine, they state that, 'There is nothing magical about switching between roles. It is something we do all the time and can literally be done at the blink of an eye' (Pargman and Jakobsson 2006).

Even though these reconfigurations of the magic circle assist in uncovering the ambiguous qualities of games and game play, I still find the concept and metaphor of the magic circle problematic in two ways. Conceptually, the magic circle refers to a pre-existing artificiality of the game space, which creates a dichotomy between the real and the imaginary that hides the fact that digital play is a material practice which is deeply anchored in everyday life. The metaphor of the magic circle makes the boundary between 'game' and 'non-game' even stronger because it represents the game space as an isolated magical wonderland which seems to be almost impossible to grasp rationally. In order to discuss the relation between fantasy and reality, scholars have opted for a counter-rhetoric that includes breaking or blurring the boundaries between the inside and outside of a game. MMORPG researchers have, for instance, argued that the magic circle of MMORPGs becomes porous when we consider the sale of virtual items and gold on eBay (Castronova 2005; Taylor 2006). In order to understand this paradox of the magic circle, in which games can be both open and closed, we have to engage more critically with Salen and Zimmerman's *Rules of play* and Huizinga's *Homo ludens*.

The play element of culture

Huizinga wrote his definition of play in relation to his overarching argument that culture is *sub specie ludi*: civilization arises and unfolds in and as play. His main goal was not to analyze the play element *in* culture, but to understand the play element *of* culture; how culture itself is formed through the process of play. Therefore, Huizinga argued that even though 'play is distinct from "ordinary" life both as to locality and duration', at the same time, it is an important part of daily life: 'play presents itself to us in the first instance: as an intermezzo, an *interlude* in our daily lives. As a regularly recurring relaxation, however, it becomes the accompaniment, the complement, in fact an integral part of life in general' (Huizinga 1938, ed. 1955, 9). In his analysis of *Homo ludens*, Hector Rodriquez argues that Huizinga underscores that the concept of play often cannot be circumscribed within precise conceptual boundaries. 'His entire study can be seen as an effort to speak as precisely as possible about categories and distinctions that cannot be neatly demarcated' (Roderiquez 2006). That many game scholars focus on Huizinga's bounded definition of play instead of his more ambiguous cultural interpretation of play might also be due to the fact that against Huizinga's will, the English subtitle of his book became 'A study of the play element *in* culture' instead of '*of* culture', thus hiding the nature of his overarching argument.

A closer look at Salen and Zimmerman's work reveals that they also deal with this paradox of play. Building on Huizinga's idea that games are 'temporary worlds within the ordinary world', Salen and Zimmerman argued that games can be open or closed systems depending on the perspective that we choose. They distinguished between three primary perspectives: rules (formal perspective), play (experiential perspective), and culture (cultural perspective). Salen and Zimmerman claimed that the formal systems of games are closed, whereas if we consider games as play, the magic circle can be either open or closed and considered as culture; games are extremely open systems. Salen and Zimmerman even argued that the study of game phenomena that cross the borders of the magic circle (such as computer-mediated and analogue role-playing games, player-generated mods [modifications] and hacks, level editors and tools designed for players, games created as open-source systems, games that are played within and across multiple platforms, and self-organizing social networks) are essential for the future of innovative game development. As Huizinga's overarching argument is formulated from a cultural perspective, Salen and Zimmerman – based on their categorization of rules, play and culture – would probably argue that he considers games to be open systems. Also taking into account the strong metaphor, I propose to withdraw from the magic circle (Copier 2005, 2007). I suggest we shift our focus from a study of games *in* culture to a study of game-play as one of the play elements and producers *of* culture.

Exploring ethical choices in relation to games and players, Mia Consalvo argues that we should build a theoretical framework that transcends 'the place apart' that games are often constructed as: 'For many players, playing games is, in some measure, a playing with rules and their boundaries' (Consalvo 2005, 10). Those rules and boundaries construct a specific game context. In turn, this context only exists in relation to other contexts, rules and boundaries. Play is thus always a negotiation of rules and boundaries both in the specific context itself but also in relation to other rules and boundaries. Defining pervasive gaming, Montola states that the genre explores the magic circle in spatial, temporal and social dimensions. He adds that the spatial, temporal and social dimensions can provide new ways of analyzing 'traditional' games as well, as even non-pervasive games do not exist in isolation (Montola 2005, 3). Instead of looking for the boundaries of the metaphorical magic circle, we can use a network perspective to map how every game and game experience is *negotiated spatially, temporally and socially*. Considering the above auto-ethnographic fragment in terms of the magic circle, ArgentArchives.org would not be part of the game experience as it has a different online place and rules. However, from the network perspective, I would analyze that WoW creates a specific context and rule set which is for instance negotiated spatially (by a website outside of the game), temporally (by players who are for instance adding information to the website while at work) and socially (by players who stop playing WoW, but are still roleplaying through their profiles on ArgentArchives.org).

From the network perspective, role play is especially interesting as it underlines in many ways how game play can be negotiated. I consider the role-play game mode to be a highly 'contested' form of play, even on RP servers. Technically, role play is 'optional', the effect of this is that there is a constant negotiation process going on between players regarding the type of game-play and behavior that is acceptable. Besides this, role play in itself is a play mode which revolves around negotiation. This contested relationship between instrumental game play and role play in WoW can be traced back throughout the code and culture to previous digital and analogue Fantasy role-playing games (Copier 2007). Role play is a collaborative experience; by playing the role of their characters, players are creating a 'shared fantasy' (Fine 1983) or 'shared imagined space' (Edwards 2004).

For example, a player who decides to roleplay a gnomish innkeeper needs other players who are willing to enact their characters to be his personnel or guests in his tavern. Players who theorize tabletop role play called this the 'lumpley principle', after the nickname of the independent game designer, Vincent Baker. Baker stated that the essence of role play is negotiating which situations or events can be part of the shared fantasy (Edwards 2004). This negotiation process, and its constantly morphing outcome, is shaped by a wide range of explicit and implicit factors such as the 3D graphical design, rules of the game, Warcraft lore, character backgrounds, character performance, player motivations, and the interpersonal relationships between both the characters and the players. Our gnomish innkeeper has to deal with two types of negotiations: players who come in with no intention of pretending that their character is a guest in a tavern, and players who act as if they are in a tavern and, for example, may roleplay their character as a friendly customer. Through negotiation, role players create a shared fantasy in which they not only form their characters, but through which they also conceptually blend conventions, identities, and interpersonal relationships. As there are thousands of player-characters on one RP server, there is not just one shared fantasy; instead, there are multiple fantasies that are continually negotiated as well. Using ANT we can study the functioning of these negotiation processes as well as the in-character and out-of-character roles, conventions, identities, and interpersonal relationships that self-proclaimed role-players negotiate in and through the systems of the commercially distributed game WoW. It is precisely the 'contested' and 'negotiated' characteristics that make role play very useful in uncovering the functioning of the systems that MMORPGs are and the cultures in which they are embedded.

A shift from games to the play element of culture, in other words to game play from a cultural perspective, is also what differentiates the work of Fine from most recent scholarship on digital games. By building on the work of Goffman and Fine, Pargman and Jakobsson's 'weak-boundary hypothesis' also focuses on play instead of games, which separates their alternative from, for instance, the 'porous membrane' (Castronova 2005). A focus on play as social interaction within a specific context opens up possibilities to discuss the ambiguity and variability of game play, for instance with regard to the relation between the real and the imaginary, not in terms of a 'closed' and 'magical' circle but as constructs that are under constant negotiation. Rules are also one part of these constructs that can be negotiated and (re)constructed. The role-play experience is shaped by (re)constructions and negotiations between various real and imaginary frames, between what I call the 'code and culture' of the game.

Conclusions

To recapitulate, the concept of the magic circle refers to a pre-existing artificiality of the game space that, combined with the strong metaphor, creates a dichotomy between the real and the imaginary which hides the ambiguity, variability, and complexity of actual games and play. I propose to withdraw from the magic circle and suggest we shift our focus from a study of games in culture to a study of game-play as one of the play elements and producers of culture. A network perspective allows us to understand how every game and game experience is negotiated spatially, temporally and socially.

As networks of human and nonhuman actors, online role-playing games are simultaneously tied in with other networks of production, power, and experience. Together, these networks make up what Castells called the network society. From the network perspective, role play is especially interesting. Role play is a contested and negotiated style of play, which makes it useful to uncover the rules, play, and culture that are constructed through online role-playing games. Additionally, because role-players consciously engage in the process of constructing and negotiating roles and frames, it becomes very visible how, through MMORPG play, pre-existing roles and frames are negotiated and (re)constructed, while at the same time new roles and frames are being constructed. These roles and frames can simultaneously be related to what we consider to be real and imaginary, game and non-game, online and offline. For various situations we construct different roles and cognitive frames, but these identities and frames exist simultaneously, they are porous and never fixed. These roles and frames can never be fixed because they are continually being negotiated and (re)constructed, as both Huizinga and Goffman suggested, often through play-like processes. Games are merely one of the settings in which these processes take place.

Notes

1. 'Fantasy' as a genre of imaginative fiction is capitalized in order to differentiate from fantasy in general, meaning the creation of the imaginative.
2. For a critical discussion of the issue of the magic circle in relation to pervasive games, see the chapter by Eva Nieuwdorp in this book.

References

Callon, Michel, John Law, and Arie Rip. 1986. *Mapping the dynamics of science and technology: Sociology of science in the real world.* Houndmills: Macmillan.

Castells, Manuel. 1998, 2000. *End of millennium.* Cambridge, MA: Blackwell Publishers.

—. 1997, 2000. *The power of identity.* Cambridge, MA: Blackwell Publishers.

—. 1996, 2000. *The rise of the network society.* Cambridge, MA: Blackwell Publishers.

Castronova, Edward. 2005. *Synthetic worlds: The business and culture of online games.* Chicago: University of Chicago Press.

Consalvo, Mia. 2005. Rule sets, cheating, and magic circles: Studying games and ethics. *International review of information ethics* 4. http://www.i-r-i-.net/inhalt/004/Consalvo.pdf.

Copier, Marinka. 2005. Connecting worlds: Fantasy role-playing games, ritual acts and the magic circle. Paper presented at *Changing Views: Worlds in Play – Digital Games Research Conference.* Vancouver, Canada.

—. 2007. *Beyond the magic circle: A network perspective on role-play in online games.* PhD thesis, Utrecht University.

Copier, Marinka, and Martin Ramstedt. 2006. Converging plays of identity. Paper presented at *Strange convergences: Performance and performativity in Fantasy game cultures, the Gothic milieu, and pagan spirituality.* Amsterdam, the Netherlands.

Edwards, Ron. 2004. The provisional glossary. *The Forge.* http://www.indie-rpgs.com/_articles/glossary.html.

Fine, Gary Alan. 1983. *Shared fantasy: Role-playing games as social worlds.* Chicago: University of Chicago Press.

Geertz, C. 1973. Thick description: Toward an interpretive theory of culture. *The Interpretation of Cultures,* 3-30.

Goffman, Erving. 1961. *Encounters: Two studies in the sociology of interaction.* Indianapolis: Bobbs-Merrill.

Huizinga, Johan. 1938. *Homo ludens: Proeve eener bepaling van het spel-element der cultuur.* Haarlem: Tjeenk Willink.

—. 1955. *Homo ludens: A study of the play-element in culture.* Boston: Beacon Press.

King, Brad, and John Borland. 2003. *Dungeons and dreamers: The rise of computer game culture from geek to chic.* New York: McGraw-Hill.

Lammes, Sybille. 2006. Spatial regimes of the digital payground: Cultural functions of spatial identification in post-colonial computergames. In *Conference proceedings Mediaterr@ – Gaming realities: A challenge for digital culture*, ed. Manthos Santorineos, 236-43. Athens, Greece: Fournos Centre for Digital Culture.

Latour, Bruno. 1987. *Science in action: How to follow scientists and engineers through society.* Cambridge, MA: Harvard University Press.

—. 2005. *Reassembling the social: An introduction to actor-network-theory.* Oxford: Oxford University Press.

Law, John. 1987. Technology and heterogeneous engineering: The case of Portuguese expansion. In *The social construction of technological systems: New directions in the sociology and history of technology*, eds. W. E. Bijker, T. P. Hughes and T. J. Pinch. Cambridge, MA: MIT Press.

Montola, Markus. 2005. Exploring the edge of the magic circle: Defining pervasive games. Paper presented at *Digital experience: Design, aestethics, practice conference.* Copenhagen, Denmark.

Nieuwdorp, Eva. 2005. The pervasive interface: Tracing the magic circle. Paper presented at *Changing views: Worlds in play – Digital Games Research conference*, Vancouver, Canada.

Pargman, Daniel, and Peter Jakobsson. 2006. The magic is gone: A critical examination of the gaming situation. In *Conference proceedings Mediaterr@ – Gaming realities: A challenge for digital culture*, ed. Manthos Santorineos, 15-22. Athens, Greece: Fournos Centre for Digital Culture.

Roderiquez, Hector. 2006. The playful and the serious: An approximation to Huizinga's Homo Ludens. *Gamestudies* 6 (1). http://gamestudies.org/0601/articles/rodriges.

Salen, Katie, and Eric Zimmerman. 2004. *Rules of play: Game design fundamentals.* Cambridge, MA: MIT Press.

Taylor, T. L. 2006. *Play between worlds: Exploring online game culture.* Cambridge, MA: MIT Press.

Yee, Nick. 2005. The real life demographics of World of Warcraft. *The Daedalus Project.* http://www.nickyee.com/daedalus/archives/001364.php.

—. 2006. The role-playing series. *The Daedalus Project.* http://www.nickyee.com/daedalus/archives/001524.php.

Renaissance now!

The gamers' perspective

Douglas Rushkoff

The frightening news is that we are living in a story. The reassuring part is that it is a story we are writing ourselves. Alas, though, most of us do not even know it – or are afraid to accept it. Never before did we have so much access to the tools of storytelling – yet few of us are willing to participate in their creation.[1] Gamers might be today's most likely candidates to helm what I hope will be a renaissance in our relationship to stories as well as the reality they mean to describe and influence.

We are living in a world of stories. We cannot help but use narratives to understand the events that occur around us. The unpredictability of nature, emotions, social interactions and power relationships led human beings, from prehistoric times, to develop narratives that described the patterns underlying the movements of these forces. Although we like to believe that primitive people actually believed the myths they created about everything from the weather to the afterlife, a growing camp of religious historians are coming to the conclusion that early religions were understood much more metaphorically than we understand religion today. They did not believe that the wind or rain were gods; they invented characters whose personalities reflected the properties of these elements. The characters and their stories served more as ways of remembering that it would be cold for four months before spring returns than genuinely accepted explanations. The people were quite self-consciously and actively anthropomorphizing the forces of nature.

As different people and groups competed for authority, they used their narratives quite differently. They used their stories to gain advantage. Stories were no longer being used simply to predict the patterns of nature but to describe and influence the course of politics, economics, and power. In such a world, stories compete solely on the basis of their ability to win believers, to be understood as real. When the Pharaoh or King is treated *as if* he were a god, it means his subjects are still actively participating in the sham. He still needs to prove his potency, in real ways, at regular intervals. But if the ruler can somehow get his followers to accept the story of his divine authority as historical fact, then he need prove nothing. The story itself serves as a substitute for reality.

Since biblical times, we have been living in a world where the stories we use to describe and predict our reality have been presented as truth and mistaken for fact. These narratives, and their tellers, compete for believers in two ways: through the content of the stories, and through the medium or tools through which the stories are told. The content of a story might be considered the 'what', while the technology through which the story is transmitted can be considered the 'how'. A story can vie for believers in both ways – through the narrative itself, or by changing the level of the playing field on which it is competing.

Exclusive access to the 'how' of storytelling lets a storyteller monopolize the 'what' . In ancient times, people were captivated by the epic storyteller as much for his ability to remember thousands of lines of text as for the actual content of the *Iliad* or *Odyssey*. Likewise, a television program or commercial holds us in its spell as much through the magic of broadcasting technology as its teleplay. Whoever has power to get inside that magic box has the power to write the story we end up believing.

After all, we do not call the stuff on television 'programming' for nothing. The people making television are not programming our TV sets or their evening schedules; they are programming *us*. We use the dial to select which program we are going to receive, and then we submit to it. This is not so dangerous in itself, but the less control we have over exactly what is fed to us through the tube, the more vulnerable we are to the whims of our programmers.

For most of us, what goes on in the television set is magic. Before the age of video recorders and camcorders, it was even more so. A television program is a magic act. Whoever has gotten his image in that box must be special. Back in the 1960s, Walter Cronkite used to end his newscast with the assertion, 'and that's the way it is.' It was his ability to appear in the magic box that gave him the tremendous authority necessary to lay claim to the absolute truth.

I have always recoiled when this rhetorical advantage is exploited by those who have the power to monopolize a medium. Back in college, I remember being incensed by a scene in the third *Star Wars* movie, *Return of the Jedi*. Luke and Han Solo have landed on an alien moon and are taken prisoner by a tribe of little furry creatures called Ewoks. In an effort to win their liberation, Luke's two robots tell the Ewoks the story of their heroes' struggle against the dark forces of the Empire. C3PO, the golden android, relates the tale, while little R2D2 projects holographic images of battling spaceships. The Ewoks are dazzled by R2's special effects and engrossed in C3PO's tale. The 'how' and the 'what'. They are so moved by the story that they not only release their prisoners but fight a violent war on their behalf! I kept wondering, what if Darth Vader had gotten down to the alien moon first and told his side of the story complete with his own special effects?

Similarly, television programming, like the many one-way media before it, communicates through stories, and it influences us through its seemingly magical capabilities. The programmer creates a character we like – with whom we can identify. As a series of plot developments bring that character into some kind of danger, we follow him, and a sense of tension rises within us.

This is what Aristotle, in his role as one of the first theater analysts, called the rising arc of dramatic action. The storyteller brings the character and the audience into as much danger as we can tolerate before inventing his solution – the rescue – allowing us all to let out a big sigh of relief. Back in Aristotle's day, this solution was called *Deus ex machina* (God from the machine), and one of the Greek gods would descend on a mechanism from the rafters and save the day. In an Arnold Schwarzenegger movie, that miraculous solution might take the form of a new, super-powered laser gun. In a commercial, well, it is the product being advertised. In any case, if he has got a captive audience, the storyteller can pick whichever solution he wants, and if we have been following the story into increasing anxiety, we will take it.

Television commercials honed this storytelling technique into the perfect 30-second package. A man is at work. His wife calls to tell him she has crashed the car. The boss comes in to tell him he just lost a big account. His bank statement shows he is in the red. His secretary quits. Now his head hurts. We have followed the poor guy all this way, and we feel his pain. What can he do? He opens the top desk drawer and finds his bottle of Brand A Pain Reliever! He swallows the pills as an awe-inspiring high-tech animation demonstrates to us the way the pill passes through his body, relieving his pain.

In a passive and mysterious medium, when we are brought into a state of vicarious tension, the storyteller can make us swallow any pill he chooses. Only by accepting his solution can we be freed from our despair.

Interactive media changed this equation. Imagine if your grandfather were watching that aspirin commercial back in 1955 on his old console television. Even if he suspected that he was watching a commercial designed to put him into a state of anxiety, in order to change the channel and remove himself from the externally imposed tension, he would have to move the popcorn off his lap, pull up the lever on his recliner, walk up to the television set, and manually turn the dial. That is a somewhat rebellious action for a bleary-eyed television viewer. To sit through the rest of the commercial, however harrowing, might cost him only a tiny quantity of human energy until the pills come out of the drawer. The brain, being lazy, chooses the path of least resistance, and grandpa sits through the whole commercial.

Flash forward to 1990. A kid with a remote control in his hand makes the same mental calculation: an ounce of stress, or an infinitesimally small quantity of human effort to move his finger an eighth of an inch and he is free! The remote control gives viewers the power to remove themselves from the storyteller's spell, with almost no effort. Watch a kid – or yourself – the next time he channel surfs from program to program. He is not changing the channel because he's bored. He surfs away when he senses that he is being put into an imposed state of tension.

The remote control breaks down the 'what'. It allows a viewer to deconstruct the content of television media and avoid falling under the programmer's spell. If he does get back around the dial to watch the end of a program, he no longer has the same captivated orientation. Kids with remotes are not watching television – they are watching the television, *playing* television. Putting it through its paces.

Just as the remote control allowed a generation to deconstruct the content of television, the videogame joystick demystified its technology. Remember back to the first time you ever saw a videogame. It was probably *Pong*, that primitive black and white depiction of a ping pong table, with a square on either side of the screen representing the paddle, and a tiny white dot representing the ball. Now, remember the exhilaration you felt at playing that game for the very first time. Was it because you had always wanted an effective simulation of ping pong? Did you celebrate because you would be able to practise without purchasing an entire table and installing it in the basement? Of course not. You were celebrating the simple ability to be able to move the pixels on the screen for the first time. It was a moment of revolution! The screen was no longer the exclusive turf of the television broadcasters. Thanks to the joystick, as well as the subsequent introduction of the VCR and camcorder, we were empowered to move the pixels ourselves. The TV was no longer magical. Its functioning had become transparent.

Finally, the computer mouse and keyboard transformed a receive-only monitor into a portal. Packaged programming was no longer any more valuable – or valid – than the words we could type ourselves. The addition of a modem turned the computer into a broadcast facility. We were no longer dependent on the content of Rupert Murdoch or CBS but could create and disseminate our own. The Internet revolution was a 'do-it-yourself' or DIY revolution. The people were now the content. New forms of community were being formed.

Of course this represented a tremendous threat to business as usual. Studies in the mid-1990s showed that families with Internet-capable computers were watching an average of nine hours less television per week. What is worse, Internet enthusiasts were sharing information, ideas, and even whole computer programs, for free! Software known as 'freeware' and 'shareware' gave rise to a gift economy based on community and mutual self-interest. People were turning to alternative news and entertainment sources for which they did not have to pay – and, worse, they were watching fewer commercials. Something had to be done. And it was.

Through a series of both deliberate and utterly systemic responses to the threat of interactivity, the mainstream media sought to reverse the effects of the remote, the joystick, and the mouse. Borrowing a term from 1970s social science, media business advocates declared that we were now living in an 'attention economy'.

True enough, the media space might be infinite, but there are only so many hours in a day during which potential audience members might be viewing a program. These units of human time became known as 'eyeball-hours', and pains were taken to create TV shows and web sites 'sticky' enough to engage those eyeballs long enough to show them an advertisement. Perhaps coincidentally, the growth of the attention economy was accompanied by an increase of concern over the 'attention spans' of young people. Channel surfing and similar behavior became equated with a very real but differently diagnosed childhood illness called Attention Deficit Disorder. Children who refused to pay attention were much too quickly drugged, before the real reasons for their adaptation to the onslaught of commercial messages were even considered.

The demystification of media enabled by the joystick and other tools was quickly reversed through the development of increasingly opaque computer interfaces. Whereas an early DOS computer user tended to understand a lot about how his computer stored information and launched programs, later operating systems such as Windows 95 put more barriers in place. Although these operating systems make computers easier to use in certain ways, they prevent users from gaining access or command over its more intricate processes. Now, to install a new program, users must consult 'the wizard'. What better metaphor do we need for the remystification of the computer? As a result, 'computer literacy' no longer means being able to program a computer, but merely knowing how to use Microsoft Office.

Finally, the DIY ethic of the Internet community was replaced by the new value of commerce. The communications age was rebranded as an 'information age' even though the Internet had never really been about downloading files or data but, instead, about communicating with other people. The difference was that information, or 'content', could be bought and sold, unlike real human interaction. It is a commodity. When selling information online did not work, business people turned to selling real products online. Thus, the e-commerce boom was ignited. Soon the Internet became the World Wide Web, whose opaque and image-heavy interfaces made it increasingly one-way and read-only – more conducive to commerce than communication.

Although very few e-commerce companies actually made any money selling goods, the *idea* that they could was all that mattered. News stories about online communities were soon overshadowed by those about daring young entrepreneurs launching multi-million-dollar IPOs (initial public offering of shares). Internet journalism moved from the culture section to the business pages as the dot. com pyramid scheme became the dominant new media story.

And so a medium born out of the ability to break through packaged stories was now being used to promote a new, equally dangerous one: the great pyramid. A smart kid writes a business plan. He finds a few 'angel investors' to back him up long enough for him to land some first-level investors. Below them on the pyramid are several more rounds of investors until the investment bank gets involved. Another few levels of investors buy in until the decision is made to 'go public'. This means that poor suckers like you and I can invest, too, by purchasing a newly issued stock on the NASDAQ exchange. Of course, by this point, the angels and other early investors are executing what is known as their 'exit strategy'. It used to be known as a carpet bag. In any case, they are gone, and we are left holding the soon-to-be-worthless shares.

Tragically, but perhaps luckily, the dot.com bubble burst, along with the story being used to keep it inflated. The entire cycle – the birth of a new medium, the battle to control it, and the downfall of the first victorious camp – taught us a lot about the relationship of stories to the technologies through which they are disseminated. And the whole ordeal may have given us another opportunity for renaissance.

Renaissance now?

Many considered the birth of the Internet era a revolution. My best friends – particularly those in the counterculture – saw in the Internet an opportunity to topple the storytellers who had dominated our politics, economics, society, and religion, in short, our very reality, and to replace their stories with ones of our own. It was a beautiful and exciting sentiment, but one as based in a particular narrative as any other. Revolutions simply replace one story with another. The capitalist narrative is replaced by the communist; the religious fundamentalist's by the gnostic's. The means may be different, but the rewards are the same, as is the exclusivity of their distribution. That is why they are called revolutions; we are just going in a circle.

I prefer to think of the proliferation of interactive media as an opportunity for renaissance: a moment when we have the opportunity to step entirely out of the story. Renaissances are historical instances of widespread recontextualization. People in a variety of different arts, philosophies, and sciences have the ability to reframe their reality.[2] Quite literally, renaissance means 'rebirth'. It is the rebirth of old ideas in a new context. A renaissance is a dimensional leap, when our perspective shifts so dramatically that our understanding of the oldest, most fundamental elements of existence changes. The stories we have been using no longer work.

Take a look back at what we think of as the original Renaissance – the one we were taught in school. What were the main leaps in perspective? Well, most obviously, perspective painting itself. Artists developed the technique of the 'vanishing point' and with it the ability to paint three-dimensional representations on two-dimensional surfaces. The character of this innovation is subtle, but distinct. It is not a technique for working in three dimensions; it is not that artists moved from working on canvas to working with clay. Rather, perspective painting allows an artist to relate between dimensions.

Likewise, calculus – another key Renaissance invention – is a mathematical system that allows us to derive one dimension from another. It is a way of describing curves with the language of lines, and spheres with the language of curves. The leap from arithmetic to calculus was not just a leap in our ability to work with higher-dimensional objects, but a leap in our ability to relate the objects of one dimension to the objects of another. It was a shift in perspective that allowed us to orient ourselves to mathematical objects from beyond the context of their own dimensionality.

The other main features of the Renaissance permitted similar shifts in perspective. Circumnavigation of the globe changed our relationship to the planet we live on and the maps we used to describe it.[3] The maps still worked, of course – only they described a globe instead of a plane. Anyone hoping to navigate a course had to be able to relate a two-dimensional map to the new reality of a three-dimensional planet. Similarly, the invention of moveable type and the printing press changed the relationship of author and audience to text. The creation of a manuscript was no longer a one-pointed affair. Well, the creation of the first manuscript still was – but now it could be replicated and distributed to everyone. It was still one story, but now it was subject to a multiplicity of individual perspectives. This lattermost innovation alone changed the landscape of religion in the Western world. Individual interpretation of the Bible led to the collapse of church authority and the unilateral nature of its decrees. Everyone demanded his or her own relationship to the story.

In all these cases, people experienced a very particular shift in their relationship to and understanding of dimensions. Understood this way, a renaissance is a moment of reframing. We step out of the frame as it is currently defined, and see the whole picture in a new context. We can then play by new rules.

It is akin to the experience of a gamer. At first, a gamer will play a video or computer game by the rules. He will read the manual, if necessary, then move through the various levels of the game. Mastery of the game, at this stage, means getting to the end – making it to the last level, surviving, becoming the most powerful character or, in the case of a simulation game, designing and maintaining a thriving family, city, or civilization. And, for many gamers, this is as far as it goes.

Some gamers, though – usually after they have mastered this level of play – will venture out onto the Internet in search of other fans or user groups. There, they will gather the 'cheat codes' that can be used to acquire special abilities within the game, such as invisibility or an infinite supply of ammunition. When the gamer returns to the game with his new secret codes, is he still playing the game, or is he cheating? From a renaissance perspective, he is still playing the game – albeit, a different one. His playing field has grown from the CD on which the game was shipped, to the entire universe of computers where these secret codes and abilities can be discussed and shared.[4] He is no longer playing the game, but a meta-game; the inner game world is still fun, but it is distanced by the gamer's new perspective – much in the way we are distanced from the play-within-a-play in one of Shakespeare's comedies or dramas. And the meta-theatrical convention gives us a new perspective on the greater story as well. It is as if we are looking at a series of proscenium arches and being invited, as an audience, to consider whether we are within a proscenium arch ourselves.

Gaming – as a metaphor but also as a lived experience – invites a renaissance perspective on the world in which we live. Perhaps gamers and game culture have been as responsible as anyone for the rise in expressly self-similar forms of television, such as *Beavis and Butthead*, *The Simpsons*, and *South Park*. The joy of such programs is not the relief of reaching the climax of the linear narrative, but rather the momentary thrill of making connections. The satisfaction is recognizing which bits of media are being satirized at any given moment. It is an entirely new perspective on television – where programs exist more in the form of Talmudic commentary – perspectives on perspectives on perspectives. We watch screens within screens – constantly reminded, almost as in a Brecht play – of the artifice of storytelling.

The great Renaissance was a simple leap in perspective. Instead of seeing everything in one dimension, we came to realize there was more than one dimension in which things were occurring. Even the Elizabethan world picture, with its concentric rings of authority – God, king, man, animals – reflects this newfound way of contending with the simultaneity of action in many dimensions at once. A gamer stepping out onto the Internet to find a cheat code certainly reaches this renaissance level of awareness and skill.

But what of the gamer who then learns to program new games for himself? He, I would argue, has stepped out of yet another frame into our current renaissance. He has deconstructed the content of the game, demystified the technology of its interface, and now feels ready to open the codes and turn the game into a do-it-yourself activity. This is precisely the character and quality of the dimensional leap associated with today's renaissance, as well.

The evidence of today's renaissance is at least as profound as that of the one that went before. The 16th century saw the successful circumnavigation of the globe via the seas. The 20th century saw the successful circumnavigation of the globe from space. The first pictures of earth from space changed our perspective on this sphere, forever. In the same century, our dominance over the planet was confirmed not just through our ability to travel around it, but to destroy it. The atomic bomb (itself the result of a rude dimensional interchange between submolecular particles) gave us the ability to destroy the globe. Now, instead of merely being able to circumnavigate 'God's' creation, we could actively destroy it. This is a new perspective.

DIGITAL MATERIAL

We also have our equivalent of perspective painting, in the invention of the holograph. The holograph allows us to represent not just three, but four dimensions on a two-dimensional plate. When the viewer walks past a holograph, she can observe the three-dimensional object over the course of time. A bird can flap its wings in a single picture. But, more importantly for our renaissance's purposes, the holographic plate itself embodies a new renaissance principle. When the plate is smashed into hundreds of pieces, we do not find that one piece contains the bird's wing, and another piece the bird's beak. No, each piece of the plate contains a faint image of the entire subject, albeit a faint one. When the pieces are put together, the image achieves greater resolution. But each piece contains a representation of the totality – a leap in dimensional understanding that is now informing disciplines as diverse as brain anatomy and computer programming.

Our analogue to calculus is the development of systems theory, chaos math, and the much-celebrated fractal. Confronting nonlinear equations on their own terms for the first time, mathematicians armed with computers are coming to new understandings of the way numbers can represent the complex relationships between dimensions. Accepting that the surfaces in our world, from coastlines to clouds, exhibit the properties of both two- and three-dimensional objects (just what is the surface area of a cloud?), they came up with ways of working with and representing objects with *fractional* dimensionality. Using fractals and their equations, we can now represent and work with objects from the natural world that defied Cartesian analysis. We have also become able to develop mathematical models that reflect many more properties of nature's own systems – such as self-similarity and remote high leverage points. Again, we find this renaissance characterized by the ability of an individual to reflect, or even affect, the grand narrative. To write the game.

Finally, our renaissance's answer to the printing press is the computer and its ability to network. Just as the printing press gave everyone access to readership, the computer and Internet give everyone access to authorship. The first Renaissance took us from the position of passive recipient to active interpreter. Our current renaissance brings us from a position of active interpretation to one of authorship. We are the creators.

As game programmers instead of game players, we begin to become aware of just how much of our reality is, indeed, open source – up for discussion. So much of what seemed like impenetrable hardware is actually software, and ripe for reprogramming. The stories we use to understand the world seem less like explanations and more like collaborations. They are rule sets – and only as good as their ability to explain the patterns of history or predict those of the future.

Consider the experience of a cartographer attempting to hold a conversation with a surfer. They both can claim intimate knowledge of the ocean, but from vastly different perspectives. While the mapmaker understands the sea as a series of longitude and latitude lines, the surfer sees only a motion of waves that are not even depicted on the cartographer's map. If the cartographer were to call out from the beach to the surfer and ask him whether he is above or below the forty-third parallel, the surfer would be unable to respond. The mapmaker would have no choice but to conclude that the surfer was hopelessly lost. If any of us were asked to choose which one we would rather rely on to get us back to shore, most of us would pick the surfer. He experiences the water as a system of moving waves and stands a much better chance of navigating a safe course through them. Each surfer at each location and each moment of the day experiences an entirely different ocean. The cartographer experiences the same map, no matter what. He has a more permanent model, but his liability is his propensity to mistake his map for the actual territory.

The difference between the cartographer and the surfer's experience of the ocean is akin to pre- and post-renaissance relationships to story. The first relies on the most linear and static interpretations of the story in order to create a static and authoritative template through which to glean its meaning. The latter relies on the living, moment-to-moment perceptions of its many active interpreters to develop a way of relating to its many changing patterns. Ultimately, in a cognitive process not unlike that employed by a chaos mathematician, the surfer learns to recognize the order underlying what at first appears to be random turbulence. Likewise, the surfer understands each moment and event in his world – like a toss of the I-Ching coins were once understood – as a possible reflection on any other in the entire system.

The renaissance experience of moving from game to meta-game allows everything old to look new again. We are liberated from the maps we have been using to navigate our world, and free to create new ones based on our own observations. This invariably leads to a whole new era of competition. Renaissance may be a rebirth of old ideas in a new context, but which ideas get to be reborn?

The first to recognize the new renaissance will compete to have their ideologies be the ones that are 'rebirthed' in this new context. This is why, with the emergence of the Internet, we saw the attempted rebirth (and occasional stillbirth) of everything from paganism to libertarianism, and communism to psychedelia. Predictably, the financial markets and consumer capitalism – the dominant narratives of our era – were the first to successfully commandeer the renaissance. But they squandered their story on a pyramid scheme – indeed, the accelerating force of computers and networks tends to force any story to its logical conclusion – and now the interactive renaissance is once again up for grabs.

Were I in the futurism business, I'd predict that gamers will be the next to steer the direction of our renaissance, and that they may have entirely better results. For, unlike businessmen or even politicians, gamers know that the reality they are engineering is not real. This is why cheating is not really cheating – but merely playing from a new perspective. It is all play. Where gamers may have formerly been competing from within the game, now they meet and compete on an entirely new level – and, in comparison, they fight as gods. This is a powerful perspective from which to operate, and one that may grow in popularity as games become an even more central entertainment in mass culture.

Without even a convincing business-to-business strategy on which to hang their market hopes, increasing numbers of hi-tech speculators are coming to the irrefutable conclusion that they just spent billions of their own and other people's money on a communications infrastructure that amounts, more than anything else, to a network gaming platform.

No, the Internet is not a content delivery system. It is not a way to download movies or even songs. It is a way of connecting gaming consoles. The only questions left are whether processing will be done on centralized servers or within the consoles, and how to cope with latency problems in transmission. The rest is a done deal. The gamers (remember who started this Internet craze, after all...) managed to convince the world to build them the most expensive toy in the history of civilization. To some, this might seem like a sad turn of events. I do not think it is.

Renaissances afford us the ability to rethink and redesign our world using entirely new rule sets. The shift in perspective, itself, however, is probably more valuable than where it takes us. It is an open window – a moment when the very control panel of our world is up for grabs. For as surely as it opened up, this window will close again once a sufficient consensus has been reached. We will then go on, accepting some new, albeit more dimensionalized, picture of reality as the truth, and mistake yet another map as the territory.

Our present, mid-renaissance moment, however, is a window of opportunity. It is like the peak of a mystical experience or psychedelic trip – that moment when the journeyer thinks to himself, 'how will I remember this when I am back to reality?' More often than not, the psychic traveler will scribble down some words ('I am one! It is one!') that appear nonsensical in the light of day – even though the insight they mean to communicate is quite penetrating.

So, assuming that we can even do it, what is it we want to embed in the civilization of the future? What would we want to remind ourselves of, once this little window has closed? I think, more than any ideology or narrative, the most important idea to associate with our renaissance is the notion that we are, as individuals and a collective, the writers of our own stories. And who or what might best accomplish this grand, trans-dimensional communication of autonomous, communitarian values?

I would place my renaissance bet on the gamers' perspective: the very notion that our world is open source, and that reality itself is up for grabs. For, more than anyone else, a real gamer knows that we are the ones creating the rules.

This chapter was first published in *Handbook of computer game studies*, eds. Joost Raessens and Jeffrey Goldstein, 415-421. Cambridge, MA: MIT Press.

Notes

1. For a critical discussion of the ideal of participatory culture, see the chapter by Mirko Tobias Schäfer in this book.
2. For a discussion of the importance of framing and reframing, see the chapter of Joost Raessens in this book.
3. For an in-depth discussion of the use of cartography in games, see the chapter by Sybille Lammes in this book.
4. For a discussion of how games like *World of Warcraft* are anchored in daily life, see the chapter of Marinka Copier in this book.

Screen

What you get is what you see

Digital images and the claim on the real

Frank Kessler

In 1898 Boleslas Matuszewski, a photographer and former court cinematographer of Tsar Nikolas II, published a booklet in France entitled *Une nouvelle source de l'histoire* in which he pleads for the creation of a repository for actuality films so that they can serve as historical documents for future generations. Animated photography, he argues, is unrivalled in its capacity to faithfully record historical events and thus should be collected and stored in an official archive. Matuszewski claims that cinematographic images in particular can resist attempts to manipulate them and thus are the most valuable witnesses of the past:

> Perhaps the cinematograph does not give history in its entirety, but at least what it does deliver is incontestable and of an absolute truth. Ordinary photography admits of *retouching*, to the point of transformation. But try to retouch, in an identical way for each figure, these thousand or twelve hundred, almost microscopic negatives...! One could say that animated photography has a character of authenticity, accuracy and precision that belongs to it alone. It is the ocular evidence that is truthful and infallible *par excellence* (Matuszewski 1995, 323).

Matuszewski thus offers a quite early formulation of a claim on the real, or in fact even a truth claim, that has haunted documentary film but also, for instance, news photography throughout the 20th century. Often challenged, time and again criticized and critiqued by practitioners and scholars alike, it has a tendency of popping up like a Jack-in-the-box whenever our trust in such images appears to have been abused. However, about a century after Matuszewski's optimistic assessment of the cinematograph's powers, media historian Brian Winston proclaimed the definitive end of such naïve hopes:

> Digitalization destroys the photographic image as evidence of anything except the process of digitalization. The physicality of the plastic material represented in any photographic image can no longer be guaranteed. For documentary to

survive the widespread diffusion of such technology depends on removing its claim on the real. There is no alternative (Winston 1995, 259).

According to Winston, the emergence of digital technology opens up almost unlimited possibilities to manipulate, reshape, fake and forge photographic and cinematic images which puts an end to a long tradition of endowing documentary photography and film with what has often been seen, in reference to a famous essay by film critic André Bazin, as an ontological claim on the real.[1] This claim, the privileged relationship of the photographic image to the real, is actually based upon the fact that photography can be regarded as a result of a trace of light reflected from an object that has caused a chemical reaction in the photosensitive emulsion of a filmstrip. Following a remark by Charles Sanders Peirce on the complex semiotic nature of photographs, being both *icon*, as they are 'in certain aspects exactly like the objects they represent', and *index*, as a result of their having a 'physical connection' to the referent, Peter Wollen (1998, 86) points towards the similarity between Bazin's thoughts on the ontology of the photographic image and Peirce's concept of the indexical sign.[2] In this way, indexicality has come to be considered an essential quality of conventional photo and film, and by the same token the guarantee of the 'authenticity, accuracy and precision', and thus truthfulness, which Matuszewski celebrated in 1898.[3] Interestingly, looking at that question from the point of view of new media, for Lev Manovich, cinema as such is 'an art of the index' (2001, 293), and he argues that 'as a media technology, its role was to capture and store visible reality' (307). This, however, is altered radically by the advent of digital media, and so Manovich arrives at a conclusion that is quite similar to Brian Winston's account quoted above: 'The mutability of digital data impairs the value of cinema recordings as documents of reality' (307).

Thus, the question arises of whether digital technology indeed weakens, impairs, or maybe even destroys the privileged (ontological, indexical) link between analogical photographic or cinematic images and the real. This is a vexed question, indeed, most of all because several aspects appear to be inextricably intertwined here. So in order to assess the scope of the problem, it may be useful to try and provisionally separate the different issues that are tied together in this argumentative knot, by designating them with a somewhat global character by using the following three tags: technology, indexicality and practices.

Technology: what you get

Looking at the claims put forward with regard to the specific powers of the new image technologies concerning their relationship to the real, it is interesting to note that Matuszewski as well as Winston and Manovich rely on quantitative rather than qualitative arguments. While Matuszewski emphasises the quasi-impossibility to retouch the sheer number of individual photographs contained on a filmstrip, Winston and Manovich insist on how extraordinarily easy it is to modify digital images or, as Philip Rosen phrases it, their 'practically infinite manipulability' (2001, 319). However, inverting these characterisations of the new technologies, one could riposte to Matuszewski that this relative difficulty of retouching a view taken by a cinematograph by no means guarantees truthfulness. With historical hindsight, it becomes clear such manipulations are not even that exceptional (tricks, special effects, but also the sometimes rather blunt attempts in Soviet films to conceal certain individuals who had fallen into disgrace). One could counter Winston and Manovich with the argument that manipulability is nothing new in this domain, and that the traditional claim on the real, in that respect, could only be accepted by wilfully disregarding such potentials for manipulation. The change brought about by the new image technologies, in other words, could be seen as rather less radical than the above-quoted statements suggest.

On the other hand, the possibilities to digitally manipulate images have, somewhat paradoxically, caused news photographers to scrutinize the various techniques they habitually used, in order to find out to what extent these are prone to objectionable alterations. As Dona Schwartz (2003) shows, interventions of one kind or the other are unavoidable: the photographer does have to make choices with regard to lenses, filters, the position from which the photo is to be taken, the film stock, the shutter speed, etc. Furthermore, also in the darkroom, even the most standard methods are in fact acts of interference (see also Gunning 2004, 40).

So what are the limits? What can a photographer justifiably eliminate from a picture? A reflection from a flash? The red-eye effect? Reducing a colour photo to black and white? Is a motion blur inappropriate? From the discussions reproduced by Schwartz (2003, 40-45), it is obvious that professional photojournalists are afraid of getting on a 'slippery slope' here and thus tend to ban even minor manipulations. On the other hand, however, there is no way to fix a standard that could guarantee the absolute objectivity that functions here tacitly as an ideal.

Schwartz distinguishes three strategies to establish such a norm: depicting the subject 'as the camera sees it', depicting it 'as someone present at the scene would have seen it', or to 'authorize the photographers to make decisions regarding image production consistent with the prevailing norms governing journalistic representations across communicative modes' (2003, 45-46). The first two strategies seem to be oriented towards a conception of objectivity in accordance with the scientific criterion of repeatability, namely that, given identical circumstances, a certain procedure will always have the same result, when a normative framework exists that photographers can refer back to in case of doubt. However, as Schwartz rightly states, taking 'camera vision' as a rationale would presuppose the use of standardised equipment, whereas the alignment with a human observer's visual experience raises numerous questions, in particular regarding the enormous differences between human perception and 'camera vision'. According to which parameters can a photograph be said to correspond to the way an onlooker would have perceived a situation? In a way, the third strategy admits the impossibility of unambiguous guidelines, relying instead on a set of more or less unwritten rules that can at any moment be modified or revised.

Nevertheless, these discussions show that the problem of manipulability did not arise with the advent of digital technologies, but has been an issue in photography all along. Rather, the debates generated by new media about the possibilities of intervention have led to a self-critical questioning of traditional media practices. In this respect, one may conclude that photography's claim on the real has always been rather fragile. Digitalization, in other words, not so much caused an obliteration of the privileged link between the photographic image and the real, but rather provoked a return of the repressed, namely a renewed awareness of the numerous forms of manipulation and intervention that constitute the very activity of producing and presenting (moving) pictures. This, I would argue, is actually the point Winston is trying to make as well. Given his detailed critique of documentary's claim on the real, preceding the remark quoted above, digitalization may in fact be nothing but the straw that breaks the camel's back.[4]

Indexicality: what you see

But even if, with regard to both traditional and digital photo and film, there are numerous factors that influence the way a picture is taken and how it appears on screen or as print, the question remains of whether the indexicality of the photographic image is somehow reduced or even abolished through the advent of digital technologies. In an article in which he interrogates the status of the concept of the index in recent debates on the subject, Tom Gunning (2004, 40) states that the difference, again, is certainly not absolute:

> Clearly a digital camera records through its numerical data the same intensities of light that a non-digital camera records: hence the similarity of their images. The difference between the digital and the film based camera has to do with the way information is captured – which does have strong implications for the way the images can be stored, transferred and indeed manipulated. But storage in terms of numerical data does not eliminate indexicality (which is why digital images can serve as passport photographs and the other sorts of legal evidence or documents which ordinary photographs supply).

Engaging in a discussion with Tom Gunning, David Rodowick insists on what he describes as an 'ontological distinctiveness of analogical and digital processes' (2007, 113). Rodowick refers here to the two fundamentally different ways in which they relate to the object that is represented:

If analog media record traces of events and digital media produce tokens of numbers, the following may also be asserted: *digital acquisition quantifies the world as manipulable series of numbers.* This is the primary automatism and the source of the creative powers of digital computing. Alternatively, photographic automatisms yield spatial segments of duration in a uniform substance. Both kinds of photography produce convincing representations as a result of their quality of counterfactual dependence, wherein any change in the referent is reflected as a corresponding change in the image, and in both cases this quality relies on the logic of indexicality. But they may also be qualitatively distinguished according to the types of causation involved in the acquisition of images and by ascertaining whether the causal relations between inputs and outputs are continuous or discontinuous. Here (analogical) *transcription* should be distinguished from (digital) *conversion* or *calculation* (Rodowick 2007, 116; author's emphasis).

So on the one hand, both Gunning and Rodowick agree that the 'logic of indexicality' is at work in both digital and analogue photography and film. They differ, however, in their assessment of the impact that results from the qualitative difference between the two processes. Here, for Rodowick, the ontological distinctiveness of the digital ultimately leads to an 'unbecoming of photography' (2007, 124). Using the terminology coined by Sol Worth (1981, 52-53) in the 1960s, one could say that both Gunning and Rodowick conceive the *videme*, the image-event, in similar terms, while they differ in their views on the status of the specificity that distinguishes the digital *cademe* (that which is recorded during one uninterrupted take) from its analogue counterpart.

As my concern is rather with the 'claim on the real' that is habitually based on the indexical quality of photography and film, I shall not discuss the issue of the ontological difference postulated by Rodowick further, even though I am sceptical about some of the conclusions he draws from this premise (more on this below). What needs further interrogation here is the scope of the 'claim on the real' that indexicality can actually support. What exactly is it that is truthfully rendered by a photograph or a cinematic take? Strictly speaking, of course, the indexical link between a filmic take or a photo and the real cannot go beyond the spatio-temporal segment that was recorded. And this in fact only concerns what Worth calls the cademe, as what is to be seen is in fact already the result of various forms of intervention. Yet, as Roland Barthes (1964, 47; 1980, 120) puts it, a photo is always the trace of something that has been in front of the camera. While this corresponds exactly to the idea of photographic and cinematic indexicality, one should be careful not to glide from stating the object's 'having been there' to the more global assertion that the image depicts 'how it was'. This in fact is what Barthes himself does in the earlier text, when he declares that a photograph appears as the evidence of how things happened ('*cela c'est passé ainsi*', 1964, 47).

Such a view indeed overstates the case that an indexical image can reasonably make[5], and, as a matter of fact, in his 1980 book *La chambre claire* Barthes limits photography's evidential power once more to its confirming of the object's 'having been': '*ça a été*' or, in Latin: *interfuit* (1980, 120-121).

As I have argued elsewhere (Kessler 1998), the concepts of the *profilmic* and of the *afilmic* that were coined by the French *École de filmologie* in the early 1950s can help to clarify the complex relationship between indexical images and 'the real'. Etienne Souriau (1953, 8) defines the profilmic as everything that has been in front of the camera and was recorded by it, whereas the afilmic refers to what exists in our world 'independent of the art of film or without any specific and original destiny in relation with this art' (1953, 7; author's translation). This distinction can be read as follows: while the profilmic is either photochemically transcribed or digitally coded, the afilmic remains irreducible to such a recording.[6] The indexical 'claim on the real', in other words, can never go beyond the profilmic. The afilmic, on the other hand, should not be seen as simply the spatial and temporal continuation of the profilmic but rather as a construction against, and in reference to, how the represented is understood, evaluated, judged, accepted or rejected, etc. by the viewer. The indexical image can hardly state anything else than that the profilmic 'has been'; even for it to say 'it has been there and then' requires, in most cases, additional information of some kind (think of the many infamous examples of abducted persons holding a newspaper in their hands in order to identify the date the picture was taken). Thus, I would argue that the problem in most of the debates about non-fictional photography or film lies in their conceiving them as *documentations of* the afilmic real rather than approaching them as *discourses on* it.

Through such a shift in perspective, the 'claim on the real' no longer depends on the indexical image but on the status a viewer ascribes to that discourse. Taking up John Searle's reflections on the logical status of fictional discourse (Searle 1979, 58-75) and using them in a pragmatic perspective, one can say that, in the first instance, what makes a photo or a film function as a non-fictional or 'serious' utterance is the fact that the viewer can interrogate it in terms of trueness. This makes it possible to deflate the idea of documentary's 'truth claim', as this does not mean that the utterance has to be true – it just is possible to ask the question of whether it is, or whether it could be a lie (whereas such questions would not make any sense with regard to a fictional utterance). The viewer, in other words, constructs an 'enunciator supposed to be real' (Odin 1984), an instance, thus, that is committed to the truth of the expressed proposition according to the rules underlying such a speech act (Searle 1979, 62). As this commitment concerns the discourse as a whole and not necessarily all of its elements, the indexical image need not carry the claim on the real all by itself. Quite to the contrary, as Roger Odin (2000, 127-150) shows, the functioning of a 'documentarisational' mode (*mode documentarisant*) will be upheld in spite of a vast hetero-geneity of image material (animation, simulation, CGI, staged scenes, poetic images, etc.), as long as the spectator does construct an enunciator that is sup-posed to be real. And indeed, there are countless examples of documentaries as well as educational, scientific, or even news films that incorporate diverse forms of non-photographic imagery without their 'claim on the real' being impaired in any way.[7] Even recreations such as the *actualités reconstituées* in early cinema, but also more recent examples such as United 93 (Paul Greengrass, USA 2006) can be read as serious utterances that do not present indexical recordings of the 'there and then' that their discourse refers to.

In the context of such a discourse on the afilmic real, indexical and other types of images can be used in many different ways. Being contextualised, arranged, oriented, discursively framed, no picture 'speaks for itself'. Viewers have to judge for themselves whether to go along with the discourse proposed by the images or read it differently: they can either trust or reject it, and the meanings that are explicitly or implicitly presented can be assessed, negotiated, evaluated and inter-preted. The indexical has to be taken into account here, certainly, but it does not guarantee anything. Or, as a text title in Jean-Luc Godard's *Vent d'Est* (1969) pro-claims: '*Ce n'est pas une image juste, mais juste une image.*'

Practices: what you get to see

Paradoxically, one might assert that new media have brought forth a proliferation of practices that foreground the indexical properties of digitally recorded images. From *JenniCam* to pet portraits on personal websites, from image-sharing sites such as *Flickr* or *YouTube* (not to mention their pornographic versions), from celeb-rity pictures to rather infamous examples like the execution of Saddam Hussein or the Abu Ghraib photos, from the most scandalous revelations to the most mun-dane documents of people's everyday lives, the uses of digital photography and video in innumerable cases rely on the indexical qualities they undoubtedly have.[8] And indeed, one would rather hope that the x-ray photos taken by one's dentist, even though they are produced and viewed as digital images, do have a justified 'claim on the real' – even though, as many may have found out in a painful way, there is no guarantee that the dentist reads them properly.

Furthermore, digital media – CD-ROM, DVD, the Internet – provide new chan-nels of distribution, either for historical non-fiction films or for new productions, but also enable filmmakers (the term seems a bit out of place here) to experiment with new documentary forms, making use of hypertext structures, non-linear pre-sentation, interactive elements, etc. Online archives and platforms make a large amount of documentary images accessible, and nothing indicates that people treat them any differently than conventional photochemical images.

For David Rodowick, however, these new forms of distribution and circulation are not so much a continuation of earlier practices but rather part of the 'ontological distinctiveness' of the digital image:

> In worrying about the capacity of computers to transform images, we nearly forget their more powerful and prosaic will to copy and transmit. Digital-capture documents and digital documentation express new powers – not only deep and superior copies, but also an increasing ease and velocity of dissemination. (...) One key difference, though, is that digital images may no longer be capable of producing the existential or ontological perplexity of which both Barthes and Cavell were so keenly and philosophically aware. Digital photographs have become more social than personal, and more attuned to the present itself than to the present's relation to the past and future. Symbolic and notational at their core, they provoke discussion of images as *information*. In this they solicit often-healthy debates (would that all images did) about provenance, reliability, accuracy, and context (Rodowick 2007, 148-149; author's emphasis).

But here, I would argue, Rodowick's focus actually shifts from the ontology of photographic images to the level of uses and practices. Observing a move from the personal to the social, from the photograph as 'remembrance of things past' celebrated by Barthes and Cavell (1979) to their informational function, Rodowick takes this as a consequence of the 'ontological distinctiveness' of digital photography. But then again, there always have been an enormous variety of ways in which the photographic image has been used, and not for all of them a phenomenological functioning as a trace of the past saying that *ça a été* is equally relevant.[9] Here Rodowick does not quite escape the problem of identifying a medium with but one specific type of practice.

This does not mean, however, that the emergence of digital technology has hardly affected photography as a medium. The argument I am making here is a different one: by looking first and foremost at technological change alone, discussions tend to either overrate or underrate its impact. Similarities and continuities are overlooked or, conversely, overemphasised. The new is seen as either radically disruptive or as just a variant of what exists. Media change, I would argue, manifests itself rather in the way new media *dispositifs* emerge. Considering media as the interrelation between the different affordances of a material technology, the positions it provides for the viewer or the user, and the textual forms it produces may help to understand media change differently, to be precise as reconfigurations of such dispositifs, keeping intact some of its aspects and modifying or even completely reshaping others (Kessler 2002, 2006). It is quite evident that an initially photochemical image that is remediated in a digital medium functions within a dispositif that is different from its traditional manifestation as a printed picture. So we need to analyse the dispositif in order to understand the functioning of the image.

As for the potential threat that digital manipulability poses to the documentary value of photography and film, the problem is addressed in a too one-sided way by just looking at the technology instead of taking into account the practices it is embedded in. As Dai Vaughan so convincingly put it, there is indeed a chance that digitally manipulated imagery will eventually have become so omnipresent that our trust in the photographic image gets lost in something like a 'catastrophe model, where a seemingly innocuous curve takes a sudden nosedive, an irreversible switch into another state' (1999, 189). But this would then be the result of the discursive practices in which these images are used, not of the technology as such. In the end, what is needed, and will become increasingly important, is a general level of media literacy that enables viewers and users to interrogate and critically assess in what way a digital image may have a claim on the real.

Notes

1. The reference here is of course to André Bazin's 'Ontologie de l'image photographique' (Bazin 1958, 11-19).
2. For a discussion about the relation between Peirce's and Bazin's ideas, see Rosen (2001, 18-23 et passim) and Gunning (2007, 29-33).
3. Furthermore, from very early on photography has been considered a potential scientific instrument as well. Already in his 1839 report on the daguerreotype the French scientist Dominique-François Arago (1995) stresses its usefulness for that domain. See also Winston (1993).
4. Elsewhere Winston's critique concerns in particular observational documentary films and their 'inflated claim on the real', and he quite favourably discusses classic documentaries and their strategy of 'honest, straightforward re-enactment', as Joris Ivens called it (Winston 1999).
5. This became painfully clear when the Rodney King videotape was presented as evidence in court. Bill Nichols (1994, 17-42) gives a brilliant analysis of this event.
6. Souriau's definitions are not without ambiguities. They also allow a different reading according to which everything that is destined to be filmed belongs to the realm of the profilmic, in particular studio sets, costumes, etc., while everything that has an existence outside the institution of cinema is considered afilmic. In this perspective the profilmic is sometimes even exclusively linked to fiction film, whereas documentary is associated with the afilmic. Jean-Luc Liout (2004, 41-51) calls everything in its actual existence afilmic, regardless of whether it is being filmed (such as the silhouette of a mountain, for instance), and everything profilmic that is intentionally linked to the act of filming (not only the abovementioned studio elements such as sets and costumes, but also, for example, the staging of an interview for a non-fiction film). While Souriau's formulations do authorise such readings, I would argue that on the basis of what one sees in the image, it is not always possible to determine whether or not it has been arranged intentionally to be filmed, and thus the difference between both concepts becomes relative and also artificial, as all the aspects of the profilmic that Liout lists do obviously exist in the afilmic world as well.

7. A case in point might be the documentary mode that Bill Nichols (1994, 92-106) describes as 'performative'. See also Plantinga (2005) who defines documentary as 'asserted veridical representation', referring also to its overall discursive status in an attempt to account for the complex interaction of different types of representational strategies, imagery, sound, and speech.
8. Rubinstein and Sluis (2008) describe the current developments in what they call 'the networked image' even in terms of 'a life more photographic'.
9. Including some in which the indexical quality is of lesser importance, such as in certain artistic practices, but also, at the other end of the spectrum, in stock photography used for illustration and advertisement. For the latter, see Frosh (2003).

References

Arago, Dominique-François. 1995 (orig. 1839). *Rapport sur le Daguerréotype*. Reprint, La Rochelle: Rumeur des Ages.

Barthes, Roland. 1964. Rhétorique de l'image. *Communications* 4: 40-51.

—. 1980. *La chambre claire*. Paris: Gallimard/Cahiers du Cinéma.

Bazin, André. 1958. *Qu'est-ce que le cinéma? I. Ontologie et langage*. Paris: Cerf.

Cavell, Stanley. 1979. *The world viewed: Reflections on the ontology of film*. Enlarged edition, Cambridge, MA: Harvard University Press.

Frosh, Paul. 2003. Digital technology and stock photography: And God created photoshop. In *Image ethics in the digital age*, eds. Larry Gross, John Stuart Katz, and Jay Ruby, 183-216. Minneapolis: University of Minnesota Press.

Gunning, Tom. 2004. What's the point of an index? or, faking photographs. *Nordicom Review* 1-2: 39-49.

—. 2007. Moving away from the index: Cinema and the impression of reality. *Differences: A Journal of feminist cultural studies* 18 (1): 29-52.

Kessler, Frank. 1998. Fakt oder Fiktion? Zum pragmatischen Status dokumentarischer Bilder. *Montage/AV* 7(2): 63-78.

—. 2002. *Het idee van vooruitgang in de mediageschiedschrijving*. Utrecht: Universiteit Utrecht.

—. 2006. The cinema of attractions as *dispositif*. In *The cinema of attractions reloaded*, ed. Wanda Strauven, 57-69. Amsterdam: Amsterdam University Press.

Liout, Jean-Luc. 2004. *À l'enseigne du réel: Penser le documentaire*. Aix-en-Provence: Publications de l'Université de Provence.

Manovich, Lev. 2001. *The language of new media*. Cambridge, MA: MIT Press.

Matuszewski, Boleslas. 1995. A new source of history [1898]. *Film History* 7 (3): 322-324.

Nichols, Bill. 1994. *Blurred boundaries: Questions of meaning in contemporary culture*. Bloomington, Indianapolis: University of Indiana Press.

Odin, Roger. 1984. Film documentaire, lecture documentarisante. In *Cinémas et réalités*, eds. Jean-Charles Lyant and Roger Odin, 263-278. Saint-Etienne: CIEREC.

—. 2000. *De la fiction*. Brussels: De Boeck.

Plantinga, Carl. 2005. What a documentary is, after all. *The Journal of Aesthetics and Art Criticism* 63 (2): 105-117.

Rodowick, David. 2007. *The virtual life of film*. Cambridge, MA: Harvard University Press.

Rosen, Philip. 2001. *Change mummified: Cinema, historicity, theory*. Minneapolis: University of Minnesota Press.

Rubinstein, Daniel and Katrina Sluis. 2008. A life more photographic: Mapping the networked image. *Photographies* 1 (1): 9-28.

Schwartz, Dona. 2003. Professional oversight: Policing the credibility of photojournalism. In *Image Ethics in the Digital Age*, eds. Larry Gross, John Stuart Katz and Jay Ruby, 27-51. Minneapolis: University of Minnesota Press.

Searle, John R. 1979. *Expression and meaning: Studies in the theory of speech acts.* Cambridge: Cambridge University Press.

Souriau, Etienne. 1953. Préface. In *L'Univers filmique*, ed. Etienne Souriau, 5-10. Paris: Flammarion.

Vaughan, Dai. 1999. *For documentary.* Berkeley: University of California Press.

Winston, Brian. 1993. The documentary film as scientific inscription. In *Theorizing documentary*, ed. Michael Renov, 37-57. New York: Routledge.

—. 1995. *Claiming the real: The documentary film revisited.* London: British Film Institute.

—. 1999. 'Honest, straightforward re-enactment': The staging of reality. In *Joris Ivens and the documentary context*, ed. Kees Bakker, 160-170. Amsterdam: Amsterdam University Press.

Wollen, Peter. 1998. *Signs and meaning in the cinema.* Expanded edition, London: British Film Institute.

Worth, Sol. 1981. *Studying visual communication.* Philadelphia: University of Pennsylvania Press.

The pervasive interface

Tracing the magic circle

Eva Nieuwdorp

Imagine you and your colleagues are invited to participate in a game to enhance team-building. You are divided into teams, each of which receives a lunchbox containing a city map, a digital camera and a web-enabled mobile phone. You are then sent out into the street, to wait for instructions. The mobile phone signals that you have received a message. On the screen it reads: 'Sometime today you will be approached by the Speaker. The Speaker could be anyone, anywhere... all we know is that the Speaker will say something to you. It could be anything, and you'll only know it's the Speaker if you form a circle around him or her and dance wildly...' (McGonigal 2003). Following this ambiguous clue, you have to complete a mission that consists of locating an unspecified person. He or she could be anywhere and anyone around you. It is your task to look for hints, forcing you to shift your perception of the surrounding environment. You are now playing *The Go Game* (www.thegogame.com), a pervasive game.

Pervasive games are steadily emerging as a new genre of digital games. Examples such as *I Love Bees* (2004, www.ilovebees.com) and *Botfighters* (2001, www. botfighters.com) broaden the game world to include elements of everyday life, subsequently also bringing rules of play into the public sphere of, for example, the street and the workplace. Unlike other games, the mobile nature of pervasive games is unique by allowing an ambiguous wavering between fantasy and reality when played. In this chapter, I will argue that it is exactly this ambiguity that is at the core of the player's experience and indeed at the construction of the game world itself. Set against the backdrop of the physical reality of everyday life, the thin line between the evident 'real' world and the institutionalised fantasy of the game becomes the crux to which the pervasive game owes its existence. The pervasive game interweaves the concept of reality and fantasy, thus transforming our everyday environment into a world in play. This complicates the notions of reality and fantasy (fantasy referring to the game). Furthermore, within the game world, Roger Caillois's terms *ludus* and *paidia* (2001) are set off against one another. As will be discussed later on, the concept of childlike 'play' or *paidia* positions itself in a similar way in relation to its more formal counterpart, *ludus* or 'game'.

Hence, not only does the world of the game reiterate its own status as a fantastical artefact through the continuing juxtaposition with the 'real' physical world of everyday life, the nature of play is also of a freer and more open character that resembles child's play.

But what happens at the crossroads of these intermingling phenomena? What are the instances that incite the merging of fantasy and reality, and how can we best define this fusion? In this chapter, I will investigate these questions by looking at the applicability of the term 'interface' to the co-existence of supposed antagonistic forces in pervasive games. I argue that the status of the interface as an intermediary between the user and the (technological) system makes it the most important focus to determine which border is being crossed from reality to game. By asking the questions of where and how the interface comes into being in pervasive games, I offer a first insight into what the limbo between reality and the game is, as well as specifying the relationship between ludus and paidia that is so characteristic of pervasive games.

The role of the player forms an important part of this chapter, as I state that players form the most crucial kind of interface in this type of play. Pervasive games exist by the mercy of players, and without them the streets will inevitably return to their everyday status. I will therefore argue that the interface I am trying to define can be partly located in the thoughts and imagination of the player, thus acquiring a more cultural and symbolic meaning. Two important notions in this equation are the 'real' and the 'virtual'. They should be conceived as the opposition between cultural conventions that are normally present in everyday life (such as going to work or walking on the street) and the fictional game world that is generated by means of computer technology. Further on in this chapter, this distinction between 'real' everyday life and the game world will be addressed in more detail, and will be respectively denoted by the terms 'telic' and 'paratelic' (Apter and Kerr 1999).

Pervasive gaming

For a term as up-and-coming as pervasive gaming, it may seem surprising that the definitions remain vague. A common approach is lacking, and it remains unclear how pervasive gaming differs from neighbouring phenomena such as ubiquitous gaming, augmented reality gaming and mobile gaming (Nieuwdorp 2007). Pervasive games are in general described as inducing a mixture of the real and the virtual, in particular creating virtual worlds of play in everyday environments through the use of different ubiquitous applications of technologies (media) (Davidsson, Peitz and Bjork 2004; McGonigal 2003). In a temporal, spatial and social sense, the game world encompasses everyday physical environments, which the player can interact with in real time through multiple media platforms (Sotamaa 2002).

When investigating the nature of pervasive play, the borders between the different elements of fantasy and reality must irrevocably be sought out, which leads us to the interface. Applied to digital games, the interface is invariably made equivalent to either the hardware (controllers and the like) or the software (visual elements of the game world) that generate human-computer interaction (HCI). The screen captures both aspects, as it is both part of the hardware while at the same time visually representing the 3D game world through software. It functions as a veritable Alberti's window through which the user can step from physical reality into the virtual universe of the game. The screen can be viewed as a translucent membrane, an intermediary, which translates digital signs into actual player experience and parallels the player's physical actions to manipulation in the digital realm. In the field of HCI, the concept is taken to mean the human-computer interface with its desktop metaphor or hardware connotations. When applied to digital games, the interface is determined as a fixed screen and gaming device (Manovich 2001) and is increasingly seen as a potential obstacle to immersive qualities of the gaming experience (Cheok et al. 2002). But is this notion of the interface in digital games satisfactory for understanding pervasive games? In pervasive games, visual representations are no longer dominated by the screen. This challenges current concepts of the interface. Both from the perspective of the game, which is ambivalent in its player-game interaction and reality/game status, and from the perspective of the interface, which is no longer limited to the hardware and software, it is interesting to see how these two terms can be defined in relation to one another. In the area of HCI as well as in digital games theory, the screen is conceived of as the ultimate interface (Johnson 1997; Laurel 1991; Manovich 2001). Especially in HCI, the interface is seen as the tip of the iceberg of the programming language that is needed to make an application work (Meyer 1988). This makes the interface primarily a graphical and tangible concept. Both hardware and software interfaces are tailored to make the interaction as easy as possible. The focus is thus put on designing and testing, and keeping the concept consistent.

Yet when we hark back to our definition of pervasive games as stated above, we see that the virtual (the synthetic artefact as generated by a computer) also intertwines on a social and cultural level with everyday life. This necessitates a different approach to the concept of the interface, as the social and geographical surroundings of the technology used are now open to change due to the mobility of the player, who interacts with more than just a PDA or mobile phone.

Although in interface theory the emphasis has been primarily placed on the graphical and the tangible, several attempts have been made to extend the concept to social and cultural realms. As computer scientist Grudin already foresaw (1989; 1990; 1993), we need to customize the concept of the interface to apply the social and spatial environments of interaction. Recently, the interest in defining the practice of computing in relation to users and their environment has increased. Users bring a personal history and setting along, which is comprised of prior knowledge and experience. This is what Paul Dourish (2001) calls 'embodied interaction'. When players participate in a pervasive game, they are actively creating meaning, and as we will see later on, they often need to reinterpret common conventions about meaning. After all, as the spatial qualities of the environment are shared with the existing setting of an already familiar environment (such as the streets), the player must bring along a concept not unlike the willing suspension of disbelief in film to engage meaningfully in the game. The game world must be accepted as somehow different from everyday life, and thus conventions in everyday life are challenged. Therefore, the facilitating factors for playing a pervasive game lie not solely within hardware and software, but also in the player.

Semiotic domains

Before examining the membrane that separates the game world from everyday life, the specifics of both terms need to be ascertained. Only after the two different domains are fenced off can we see what the fence is made of. What makes a pervasive game? What makes it come into being? To answer these questions, a closer look at the practice of signs and semiotics is needed.

As a pervasive game takes place partly in an already existing environment with its own laws and conventions, it is important to look at the elements that actually change when the game world comes into being. Knowing the conventions of the real world makes it easier to observe what changes in the arena of play. These cultural conventions, which are agreed upon socially but are implemented on a personal scale, are the focus of the interface in pervasive game-play.

I would like to illustrate this with an example. Imagine you are a participant in The Go Game, a pervasive game that is played with a mobile phone in an urban environment. You are walking on the street when you receive a text message: 'Sometime today you will find the Mystery Key. It won't look like a key, but it will work some kind of magic when you encounter a locked door later in the game. So make sure you take with you any unusual objects you find along the way...' (McGonigal 2003).

In a 'normal' situation, one would know a key when seeing one, whilst now the only thing you do know is that the key in question could be *anything but* a conventional key. Instead of going to a locksmith, you will need to consider all objects that do not fit the conventional context of everyday surroundings as potential keys. In other words, you need to view familiar environments with different eyes. This is only one example, and perhaps an exaggerated one, but it does point to a characteristic of all pervasive games. Whether brought about by vague missions or the situation that the street has changed into a battlefield, the fact remains that, no matter the degree of intensity, the player always needs to shift focus from the everyday world to the conventions and rules of the entered game. The example above demonstrates how different the approach to environments then needs to be.

What changes is the correlation between an entity and its meaning. This is very apparent in the form that the key takes in the example: instead of the word 'key' pertaining to a specific object, it now relates to anything but that object. What is put under strain is the semiotic relationship between the Saussurian 'signifier' and 'signified', where the former refers to the linguistic sound image of a thing, and the latter to the mental concept of a thing (Hawkes 2003). The relationship between an object and its accepted conventional meaning alters in pervasive games. Surely, in everyday life it is always possible to approach an object or situation in different ways according to context and personal goals, but in pervasive games this relationship is more purposefully challenged.

One could argue that we transgress into another mental state that makes us accept new rules and conventions when shifting from practices of everyday life to the ludic space of the pervasive game world. But how does this happen? Semiotics can help us to answer this question. According to James Paul Gee (2003) video-games can be perceived as distinct semiotic domains. In pervasive games, we can then approach the game world as a semiotic domain with its own constructed meanings. This world can be seen as separate from the semiotic domain of every-day life, which Gee calls the 'lifeworld' domain. When deciding to play a perva-sive game, one crosses from one semiotic ('lifeworld') domain into another do-main, thus adopting and adapting to a distinctive set of conventions and meanings. But where does this border reside? To answer this question I will take a closer look at the concept of the magic circle and the metaphor of the cell mem-brane.

The magic circle and the metaphorical membrane

A concept that is often employed to describe the soap bubble of the game world is that of the magical circle, as introduced by Dutch historian Johan Huizinga (1955).[1] Relating this term to the interface in pervasive gaming, the thin line be-tween this ludic circle and the practice of everyday life becomes the main focus. It is this border, this threshold, which needs to be crossed in order to enter the game world. And thus, tracing the contours of the magic circle is indeed closely related to tracking down the several levels of the pervasive interface. As pervasive games force us to reinterpret meanings ascribed to everyday settings and objects, this border becomes more apparent than in any other type of game.

The magic circle must not be viewed as a rigid sphere that can be superim-posed on everyday reality. Instead, it should be seen as a nearly organic entity that changes, develops and interacts with its surroundings as the pervasive game comes into being through play. In this sense the magic circle becomes a perme-able membrane where conventional meanings, psychological artefacts and environments, and players alike can slip through. This reasoning is supported by Erving Goffman (1961), who argues that a permeable screen-like boundary demarcates games from the world at large. Yet the relationship between reality and game is more intricate than a crude juxtaposition of terms. The very notion of a cell membrane points to the two-way direction of exchange between the game world and everyday life.

But how can we delineate the border between everyday life and the domain of the pervasive game? According to Goffman specific boundary-maintaining mechanisms can be distinguished that govern the shape of the magic circle or ludic cell membrane of a game. Goffman asserts that these mechanisms can be categorised as follows:

1. rules of irrelevance: players renounce material, emotional or aesthetic values when playing a game;
2. transformation rules: these rules denote the amount of influence on the status of the game a non-game element has that for some reason enters the magic circle;
3. realised resources: all possible moves that can be made in the game that are open to all players.

All of these factors play an important role in pervasive games. Transformation rules tell us what effect external aspects can have in the game world. Thinking back to the example of *The Go Game*, it is clear that the transformation rules are very loosely defined in that game, making it difficult for the player to discern what is part of the game world and what is not. This means that the realised resources in the game world seem almost infinite to players, since they cannot be sure what objects are intended for the game world. Both the transformation rules and the realised resources can then be seen to depend on the acceptance of the game world as an omnipresent and persistent realm of which everything could possibly be part. This is what Goffman calls rules of irrelevance: a selective disregard of certain values that have a meaningful place in the life world domain, but which do not agree with the cultural conventions of the game world. These rules facilitate the state of mind that is needed to accept the game world as an arena of play. How this state can be described and takes shape will be discussed in the next section of this chapter.

Now it has become clear that the pervasive game world is in fact a semiotic domain with its own rules and conventions and that the coming-into-being of this game world requires an active mental shift from players in relation to their environment, we can direct our attention to a description of the shift that the player has to make to acquire a state of playing.

So far, little research has been conducted in the field of players' attitudes from a formal perspective. Some attempts have been made, notably by Bernard Suits

(1990) and Satu Heliö (2004) who speak of 'lusory attitude' and the 'gaming mindset', respectively, but both of these terms are related to the way a player views the game world 'in play'. They do not refer to the instance when this change in mental state actually occurs, which, so to speak, 'announces' the coming-into-being of the game world. This is where the notion of the interface comes in.

The liminal interface: paratelic and paraludic

I have already shown that interfaces, which facilitate the game world to take form, are not merely located in hardware and software, but also in the mind of the player. I have called this the *liminal* interface, liminal referring to the status of the interface as threshold or transitional stage. As a term coined by anthropologist Victor Turner, the liminal has been used to describe the phase of transition to play (Ericsson 2004; Brian Sutton-Smith 1997). The liminal interface, then, is the aforementioned interface that is located in the mind of the player and refers to the semiotic switch that has to be made between the sphere of everyday life and the semiotic domain of the pervasive game. This interface consists of two sub-categories: the *paratelic* and the *paraludic* interface.

The following theory is based on a combination of views in psychology about adult play (Apter et al, 1991), and classifications of playing and gaming as devised by Bo Kampmann Walther (2003). Walther discerns two different transitions: first between the initially serious state of mind (non-play) into play, and secondly the subsequent transition to accepting the rigid rules of a game (from play to game). The terms 'play' and 'game' correspond to Caillois's (2001, 13) terms paidia and ludus, respectively. He described paidia as 'an almost indivisible principle, common to diversion, turbulence, free improvisation, and carefree gaiety' and ludus as 'a tendency to bind [paidia] with arbitrary, imperative, and purposely tedious conventions.' Paidia then refers to free play such as that of children, while ludus indicates the institutionalized game with its rules and regulations.

Let's first focus on the transgression from non-play into play. This first initiation into the pervasive game, and indeed into all games, can be called the paratelic state. Coined by psychologists Apter and Kerr (1991), it refers to a playful state of mind as opposed to one in which the 'seriousness' of everyday life takes pride of place. In the paratelic state, a person becomes playful and lets go of the restraints and cultural conventions that apply to work and other activities in which the end justifies the means. The paratelic state of 'play' must be conceived in Caillois's sense of the word, and corresponds to paidia. The decision to play, and thus entering a game world, implies the necessary rejection of particular conventions and practices that are prevalent in the domain of everyday life (Apter and Kerr

1991). This is what Goffman referred to as rules of irrelevance: letting go of the practices of everyday life to prepare one's mind for play.

When we look at pervasive gaming, the paratelic interface becomes relevant at the moment that a person rejects the practices and conventions within the semiotic domain of everyday life in order to enter a more playful realm. In my view this has everything to do with a temporary and reversible attention shift, in which the conventions of the semiotic domain of play prevail over those in daily life. It is important to keep in mind here that the term 'para' refers to the two-way direction between reality and play and that the player can oscillate between these positions. The fact that the conventions of the 'lifeworld' domain are left behind through rules of irrelevance does not mean that reality is pushed out of the picture. In fact, quite the contrary is happening, as play actively needs reality to reiterate its own status (Walther 2003).

However, to complete the transition of moving into a game world with its own set of rules, more is needed than the rejection of conventions that are predominant in everyday life. Additionally, game rules need to be accepted as the laws of the new semiotic domain that is entered. Put in Gee's vocabulary, the player would otherwise not be able to understand the signs that govern the realm that is entered (Gee 2003). This is why a second transition is needed (the paraludic interface).

Once players have crossed the threshold to enter the paraludic state, the rules of the game need to be learned. Gaining knowledge of its semiotic conventions enables players to develop a literacy that is needed to become part of the game world. Again, however, we must take into account the two-directional relation of the two states of play and game (Walther 2003). As the player enters the game, play is never far away. Thinking back to *The Go Game*, it is clear that a playful attitude can very much be a part of the game, for example when assignments are open to interpretation.

These shifts from non-play to play into game require a very active stance of the player, who needs to realise on a meta-level the qualities of play, game and reality at once: something is play because it is not reality, something is a game because it is not play and consequently not reality. This constant threefold reiteration of the status of a game means that the player of a pervasive game will always in some form be reminded of the game being a construct. At the same time, accepting the game world as a separate semiotic domain implies shifting one's focus and accepting the conventions within that domain as dominant and thus as 'real'.

Conclusions

Pervasive games are a special type of game in which the relation between reality and game is emphasized. Due to the fact that the pervasive game is set both spatially and temporally in the 'lifeworld' domain, it is important to scrutinize how the game world can be distinguished from daily life. In this chapter I have investigated this by looking at the status of the interface.

In general, I can conclude that the term interface is mostly exclusively consigned to the screen, since it is often apparent in hardware or software applications. However, I have argued that the pervasive game challenges this notion of the interface by its ubiquitous and mobile nature. Literally taking the game world to the streets, it mixes the semiotic conventions that exist in the 'lifeworld' domain and the pervasive game world. I have introduced the notion of the liminal interface to account for the fact that through a mental shift the player stays aware of this mixture and is able to distinguish between these two realms. The liminal interface can be seen as the edge of the magic circle or the metaphorical membrane that is entered when accepting the rules of irrelevance.

The liminal interface consists of two levels: the paratelic interface, which refers to the player's shifting focus when leaving the conventions of the 'lifeworld' domain behind, and the paraludic interface, which makes the player accept the new conventions of the game world. In pervasive games these shifts are foregrounded by the unrelenting presence of the everyday world: the player needs to accept the game world as an omnipresent, persistent and consistent universe of which everything can be part, otherwise the interface, the edge of the magic circle, will become damaged – obliterating the very existence of the pervasive game.

Note

1. For an in-depth discussion of the term magic circle, see the chapter by Marinka Copier in this book.

References

Apter, Michael, and John Kerr, eds. 1991. *Adult play: A reversal theory approach*. Amsterdam: Swets and Zeitlinger.

Caillois, Roger. 2001 (orig. 1958). *Man, play, and games*. Champaign: University of Illinois Press.

Cheok, Adrian, D., Xubo Yang, Zhou Zhi Ying, Mark Billinghurst, and Hirokazu Kato. 2002. Touch-Space: Mixed reality game space based on ubiquitous, tangible and social computing. *Personal and ubiquitous computing* (6): 430-442.

Davidsson, Ola, Johan Peitz, and Staffan Björk. 2004. Game design patterns for mobile games. *Project report to Nokia Research Center, Finland*. http://www.gamedesignpatterns.org.

Dourish, Paul. 2001. *Where the action is: The foundations of embodied interaction*. Cambridge MA: MIT Press.

Ericsson, Martin. 2004. Play to love: Reading Turner's 'Liminal to limonoid, in play, flow, and ritual: An essay in comparative symbology'. In *Beyond role and play: Tools, toys and theory for harnessing the imagination*, eds. Montola, M. and J. Stenros, 15-31. Ropecon ry, Helsinki.

Gee, James P. 2003. *What video games have to teach us about learning and literacy*. New York: Macmillan.

Goffman, Erving. 1961. *Encounters: Two studies in the sociology of interaction*. Indianapolis: Bobbs-Merril.

Grudin, Jonathan. 1989. The case against user consistency. *Communications of the ACM* 32 (10): 1164-1173.

—. 1990. The computer reaches out: The historical continuity of interface design. *CHI '90 Proceedings*, 261-268.

—. 1993. Interface. *Communications of the ACM* 36 (4): 112-119.

Hawkes, Terence. 2003 (orig. 1977). *Structuralism and semiotics*. New York: Routledge.

Heliö, Satu. 2004. Role-playing: A narrative experience and a mindset. In *Beyond role and play: Tools, toys and theory for harnessing the imagination*, eds. Montola, M. and J. Stenros. Ropecon ry, Helsinki.

Huizinga, Johan. 1955 (orig. 1938). *Homo Ludens: A study of the play element in culture*. Boston: Beacon Press.

Johnson, Steven. 1997. *Interface culture: How new technology transforms the way we create and communicate*. San Francisco: Harper.

Laurel, Brenda. 1991. *Computers as theatre*. Boston: Addison-Wesley Publications.

Manovich, Lev. 2001. *The language of new media*. Cambridge, MA: MIT Press.

McGonigal, Jane. 2003. A real little game: The Pinocchio effect in pervasive play. In *Level up: Digital games research conference*, eds. Marinka Copier and Joost Raessens. Utrecht: Utrecht University.

Meyer, Bertrand. 1988. *Object-oriented software construction*. New Jersey: Prentice Hall.

Nieuwdorp, Eva. 2007. The pervasive discourse: An analysis. *ACM Computers in Entertainment (CIE)* 5 (2): n.p.

Salen, Katie, and Eric Zimmerman. 2004. *Rules of play: Game design fundamentals*. Cambridge, MA: MIT Press.

Sotamaa, Olli. 2002. All the world's a Botfighter stage: Notes on location-based multi-user gaming. *CGDC Conference Proceedings*. Tampere University Press, 35-44.

Suits, Bernard. 1990. *Grasshopper: Games, life and utopia*. Boston: David R. Godine.

Sutton-Smith, Brian. 1997. *The ambiguity of play*. Cambridge, MA: Harvard University Press.

Walther, Bo Kampmann. 2003. Playing and gaming: Reflections and classifications. *Game Studies: The International Journal of Computer Game Research* 3 (1). http://www.gamestudies.org/0301/walther.

Grasping the screen

Towards a conceptualization of touch, mobility and multiplicity

Nanna Verhoeff

In 2004 Nintendo released the DS. With this new handheld console Nintendo updated and expanded the commercially successful Gameboy (1989) and its successors, the Game Boy Color (1998) and the Game Boy Advance (2001). The DS is marketed as a revolutionary console, because it allegedly offers radically new possibilities for game play. The new 'specs' or technological features of the DS are, indeed, various: voice-control options, WiFi connectivity, touch-screen technology, and last but not least, multiple screens.

Figure 2: *The Nintendo DS Lite with screenshots of the game* Wario: Master of Disguise. (*Courtesy of Nintendo, Benelux*)

I chose this handheld game console as the object for my inquiry into the status of the mobile screen to answer historical as well as theoretical questions. In the midst of a continuous push for innovation and development, accompanied by ubiquitous marketing, it is the historical status of the gadget that is my first point of interest. With its specifications the DS console offers a distinctive interface and enables quite diverse possibilities for engaging and interacting with its screens and their on-screen content. This makes the DS an appealing case for my purpose: to explore the complex issues that emerge from a 'theoretical object' approach to the Nintendo DS as a time-bound piece of material screen technology. Specifically, I am interested in the way innovations of technological objects – such as this gadget – inspire, and make necessary, applications that explore the possibilities and limitations offered by the interface for the use of the object as 'screen practice'.

A theoretical reason for my choice of the DS as object is that it is a screen-based *console* – a term I consider significant, literally as well as metaphorically. As a console, the DS is a platform or interface for the games that can be played on it. Like any screen-based apparatus, its technology and the ensuing possibilities for its users both prescribe and need content. It requires an on-screen image or application, on the one hand, and the actual viewing or handling of the screen on the other. This dual need makes it necessary to consider the DS as more than an object; it must be seen as a *practice*. Screening as practice involves technology, content or application, and use. When we take the gadget not simply as a material object but as a time-bound object-in-practice, it becomes productive to consider a handheld console like the DS a theoretical object – or, as I argue below, a theoretical console.[1]

The DS can be taken as an instance of issues that emerge from the integrated examination of screen, application, and use. The DS is a mobile dispositif: a screening arrangement that encompasses both the positioning of the screen's user and the physical set-up for interactive interfacing by the screen's use. Its mobility is multiple – a mobility of screen, user, and image – and raises questions about the mobile screen as related to movement, touch, and the process of spatial transformation.

To demonstrate the usefulness of this take on a somewhat banal object such as the Nintendo DS, I will zoom in on three of its features that make up its particular mobility – the mobility of the screen, the touch control of the screen, and the doubling or multiplicity of the screen – to explore the range of historical and theoretical questions that emanate from that mobility.

A new gadget

Even though the screen features of the DS (Dual Screens) are central in the console's marketing campaign, the use of a multiscreen format is not new for Nintendo gaming devices. A clamshell case was already used in the Game & Watch series (1980-1991). There are, however, some important differences between earlier portable games and the DS console. Firstly, the Game & Watch series offered single games – of which Donkey Kong is perhaps the best known – rather than operating as a platform for multiple games on interchangeable game cartridges, as does the DS.

A second difference is that the screens of these older games were partly pre-printed with both a foreground and background setting. These preprints situated the versatile on-screen game characters within a fixed spatial environment. Moreover, the double screens offered only one possibility: the player was able to move the game characters from one screen to the other, creating a linear spatial continuity between the two screens. On the DS the two screen spaces can be related to each other in a variety of ways in each game.

Thirdly, the user controls the lower screen by touch. The touch screen is operated by a fundamentally different kind of 'handling' than the traditional button controls for the upper screen. Rather than a singular object, as a console, the DS is a platform of a whole array of games that each provides different applications of the dual screens and the touch screen capabilities.[2]

This dual-screen element gives the company's advertisers an argument to enhance newness. On the Nintendo DS consumer service website, the producers stress that the letters DS, in addition to being an abbreviation for Dual Screens, have another meaning: '[t]o our developers, it stands for "Developers" System', since we believe it gives game creators brand new tools which will lead to more innovative games for the world's players.'[3] In spite of the obvious rhetoric of hyperbole deployed to accentuate innovation and global scale, the producers do have a point. The two-screen features that distinguish this console from other portable, hybrid or convergent game systems such as Sony's PSP (PlayStation Portable) or Nokia's N-Gage invite newly designed games or modifications of older games. Conversely, these games explore the particular possibilities of the DS screens.

Moreover, with the double screens, different screen functions converge. Read the combination of the following statements from the Nintendo website, for example:

> With Nintendo DS, dual screens and touch-screen technology allow you to interact with games like never before. Wireless communication allows you to experience real-time multiplayer game play, while built-in PictoChat software gives you the power to draw, write and send messages wirelessly.

> Two LCD screens offer one of the most groundbreaking gameplay advances ever developed. (...) In a racing game, you might see your own vehicle's perspective on one screen and an overall track view on the other. Soon, games

could be created allowing you to play games on one screen while sending text messages on the other.

The lower screen offers something never before provided by any dedicated game device: touch-screen capabilities. You no longer have to rely on just buttons to move your character or shift perspectives. Navigate menus or access inventory items simply by touching the screen with a stylus or fingertip.[4]

These statements each foreground precisely the different aspects I intend to focus on: a vision of what the screen is, what we can do with screens, and what makes a particular screen-based device stand out as new. They address the temporality, the real-time aspect of communication through wireless connectivity and touch-screen interaction; the spatial multiplication when they speak of multiple perspectives enabled and visualized by the double screens; and practice, with the suggestion of more intuitive interaction with the screen by direct touch.

In addition to that analysis of newness, the quoted passages bring us closer to a triple theoretical point the DS makes concerning the status of the gadget as object. The gadget as object is *material*. Moreover, a screen-based gadget is temporal as well as temporary, or ephemeral. Therefore, the status of the gadget in the history of media is at issue. This status is both comparative and historical, concerning synchronic differentiations and confluence, as well as transformation over time. Herein lies its *historical* status. Lastly, the gadget's *functionality* is determined by the way any screen-based object embodies possibilities of multiple interfaces. This is why such multifaceted objects should be considered theoretical *consoles* rather than theoretical *objects* (singular). The issues the gadget raises offer a constellation of concepts for use in media history and theory together.

The first issue raised is one of method: how can we study it from a media-archeological perspective? Within media history, a gadget is a commercial and vernacular technological object that is designed as an interface and platform for multimedia applications. Its market value is primarily determined by its innovative character, its newness. Paradoxically, however, its innovation is recognizable through its similarity to other, previously marketed gadgets. The fact that we speak of *generations* of mobile phones, mobile game consoles, or media players indicates this assumption of a family resemblance and a lineage among gadgets. More specifically, a gadget is a small, pocket-sized, handheld object designed for individual, daily use. Its status lies somewhere between practical tool, fun object, and shiny piece of technology. As Lev Manovich stresses, it is also an aesthetic object in which such different functions and meanings converge as 'friendly, playful, pleasurable, aesthetically pleasing, expressive, and fashionable; signifying cultural identity, and designed for emotional satisfaction' (2006, 1).

As a technological *moment* the gadget provides a historical anchoring of technology. In this in-between-ness of the gadget – between apparatus, device and appliance – a convergence becomes visible. Convergence is a useful notion to account for the other side of history, namely the momentary synthesis of a particular moment, a synchronic slice of time where different issues, possibilities and desires come together. Here, the convergence is the synthesis of media technologies and therefore of media uses. However, in the case at hand the issue is not that different technologies come together in one appliance, but that a singular constellation of technologies emerges in one console. This mixture offers a platform – console – for a whole array of possibilities for the gadget's applications. It is not a singular medium; it is, rather, a composite, a convergence of screen paradigms within a single dispositif. Therefore, the features of the screen that both *converge* and *transform* in this apparatus bind synchrony to diachrony and thus embody its status as theoretical console. This warrants a closer look at the many-sided screen of the DS: the touch screen, the mobile screen, and the double screen.

Touch screen

The first element in this convergence of screen paradigms is touch. The haptic element of touch screens primarily meant for viewing inflects the notion – and action – of viewing itself. This haptic form of 'viewing' bears consequences for the way the screen enables the viewer/user to virtually travel through the screen. This feature is, again, both new and old. This traversing has a long-standing status as metaphor for screen-based viewing. The idea, or conceptual metaphor, of moving *through* has been dominant in our way of perceiving how visual screen media work.

Seeing has a longstanding cultural meaning metaphorically expressed in the window. Not coincidentally, the Nintendo DS promotes itself in the terms of 'thing theorist' Bill Brown – as a dirty window:

A boy approaches the dirty rear windows of a van and writes 'GO' with his fingers, upon which the van drives away. This short evocative clip speaks of the main feature of the touch screen technology: like on a dirty window, on the touch screen we can write commands. The analogy between a dirty window and touch screen, here deployed as a visual comparison, suggests two directions in which to consider the two elements. From window to touch screen, it says both simplicity and general availability. From touch screen to window, the clip suggests a sense of magic conferred upon the everyday; things will happen when we touch the opaque glass shield. Far from being transparent, the screen becomes, emphatically, a thing.

The comparison between the screen and the window, so utterly commonplace, demonstrates what is at stake here. When a window is dirty, is it the window we actually see: it is the impossibility of seeing *through* the window, its opacity, that marks its presence as a thing. This is how Bill Brown explains what he calls thingness. He refers to a novel by A.S. Byatt: 'the interruption of the habit of looking *through* windows as transparencies enables [Byatt's] protagonist to look *at* a window in itself in its opacity' (Brown 2004, 4).

When the screen functions as a transparent window, it is invisible as an object. When it is opaque, its materiality or thingness, surfaces. This paradox of non-functionality that correlates to visibility and thingness is particularly intriguing in the case of the screen. Unlike the window, the operation of this screen necessitates opaqueness for virtual transparency: it needs the surface to reflect the images *on* the screen.

Heidi Rae Cooley also invokes the difference between the screen as transparent window and the screen as opaque surface. Cooley defines what she calls tactile vision, a vision 'activated by the hand' and 'a material and dynamic seeing involving eyes as well as hands and a MSD [mobile screenic device]' (2004, 137). With this term she does not refer to touch-screen technology in a strict sense, but to the more general manual 'handling' of mobile screens – the 'touched-screen' as we may call this broader category. Tactile vision, according to Cooley, is based on the principle of the fit: 'the particular relationship between a hand and a MSD, which opens onto a relation of interface through which vision becomes and remains tactile' (ibid., 137).

While Cooley rightly argues for a tactile notion of *interfacing*, I would derive a stronger point from this tactility. The haptic nature of the touch screen technology transforms the *practice* of screening; it foregrounds the temporal collapse between making and viewing images. Using the screen of the DS is a physical and performative activity. Viewing is no longer a matter of perceptually receiving images. It entails movements with the hand that holds the stylus. There are no images prior to the moment the user conjures them up by touch. This simultaneity of touching, making, and viewing connects the viewing experience to the *liveness* of television, and to the physical and creative experience of drawing. This temporal aspect is clear in the ad, where looking and doing occur at the same moment – are, in fact, one act. The activity, or performance, of making shifts the focus from receptivity to production.

As part of a body that can move around, the hand that touches the screen of the DS gadget can also take the gadget to different places. I turn now to the mobility that results from this aspect as a second, fundamentally new, yet also continuous aspect of the gadget. As I argue below, multiple takes on mobility – of device, screen, and user – can be brought to bear on the particular touch screen interface.

Mobile screen

As a handheld device the DS can be taken anywhere. The portability of the device makes it a mobile medium but because of its pocket size also a very individual one. Yet, as stressed in the marketing of the DS, sharing is part of the fun – of its social ecology. Sharing concerns the way the mobile screen as a handheld object can be passed around, a mobility not of space only, but also a mobility of use and even property. Although mobile gadgets are often also called 'personal electronic devices', the DS ad campaign explicitly targets connectivity, communal play, and media use.

Consider the following commercial for the DS, called Gravy. Five young people in a restaurant play with their food. Shots of them seem to be unrelated, until we understand that they are, in fact, connected, communicating with each other. 'Game?' is the question a boy writes in a pool of gravy on his plate. 'I'm in,' a girl writes on her frosted glass. This commercial plays with a magical idea, especially appealing to children who hate to be forced to finish their dinner. The medium, enabling the bored child to break his solitude, allows what can be called space-binding – the particular characteristic of televisual connections between spaces that fundamentally alters the experience of time within a place, as Anna McCarthy has pointed out (2001, 74). This telewriting invokes the association with the mystic writing pad, which was also alluded to in the dirty-windows ad. There, the potential opaqueness visually was offered to the use of performative writing – the command that took immediate effect. Here, the magic of the mystic writing pad appears in the writable gravy.[5]

This is a form of ghost writing: someone else, invisible to you as if on the other side of the screen, makes things visible on your screen. The fact that someone else, who is elsewhere, manages your screen turns that screen into a shared space. The screen gains liveness, as the process of writing is simultaneous with viewing, like in live animation. This ad suggests that different perspectives and agencies run into one another on one single screen. Connectivity not only multiplies screen space, it also turns multiple screens into one. The gadget is thus positioned as tool and as site for private, yet collective, mediation.

In addition to the possibility of passing around the whole gadget, hence, the whole screen, the feature of connectivity enables another way of sharing. Through wireless connection the user/player can share screen space, simultaneously in multiple-player games or alternately by sending messages. Screen space is something else than, literally, the space of the hand that holds the screen. Instead, the experience of space can be considered in terms of a spatial continuity of eyes, hand, screen, and screened space. In response to earlier screen technologies, the mobility of the gadget is therefore perhaps best understood as the spatial extension not beyond the screen (into the screened space) but in front of the screen (between eye and screen). More intimate than a distant screen, more individual than a large screen, more intuitive than a separated screen, the handheld aspect of the mobile screen emphasizes the continuity between spaces.

This brings me to another aspect of spatial continuity, namely the impact of time on space. Continuity is spatial but inevitably also temporal. Simultaneity and the sharing of screen space is a way of temporalizing space. The gravy ad takes time and represents time: the time of boredom, and the time in which boredom is interrupted by the initiative to play. This is why media of mobility are so attractive: they play with *and* naturalize the time-space continuum.

Continuity, and in its wake sharing, are not only clarifying but also mystifying terms. They suggest a social advantage, an overcoming of individualism and loneliness. When speaking of the 'bi-located psyche' of the player, Parikka and Suominen (2006) point out how this discourse of connectivity does not disrupt the traditional separation between public and private domains. Instead, this discourse expands on another trope, namely that of virtual mobility. Sharing and connectivity concern transport. Space itself is transported: the expansion of space through the media device, whether or not with clean windows, allows the player to do something else, somewhere else. Thus, the mobility of the device comes to stand for the mobility of the medium.

It follows that mobility operates on different levels: the mobility of the device, the mobility of the player/user, and the mobility between places and users. What is most significant for the mobile game console, then, is the way the mobility *of* the screen relates to the virtual mobility that the screen 'images'. Drawing attention to that double-edged mobility turns the console as gadget once more into a theoretical console.

There is, however, a paradox at the heart of this mobility: that of the immobile spectator. Anne Friedberg has pointed out this paradox of the cinematic viewing arrangement in her thought-provoking analysis of screen media and their virtual mobility (2006). The virtual mobility of the medium is made possible precisely in the space between the immobile (cinema) viewer, the static screen or frame, and the mobility of the images on screen.

In the case of the DS, the spectator is a player, a user, and is physically engaged when using the console. The touch screen is screen and controller in one and requires physical action, and such action entails movement. But movement is not mobility; moving one's hand is not the same as moving around. This brings me, once more, to the 'old' aspect of this gadget. The immobility of the spectator is required for the classical screen, of which the film screen is the paradigmatic example. The newness resides in the fact that mobile screens not only allow, potentially, for mobility of both body and screen, they also position the mobility of the body within a number of relationships. The DS embodies an aspect of newness it shares with many other contemporary gadgets. This further develops its status as a theoretical console. As Ingrid Richardson argues, they set up a distinctive relationship between body, screen/technology, and environment/space:

> The idea that embodiment is possible relies largely on the supposition that our engagement with screen media requires a stationary body, such that one's awareness of the corporeal recedes. Yet, as I have suggested mobile media

complicate this relation, and facilitate a physical mobility of the body, whether pedestrian or vehicular, partially returning one's attention to physical location and the navigation within and around the material environment (2005, np).

This mobility is most emphatically demonstrated in the case of navigation screens. There, our literal being in the world, our physical occupation of space and the inherent coordinates, make on-screen navigation possible. Therefore, we are becoming familiar with the principle that not only the body can become mobile, but that it has to move in order for the screen to function.[6]

This mobility is similar to the movement of the avatar as a representation of the player on the screen of racing games. In those cases the cars even represent the vehicle, which virtually transports the player through the virtual space of the racing track. There is a difference here. The navigation of the screen itself – in the hands of the user or in the car/vehicle that transports both user/viewer and device/ screen – 'pulls' the avatar through the represented space on the screen of the navigation device. In contrast, the movement of buttons, finger or stylus 'pushes' the avatar across the screen space in the case of racing games.

All these aspects of mobility over-determine the simple but significant fact that the gadget itself, as a thing, can be transported wherever the user wishes to go. It is pocketsize, handheld, and lightweight. This mobility could not even be imagined in the days of old media. But clearly, this mobility of the thing *qua* thing is only the outer shell of something of which the mobility is multiple and constantly shifting. The fascination, in the end, is with mobility as such, old and new. As it provides us a freedom within space-time that no longer holds us but that we, as owner of this gadget, can hold, it is new in relation to the old. Rather than a screen-window through which we can look outside, the gadget is like a remote control for the subject itself. Like a pocket teleporter, it transports us while being on the move.

Double screen

In combination with the tactile and the mobile screen, the DS raises the stakes of screen technology through the doubling of the screen. It doubles the screen not only literally, by offering two related screens that split up screen space, but also conceptually, thus thickening its potential as a theoretical console even more. As a material site for interfacing, the screen can be multiplied. This can be done in order to combine different interfaces. This is how the screen has become a convergent medium. Looking at the DS, the clamshell case not only makes closing the screens possible, but also divides them: splitting up single-screen space into two separate screens. Again, theoretical implications cross historical ones, as the newness meets its past.

Figure 2: Simultaneous screens of Mario Kart DS, a racing game for the DS (Courtesy of Nintendo Benelux)

Obviously, screens within screens, or perhaps more appropriately, frames within frames have a longer history than Nintendo's invention. Split screens, inserts, *mise-en-abymes*: we have seen it all in cinema – and before that in painting. Yet the primary difference here is the aspect of navigation. In her section on multiple frames and screens, Anne Friedberg has pointed out how the digital, multiple screen allows for multitasking. This implies a temporal simultaneity of different activities in parallel spaces (2006, 233). Following the historical metamorphoses of the screen, which Friedberg helps us to investigate, a temporal and spatial doubling of multiple screens is perhaps the most significant newness of the digital screen. In this vein, I focus here on the fractured, yet connected, spatial arrangement of screen-based activity; the exploring of or navigating within one screen space, for example, which results in a representation of that process in another space.

Through its multiple screens – material screens, in the case of the DS, not just multiple frames within the larger frame of a single screen – the DS makes connections between multiple (virtual) spaces but also to multiple interfaces possible; and it makes that possibility visible. The games developed for the DS explore these possibilities for double vision. One of the clearest cases of related interfaces is that of racing games. Since the early days of racing games we have known the screen insert with a little map of the racing track in the upper or lower corner of the frame. These maps show little arrows, or avatars that resemble the cars that are driven in the game. On the larger screen we see a first-person perspective from a car on the racetrack.

These representations are excellent examples of what Michel De Certeau (1984) calls map and tour paradigms. While tours are visual narratives, maps are visual abstractions of space. These two forms of space-making announce what double screens make possible. De Certeau was talking about traditional cartography, but in the case of interactive digital maps, shifting perspectives and navigation on screen are at issue. The virtual movements of the avatar on screenic maps allow for a *haptic navigation* – navigation based on the transfer of physical movement to another spatial realm. When the navigator moves, the avatar moves along. The continuity between spaces makes navigation between the converged mapping paradigms possible. This is what the DS demonstrates, proposing for our reflection the implications of mapping according to De Certeau, the way these implications respond to the old cartographies, and to what extent the newness, with all its rhetoric of sharing, truly innovates the ecology of screen technology.[7]

Console

As a theoretical console, the Nintendo DS offers us insight into the mobile screen as gadget where history and theory cross. As an instance of commercial gadgetry, the object represents the state of the art of applied technology available for the average consumer. Its commercial value lies in the discourse of an ever-moving or changing horizon of technological development. As Baudrillard put it in his critical analysis of the system of fashionable objects, this discourse is even embedded in the technological make-up of the object itself (1996, esp. 115-138). In the 'permanent state of revolution' of technology, it is the object that 'speaks' its *time* (ibid., 9; emphasis in text). With its historical status it suggests the interrogation of the gadget as 'speaking its time' through its combination of recognizable 'old' and exciting 'new' features. Theoretically, it encourages the exploration of its possibilities as a console, a polymorphous 'screenic' platform for a variety of applications and practices. When we separate the thing – the DS in its material form – from the object – the thing that asks us what it is – we create what in science is denoted by the term 'theoretical object': a temporary construction. The object – here a particular screenic device – is imagined, constructed, in order to interrogate the meaning of the object that is theorized 'about'.

In addition to the many faces of the console, the specific characteristic of the portable system as a piece of technology, as hardware, the very materiality, its thingness, raises questions about the gadget status of the apparatus. As such, the gadget is more than an object: it is a tool for the user/player to do things with it. In this respect, the gadget as console is best understood as a thing, place, instrument and portal at the same time. Moreover, unlike other (portable) media players, a console is, in part, an empty interface. The software application determines part of the interface, in dialogue with the hardware elements. The complex of characteristics of the portable console as a versatile object, a thing/medium, demands a theoretical grasp of the phenomenon.

As a console it is, first, a material object (the device we hold in our hands). It is also a screen we look at as well as through, and a screen we touch. And thirdly, it is an interface utility, at once an invisible and visible platform – a machine for *visual (and audio) output* of the applications one can play on it. This interfacing function of screens is fundamentally, not coincidentally, imagined as a spatiotemporal traversal. And traversal, to become concretely imaginable, takes the form of travel. Travel as a practice, then, becomes a theoretical trope. As trope, travel is a concrete and visualizable idea that harbors theoretical thoughts that a critic can engage in when analyzing objects. By the same token, things that are contemplated as objects that embody such visual forms of travel can in turn be understood as theoretical objects.

I have proposed that the DS can thus be considered as a theoretical object, but more specifically in this case, as a theoretical console. The difference between what is called a theoretical object and what I term a theoretical console is that between a thing, used and reflected upon as object, and a variety of practices performed through that thing – its 'consoleness'. As an *object*, the DS Nintendo already raises questions and suggests ideas about the status, the limits and the possibilities of the screen. This turns the object as artefact into a theoretical object. As a *console*, it works as a dispositif that compels particular practices, and thus it complicates these questions.

Notes

1. For a more developed version of this argument, see my article in *Journal of Visual Culture* 8, 2 (forthcoming, August 2009).
2. Digitally animated and interactive games are not the only applications for the DS. An Internet browser, movie and music players and e-book readers have been developed, both by Nintendo, third-party commercial producers, as well as by consumers who produce so-called homebrew applications.
3. http://www.nintendo.com/consumer/systems/ds/faq.jsp.
4. http://www.nintendo.com/overviewds.
5. About Freud's essay on the mystic writing pad as metaphor for memory and the relationship with screen time, see Mary Ann Doane (1996; 2002). In a slightly different vein, Maureen Turim considers the children's toy Etch-a-Sketch as a pre-digital *Wunderblock* (1999, 49). Thanks to Ann-Sophie Lehmann for bringing this essay to my attention.
6. Elsewhere (2008), I have argued about separate, yet connected spaces of navigation devices, that the on-screen representation of navigation is, in fact, the means for navigating off-screen space. This simultaneous onscreen and offscreen navigation can be conceptualized as the construction of *screen space*: a hybrid space between onscreen and offscreen space.
7. On De Certeau's notion of space and maps, see also the essay by Sybille Lammes in this volume.

References

Baudrillard, Jean. 1996. *The system of objects*. Translated by James Benedict. London, New York: Verso.

Brown, Bill. 2004. Thing theory. In *Thing*, ed. Bill Brown, Chicago: The University of Chicago Press.

Cooley, Heidi Rae. 2004. It's all about the fit: The hand, the mobile screenic device and tactile vision. *Journal of Visual Culture* 3 (2): 133-155.

Certeau, Michel de. 1984. *The practice of everyday life*. Berkeley, CA: University of California Press.

Doane, Mary Anne. 2002. *The emergence of cinematic time: Modernity, contingency, the archive*. Cambridge, MA: Harvard University Press.

Doane, Mary Ann. 1996. Temporality, storage, legibility: Freud, Marey, and the cinema. *Critical Inquiry* 22 (2), Winter: 313-343.

Friedberg, Anne. 2006. *The virtual window: From Alberti to Microsoft*. Cambridge, MA: MIT Press.

Manovich, Lev. 2006. Interaction as an aesthetic event. *Receiver* (17). http://www.vodafone.com/flash/receiver/17/articles/index09.html.

McCarthy, Anna. 2001. *Ambient television: Visual culture and public space*. Durham and London: Duke University Press.

Parikka, Jussi and Jaakko Suominen. 2006. Victorian snakes? Towards a cultural history of mobile games and the experience of movement. *Game Studies* 6 (1). http://gamestudies.org/0601/articles/parikka_suominen.

Richardson, Ingrid. 2005. Mobile technosoma: Some phenomenological reflections on itinerant media devices. *Fibreculture* (6). http://journal.fibreculture.org/issue6/issue6_richardson.html.

Turim, Maureen. 1999. Artisanal prefigurations of the digital: Animating realities, collage effects, and theories of image manipulation. *Wide Angle* 21 (1): 49-62.

Verhoeff, Nanna. 2008. Screens of navigation: From taking a ride to making the ride. *Refractory: A Journal of Entertainment Media* 11. http://blogs.arts.unimelb.edu.au/refractory/2008/03/06/screens-of-navigation-from-taking-a-ride-to-making-the-ride.

Terra incognita

Computer games, cartography and spatial stories

Sybille Lammes

In this chapter I will examine computer games in which both mapping and spatial progress are important organizing principles. Games such as *Age of Empires* (1997-2005), *Rise of Nations* (2003), and *Civilization* (1991-2005) invite the player to go on an imaginary expedition, where traveling through landscapes creates a story. During this process maps and landscapes are mutable instead of fixed, changing appearances according to where the player travels and what is being altered in environments (e.g. mining, founding trading posts or towns, expanding borders). Right through this explorative journey, the player develops a spatial story with herself or himself as the main character as well as being an imaginary cartographer who interacts with maps and changes them according to the spatial advancements that are made. As I will show in this chapter, cartographical practices in such games augment the spatial awareness and reflection of players by inviting them to play with maps and change them according to their spatial advancements. Players themselves create spatial formations, thus generating a particular sense of place and space.

To specify how the relationship between transformative cartography and spatial progress can be understood, I will approach them as spatial stories, a term that has been theorized by De Certeau (1984). Although I am aware of the fact that De Certeau is a nonconformist in how he uses terms such as space and place, his theories are pertinent to my argument because of the emphasis that he puts on the relation and oscillation between the map and tour when we create spatial stories.[1]

Clearly, in the games that are central to this chapter, mapping is combined with touring when moving through the game space. De Certeau's theories, if used critically, can thus facilitate an understanding of how spatial stories are being developed in such games, and how maps function in this process.

In this context it is particularly interesting to see how spatial stories in computer games differ from conventional spatial stories, due to the use of digital instead of analogue mapping techniques. It has been often maintained that analogue maps – and space in general – have been ideologically constructed as fixed and objective, while they are actually socially produced (Lefèbvre 1991; Massey 1994), ideologically coded (Harley 1988; Harley 1989; Wood 1992; Crampton 2001; Wood 2002) and one of the main institutions for national states to 'imagine' their power (Anderson 1991). De Certeau's argument – written in the pre-digital era – also hinges on the fact that analogue maps are frozen representations. Hence, he maintains, a friction occurs between the personal and dynamic way in which people experience traveling through space in daily life and how maps (and other techno-scientific representations of space) represent environments as unchangeable and abstract. Since the digital maps under scrutiny in this chapter have lost such preset qualities, this argument needs critical reconsideration. The mutability of the digital maps that the player can manipulate prompts questions about how and to what extent spatio-cultural meanings shift when maps become more alterable.

Another reason why De Certeau offers an appealing perspective to study these games is because he speaks of spatial stories as practices (Thrift 2004). Although his writings are very much indebted to a semiotic tradition, he no longer defines stories as conventional narrative structures with a predetermined outcome and determinable positions of reader and narrator. Instead he speaks of spatial stories as performative acts in which the traveler becomes the story-maker. This is a highly important notion when trying to understand mapping and spatial progress in these games, or in fact any digital game. As has been amply discussed before, the player of a game cannot simply be theorized as a reader of or listener to a story as text, but is rather engaged in playful spatial practices through which personal stories are being developed (Juul 2001; Ryan 2002; Kücklich 2003; Jenkins 2004; Murray 2005; Frasca 2005; Jenkins 2005). De Certeau's approach offers the means to deal with games as stories, yet at the same time acknowledging their simulative and interactive qualities and the agency of the player.

Stories as playgrounds

Surely the fact that De Certeau's theories open up possibilities to look at stories in interactive terms is one of the reasons that the notion of spatial stories has so often been applied to computer games. It was especially an article by cultural theorist Henry Jenkins and literary historian Mary Fuller, *Nintendo® and new world travel writing: A dialogue*, that set this trend. Jenkins asserts in this article that Nintendo games, and even new media as a whole, may be perceived as spatial stories. He observes that games and other digital expressions can be best described in such terms because players primarily construct a narrative by traveling through space (Fuller and Jenkins 1995). Friedman took this idea on board in his writing about the game *Civilization*, presenting it as a suitable concept for understanding simulation games in which the player re-enacts and gives shape to history through the mastery of landscape (Friedman 1999).

Jenkins's and Friedman's views have since been the touchstone for many sub-sequent academic writings on games (Douglas 2002; Poblocki 2002; Lammes 2003; Newman 2004; Magnet 2006). Following the authors' example, they mostly refer to the difference that De Certeau made between space and place, and between the map and the tour, and apply these dichotomies to games. Places and maps are then perceived as abstract, timeless and stable. Space and tours, on the other hand, are seen as concrete, known and changeable and part of a more personal spatial experience.

In the following section I will first briefly re-visit De Certeau's writings on these four concepts, since they are often referred to in a rather condensed or even eroded way. I will move on to discuss how his vocabulary has been used in relation to games so far, and how it could be relevant to comprehend the cartographical practices figuring in the games central to this chapter. Additionally, I will argue that De Certeau's understanding of boundaries should be more explicitly added to this quartet to come to a better understanding of how these games treat spatial borders.

De Certeau re-visited

In *The practice of everyday life* (1984), De Certeau dedicates a chapter to the working of spatial stories. Unlike some ludologist game researchers, who would claim that games are in essence non-narrative (Frasca 2003, 2005; Juul 2004, Aarseth 2004), spatial stories are everywhere according to De Certeau. Not only do we need them to make sense of everyday life; stories are the central organizing principle for all human activity and are especially important when trying to come to grips with spatial change: '[E]very day, they traverse and organize places. (...) They are spatial trajectories' (De Certeau 1984, 115).

To understand how such spatial stories take shape, he makes the aforementioned distinction between space and place and map and tour, two concepts I will explain here in more detail.

The most important difference between place ('lieu') and space ('espace') is that the first term is about stability and an ordered configuration of elements, whilst the latter rather implies mobility and has a 'polyvalent' character. Place refers to the 'proper' order, to the way spatial positions are related in an objective account, whilst space is about how we deal with spatiality as 'a practiced place'. To explain the difference, De Certeau gives the example of walking the streets of a city. The geometrical configuration of the streets he equates with place, while the act of traversing these streets changes them into space. Thus, place is set and univocal, while the notion of space has as many meanings as there are walkers (De Certeau 1984, 117).

De Certeau speaks of both terms as constantly influencing each other. He identifies place as having the purpose to create static and lifeless objects. Space, on the other hand, presupposes a subjective purpose. It implies movement and change. In stories, these two determinations should be understood as in constant fluctuation in which a lifeless, objective, abstract place can become an animated and changeable, concrete space. Conversely, space can also be consolidated into place (De Certeau 1984, 117-21).

De Certeau introduces the difference between the map and the tour as a means to distinguish the different modes of the interplay of space and place in one of the most basic travel stories, namely spatial descriptions. From a study of how residents experience their apartments, he learned that the majority of people describe their dwellings in terms of moving about, and that only a small minority uses terms of seeing to explain how their apartments look. De Certeau links the latter to the notion of the map. A map can be described as a static representation of the world we live in. It objectifies spatial relations. The moving mode he relates to the notion of the tour. Touring is a dynamic principle that is subjective, since the point of view of the traveler is central. According to De Certeau these two conceptions of spatiality are both incongruous dimensions of contemporary culture. While being confronted with a static representation of the world we live in, we sense our space in a dynamic and more personal way. Just like place and space, maps and tours necessitate one another and come into being through a reciprocal movement. Even more so as a map always presupposes a tour; one first needs to go somewhere to give an objective spatial account of it (De Certeau 1984, 117-21).

Map/Space	Tour/Place
Objective	Subjective
'Scientific'	Personal
Abstract	Concrete
Fixed	Dynamic

Table 1: De Certeau's spatial distinctions

Although these concepts are in essence intertwined, maps have become more and more separated from the experience of tours in Western cultures. On medieval maps, where the itineraries themselves are basic and the emphasis lies on how long it would take to travel and where to stop, their interaction is still clearly discernable. But gradually the traces of the tours, which permitted the making of maps, were erased, and maps became more formal and abstract. Today, De Certeau states, we have to deal with this 'isolated (...) system of geographical places' (ibid., 121) while simultaneously experiencing space as an ongoing and mobile practice. Everyday stories help to make sense of such frictions: 'they are treatments of space' (ibid.).

New world dialogues

In the aforementioned dialogue between Jenkins and Fuller, Jenkins uses the writings of De Certeau to situate Nintendo games in the realm of popular entertainment. Additionally, his dialogue with Fuller is aimed at comparing the treatment of space and place in Nintendo games with earlier Anglo-Saxon writings on the 'discovery' of new lands. Consequently, an interesting picture emerges of the imagination of space as a popular discourse, one that is closely related to the American myth of the Wild West and new frontiers.

Jenkins finds that De Certeau's ideas on spatial stories are very apt for explaining imaginary spatial quests as stories. According to Jenkins Nintendo games are spatial stories because they cannot be easily defined in terms of an intricate plot or character. The story mainly develops by moving through landscapes, while the plot remains relatively simple (Fuller and Jenkins 1995; Jenkins 2004).

When applying De Certeau's distinction between place and space to Nintendo games, Jenkins relates place to the code that presupposes the game, while space 'happens' at the moment that the code is in the hands of the player who creates an imaginary landscape that is both personal and mobile. He then compares the paper maps that are supplied with the game to De Certeau's medieval maps, in which descriptions are less isolated from the tour that they facilitate because they supply descriptions of how to move through the game.

The assessment that Jenkins makes about the use of paper maps is of course pertinent and intriguing. Yet I would argue that maps can also be found within the games themselves, and that these maps are even less isolated than the quasi-medieval maps of which Jenkins speaks.

Ted Friedman believes that the use of maps in simulation games like Civilization III (1996) differs from Jenkins's analysis (1999). According to Friedman, such games are more about inviting the player to become a mapmaker. Interestingly, Friedman maintains that the landscape through which the player travels has cartographical qualities: when playing the game one identifies with the environment (a spatial practice) in a more abstract sense, because one constantly sees the landscape from above. Through this bird's-eye view, the player is fixed in a depersonalized frame of mind. So a story can be developed without ever bringing it to the level of individual experience. The map therefore is not merely the environment for the story; it's the hero of the story. Thus, Friedman concludes that the player has a less subjective identification with the visited landscape, and that space is experienced as mapping.

Although the observation about the cartographical disposition of landscapes in simulation games is highly relevant, it needs some reconsideration. When Friedman states that the map becomes the protagonist of the story, with whom the player identifies, he overlooks a pivotal quality of any game: in the end, it is always the player who is the hero (or the loser). Games are not pre-set texts with pre-set heroes, but interactive forms of expression. Because the player's actions are vital to the outcome of a game, a different identification process emerges in which a map cannot be a protagonist. It is rather the player who dynamically fluctuates between being a cartographer and being a traveler. Therefore, simulation games offer more than a frozen ideological representation of space, they allow us to spatially transform environments.

Figure 1: Screenshot from Sid Meier's Civilization IV (Firaxis Games 2005)

As such, identification in simulation games takes place on an even more spatial level than in the Nintendo games. Instead of touring with an avatar on foot (virtual), the player is constantly involved in mapping the space that he creates by touring with a bird's-eye view. This literal overview informs a strong interplay between mapping and touring, and the gamer is constantly and explicitly involved in making his own space, translating that into places and vice versa. The stories thus created, liberate maps from the isolated, unchangeable and static form they have gained since the Renaissance. They bring maps back (in)to life.

Friedman's argument also needs to be adjusted to the rapidly changing gameplay. Nowadays games like Civilization heavily depend on the use of so-called mini-maps. Although the environment that the player watches and masters from above has certainly cartographical qualities, the use of mini-maps in recent strategy games adds a new layer. While environments of touring obtain cartographical features and become somewhat de-personalized, mini-maps develop into more subjective playgrounds.

I would like to explain this by looking at the use of mini-maps in the game *Age of Empires III* (AOE). Here, the player is in a constant flux of moving through territory, which is translated into an expansion (filling in) of the mini-map (left corner of fig. 3). Conversely, one can click on the mini-map to move to an area on the big screen. It is even possible to click on the figure of the explorer on the main screen, go back to the mini-map, click on the area he is to be sent to and subsequently move him to that spot on the main screen. Through these actions, mapping and touring entertain a highly dynamic relationship, which somewhat complicates Friedman's claim that the player simply becomes a cartographer as opposed to a tour-maker. The player indeed becomes a mapmaker, but this cannot be described as a depersonalized endeavour. It would be more precise to call the player a cartographer on tour.

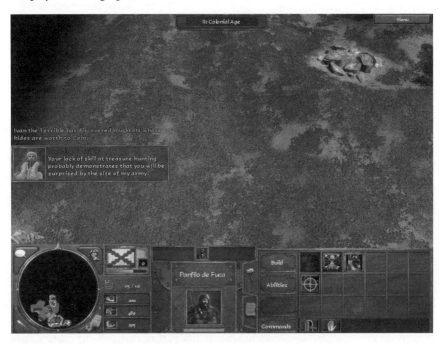

Figure 2: *Screenshot from* Age of Empires III *(Ensemble Studios 2005)*

Certainly, strategy games are the pinnacle of what De Certeau defines as spatial stories, precisely because spatial exploration is so central to them and is not hindered by plot or avatar. But it no longer suffices to maintain that they give the player the opportunity of understanding space as a map. Contemporary strategy games make such interesting spatial stories because they elicit a constant interplay between the static and the mobile, the subjective and the objective.

Rendering spatial categories fluid, these games actually seem to undermine De Certeau's argument that maps and tours have become separated realms in Western cultures. Even the activities of looking and walking De Certeau assigns to mapping and touring, respectively, become less distinct. In the example I just mentioned, looking and exploring have become inseparable processes and the oscillation between them is actually a crucial part of the game play: maps are not only transformable, but become places one can go to, while landscapes that are toured acquire cartographical qualities and become observable.

Stories and boundaries

Contemporary strategy games are not only unusual spatial stories because they entail a breakdown of the map as a means of seeing and tour as a way of going. They also accentuate two other objects important to De Certeau's definition of spatial story, namely the frontier and the bridge.

De Certeau argues that stories perform an important function in everyday life by setting limitations. By describing space, they arrange and order cultural domains. As such they not only set limits but also alter boundaries: 'one can see that the primary function is to authorize the establishment, displacement or transcendence of limits' (De Certeau 1984, 123). To describe this paradoxical quality of boundaries, he distinguishes two narrative figures in every story that have the power to fix boundaries and to revise them, namely the frontier and the bridge, respectively.

In explaining the figure of the frontier, De Certeau takes his reader on an etymological tour to prove that stories are ways of creating borders. If more scattered now than before, the 'primary role of stories' has always been to function as a playground for actions after their formation as a delineated domain. Such actions can nevertheless also transgress the limits that are first set by the story (e. g. feudal conflicts in which set borders are contested). As such, boundaries are the prerequisite for any social practice. In this process the figure of the frontier and the bridge entertain a paradoxical relationship (De Certeau 1984, 118).

In De Certeau's vocabulary the frontier should be equated with 'legitimate' domains, since it creates spatial formations such as nations and empires. The bridge, on the other hand, points to what is not part of that area, in other words to 'its (alien) exteriority', such as other nations, unconquered territories or no-man's lands. The frontier has a mediating or 'bridging' quality because it is the point of contact between the two entities it separates. In itself it does not belong to either entity (De Certeau 1984, 126-28). Frontiers are in that sense twilight zones.

Strategy games explicitly ask the player to mark off land and to create borders and transgress them in an interactive way. A player has to deal with at least two different kinds of borders at once: the border between filled-in territory and the undiscovered black space on screen, and the borders between his own territory and that of others. Interestingly, games like AOE foreground the bridging qualities of borders. Since continuous spatial transgression is so central to such games, borders have gained a semi-permeable quality. They are always crossings to 'otherlands' and never presented as hard and definite lines. In *Civilization IV* (Figure 3) for example, the player's territory spreads like liquid over a surface.

Figure 3: *Screenshot from Sid Meier's* Civilization IV *(Firaxis Games 2005)*

Certainly, the map that has to be filled in has preset limits on what Jenkins calls the level of code (1995). Yet the demarcations of the player's own territory appears rather fuzzy on screen. In AOE it is presented by different colours for different nations, and in *Civilization IV* by an opaque line that is drawn around the 'zone of influence'. While the player is involved in a constant process of defining and expanding his territory, others will try to diminish the playroom or push back the borders. This element of bridging should be seen in the light of the interactive quality of games. Because the player is able to draw and transcend boundaries and can be interactively involved in creating a spatial story, the emphasis lies on the passing of borders. Players become enactors instead of tellers of spatial stories, trying to develop a story by pushing spatial limits.

Digital mapping

Although it has been suggested that games offer us digital playgrounds to express our daily spatial experience of living in an overcrowded world with fewer and fewer places to play outside (Fuller and Jenkins 1995; Friedman 1999), sticking to such a basic explanation of the socio-spatial function of cartographies would not do justice to the games discussed here.

Jenkins places Nintendo games in the same league with early science fiction, pulp fiction and imaginary quests like *Alice in Wonderland* where stories also develop through the exploration of unknown territory while plot and character are less important. He also draws a parallel with playground attractions such as the rollercoaster. Like such attractions, Nintendo games offer the recreational sensation of sightseeing. But in contrast to these attractions, they offer the participant the opportunity to interact and transform landscapes during touring.

As Jenkins points out, such games are also part and parcel of a more widespread Western fascination with new world exploration. Although a nostalgia for being an explorer and cartographer who marks out 'new' territory has been present in, for example, travelogues and certain board games, the actual possibilities of making environments and maps have been limited (Fuller and Jenkins 1995). The discussed games are unique in that they offer players the potential of being an active explorer and mapmaker at once. Still, I would like to add, they involve not so much a spatial reproduction of being a new world explorer, but rather entail a transformation of past endeavours to map and conquer new lands. Being a new world traveler is not so much re-constructed, but rather transformed into a playful activity in which mastering space becomes more of a personal power struggle than an accurate historical reiteration of how spatial relationships have been shaped by external hegemonic forces (Lammes 2003). Games translate spatial hegemonies into play, thus necessarily changing them into something more personal and subjective. As players are given the ludic power to mark territories and empires, they can create their own (post)colonial tales by translating world histories into personal stories.

Furthermore, strategy games should also be seen within a wider contemporary development that assigns new meanings and functions to cartography. With the emergence of new media, maps in general have changed drastically. Not only do they look rather different, also the way we use them has altered significantly. Older maps may have offered some possibilities of modification (e.g. adding notes), but today users have the opportunity to interrelate with maps whilst navigating. Be it an automated navigation system that alters its itinerary when the driver chooses to drive elsewhere, or a map in a computer game that is partly created by the player(s) during the game – maps have become less fixed and are co-produced by their users.

The games discussed here are particular performances within this wider tech-noscientific network of digital cartographies. The Lithuanian writer Gailitis stated that with GPS technologies, 'the subject becomes the object, and we are nothing more than our own remote control' (Gailitis 2005, 479). Yet, as the above analysis has shown, computer games differ from GPS devices in that they do not simply present us with an objectification of our personal whereabouts but actually over-come the one-directional transformation Gailitis stresses. They are for that matter more closely related to applications like *Google Earth* that also allows users to mix observant roles with subjective and personal experiences of space (e.g. *The 21 Steps*, *Panoramio*). As playful domains, they inspire gamers to appropriate spatial practices and make sense of them in their own way, hybridizing notions of objec-tive place and subjective space.

It has been argued that new media have deprived us of a sense of spatial be-longing. Through their global and ubiquitous use and representations, they are believed to have created 'geographies of nowhere' instead (Eberle 1994; Kunstler 1994; Augé 1995). Yet this rather dystopian contention becomes problematic when one thinks of the increasing quantity of digital maps that we have to deal with. However diverse the purposes of individual technologies may be, they all point to an increasing involvement of users with their environments. As cartogra-phers on tour, players are engaged in a process that is targeted towards a perso-nal rather than a global or homogenous concept of spatiality. Such games do more than just ask a certain degree of spatial attentiveness from players to win the game. They invite them to create and transform maps and landscapes accord-ing to their individual choices. Gamers are thus actively exploring and transform-ing territories and maps in a highly personal, precise and even reflexive way. As such these games demonstrate that the global use of new media (and globaliza-tion in general) may have transformed our sense of belonging, but has not neces-sarily led to spatial homogenizations (Appadurai 2002). Our sense of place and space may indeed have changed but has not disappeared.

Note

1. For a related discussion of De Certeau's concept in the context of portable gaming devices, see the chapter by Nanna Verhoeff. For an inverted use of the terms space and place, informed by a sociological approach, see the chapter by Ann-Sophie Lehmann.

References

The 21 Steps. http://www.wetellstories.co.uk/stories/week1.

Aarseth, Espen. 2004. Genre trouble: Narrativism and the art of simulation. In First person: New media as story, performance and game, eds. Noah Wardrip-Fruin and Pat Harrigan, 45-47. Cambridge, MA: MIT Press.

Age of empires series. Ensemble Studios, Microsoft Game Studios 1997-2005.

Anderson, Benedict R. 1991. Census, map, museum. In Imagined communities: Reflections on the origin and spread of nationalism, 163-85. Rev. ed. London: Verso.

Appadurai, Arjun. 2002. Disjuncture and difference in the global cultural economy. Theory, Culture & Society 7: 295-310.

Augé, Marc. 1995. Non-places: Introduction to an anthropology of supermodernity. London: Verso.

Certeau, Michel de. 1984. The practice of everyday life. Berkeley, London: University of California Press.

Civilization series. MicroProse, Koei, Firaxis Games, 2K Games & Aspyr 1991-2005.

Crampton, Jeremy W. 2001. Maps as social constructions: Power, communication and visualization. Progress in Human Geography 25 (2): 235-52.

Douglas, Christopher. 2002. 'You have unleashed a horde of barbarians!' Fighting indians, playing games, forming disciplines. Postmodern Culture 13 (1). http://www3.iath.virginia.edu/pmc/issue.902/13.1douglas.html.

Eberle, Gary. 1994. The geography of nowhere: Finding one's self in the postmodern world. Kansas City: Sheed and Ward.

Frasca, Gonzalo. 2005. Ludology meets narratology: Similitude and differences between (video) games and narrative. Ludology. http://www.ludology.org/articles/ludology.htm.

—. Simulation versus narrative: Introduction to ludology. In The video game theory reader, eds. Mark J. P. Wolf and Bernard Perron, 221- 236. New York, London: Routledge.

Friedman, Ted. 1999. Civilization and its discontents: Simulation, subjectivity, and space. In Discovering discs: Transforming space and genre on CD-ROM, ed. Greg Smith. New York: New York University Press. http://www.duke.edu/~tlove/civ.htm.

Fuller, Mary, and Henry Jenkins. 1995. Nintendo® and new world travel writing: A dialogue. In Cybersociety: Computer-mediated communication and community, ed. Steven G. Jones, 57-72. Thousand Oaks: Sage.

Gailitis, Viestarts. 2005. Milky way. In Making things public: Atmospheres of democracy, eds. Bruno Latour and Peter Weibel, 497-98. Cambridge, MA: MIT Press.

Harley, J. Brian. 1989. Deconstructing the map. Cartographica 26 (2): 1-20.

—. 1988. Maps, knowledge, and power. In The iconography of landscape: Essays on the symbolic representation, design and use of past environments, eds. Denis Cosgrove and Stephen Daniels, 277-312. Cambridge: Cambridge University Press.

Jenkins, Henry. 2005. Computer and narrative. In Routledge encyclopedia of narrative theory, eds. David Herman, Manfred Jahn and Marie-Laure Ryan, 80-82. London: Routledge.

—. 2004. Game design as narrative architecture. In First person: New media as story, performance, and game, eds. Noah Wardrip-Fruin and Pat Harrigan. Cambridge, MA: MIT Press.

Juul, Jesper. 2001. Games telling stories. Game Studies, 1 (1) http://gamestudies.org/0101/juul-gts.

—. 2004. The Definitive history of games and stories, ludology and narratology. *The ludologist*. http://www. jesperjuul.dk/ludologist/index.php.

Kücklich, Julian. 2003. Perspectives of computer game philology. *Game Studies* 3 (1). http://www.gamestudies.org/0301/kucklich.

Kunstler, James Howard. 1994. *The geography of nowhere: The rise and decline of America's man-made landscape*. New York: Simon and Schuster.

Lammes, Sybille. 2003. On the border: Pleasures of exploration and colonial mastery in *Civilization III Play the World*. In *Level up: Digital games research conference*, eds. Marinka Copier and Joost Raessens, 120-29. Utrecht: Utrecht University.

Lefèbvre, Henri. 1991. *The production of space*. Oxford: Blackwell.

Magnet, Shoshana. 2006. Playing at colonization: Interpreting imaginary landscapes in the video game *Tropico*. *Journal of Communication Inquiry* 30 (2): 142-62.

Massey, Doreen. 1994. *Space, place, and gender*. Cambridge: Polity Press.

Murray, Janet H. 2005. The last word on ludology vs. narratology in game studies. Paper presented at the *DiGRA 2005 Conference: Changing views of worlds in play*.

Newman, James. 2004. Videogames, space and cyberspace: Exploration, navigation and mastery. In *Videogames*, 107-26. London: Routledge.

Panoramio. http://www.panoramio.com.

Poblocki, Kacper. 2002. Becoming-state: The bio-cultural imperialism of Sid Meier's Civilization. *European Journal of Anthropology* 39: 163-77.

Rise of nations. Big huge games, Microsoft Game Studios 2003.

Ryan, Marie-Laure. 2002. Beyond myth and metaphor: Narrative in digital media. *Poetics Today* 23 (4): 581-609.

Thrift, Nigel J. 2004. Driving in the city. *Theory, Culture & Society* 21 (4/5): 41-59.

Victoria: An empire under the sun. Paradox Interactive 2003.

Wood, Dennis. 2002. The map as a kind of talk: Brian Harley and the confabulation of the inner and outer voice. *Visual Communication* 1 (2): 139-61.

—. 1992. *The power of maps*. New York: Guilford Publications.

Keyboard

Conceptualizing forums and blogs as public sphere

Thomas Poell

On the morning of 2 November 2004, immediately after the assassination of the controversial Dutch film director Theo van Gogh by the young Dutch Moroccan Mohammed B., large numbers of people rushed to the Internet to share their grief, anger, insights, and opinions. On FOK!*forum!*, one of the largest web forums in the Netherlands, every minute several posts appeared. Most of them said little more than: 'Goddammit!!!', 'jesus!!!!!!!!!!!!!!', 'No! Fucking hell!', and 'let's hope he's still alive'. Later during the day, when the news spread that the assassin was Moroccan, the posts became more reflexive, but also more aggressive. For example, at a quarter past six in the evening, one message on FOK!*forum!* read: 'however you look at it, it remains a POLITICAL MISTAKE. Repeatedly, it has been indicated that there are a lot of problems in this MULTICULTURAL society. But has anything ever been done? NO!!'. A few minutes later, someone responded by claiming: 'Bull-shit, this involves one moron, who decided to kill someone because of his ideas. There will always be such types.'[1]

How should this kind of online interaction be understood? Can it be interpreted as fruitful public debate? Particularly two concepts, which are both normative and descriptive, play an important role in the discussion on the influence of online communication on public debate. Firstly, inspired by Jürgen Habermas's *Structural transformation of the public sphere* (1989; org. 1962), various new media scholars argue that the Internet can revive or extend the *public sphere*, as it is, contrary to the traditional mass media, in essence an interactive medium. Following Habermas, most of these authors refer to the concept of the public sphere as a realm separate from political, religious, or economic interests, in which citizens articulate shared opinions through public debate (Benkler 2006, 176-178; Dahlberg 2001; 2005; Knapp 1997; McNair 2006, 152-154; Rheingold 1993, 274-280). Secondly, in critical dialogue with the original Habermasian concept of the public sphere, other theorists maintain that the Internet is especially important because it facilitates the construction of *multiple alternative* or *counter-public spheres*. With this concept they allude to online communicative spaces in which social groups, which have no access to the mass media platform, can construct shared identities and interests and coordinate public actions (Bennett 2004; Dahlgren 2001, 52-53; Downey and Fenton 2003, 198-199; Hacker and Van Dijk 2000; Poster 1995).

So far, these concepts have primarily been used for general reflections on the relationship between online communication and public debate. This raises the question of whether they can also help us to understand the influence of particular forms of online communication, that is, as medium-specific materializations. This chapter tries to answer this question by examining the role of Internet forums and blogs in the intense public discussions following the assassination of Theo van Gogh. It focuses on an actual social conflict because the medium-specific characteristics of forums and blogs can be most clearly observed when the public and the various media are in a state of alert, and all focused on the same issue.

The assassination of Theo van Gogh is particularly interesting from an analytical point of view as it received an enormous amount of media attention and put the Netherlands, at least for a few days, in a state of shock. As the assassin was a young Dutch Moroccan, who claimed to have murdered Van Gogh for religious reasons, the discussions inevitably revolved around central democratic issues such as citizenship, freedom of speech, and the place of religion in a liberal democratic society (see also Boomgaarden and De Vreese 2007; Hajer and Uitermark 2008; Pantti and Van Zoonen 2006). In previous years, Van Gogh himself had become an important figure in the debate over these issues, as he had fiercely criticized Muslim practices and beliefs as well as the multicultural politics of the central government, which promoted cultural diversity (Hajer and Uitermark 2008).

For the evaluation of the two concepts, 51 blogs were investigated in the first three days after the assassination. A blog (short for web log) is a website, usually maintained by an individual, which has separately locatable entries, displayed in reverse chronological order. Most blogs offer the reader the opportunity to leave comments, which may be moderated or deleted by the blog owner. The 51 investigated blogs effectively constitute all of the retrievable Dutch language blogs commenting on the assassination. Of these 51 blogs, 46 were found through Google Blog Search, which allows one to search specifically for blog posts written on a particular date. Yet, Google Blog Search is by no means perfect; a manual search revealed that a significant part of the most well-known Dutch blogs commenting on the assassination was not available through Google Blog Search. Consequently, five extra blogs, among others the right-wing shocklog GeenStijl, were added to the selection.

In addition, four Internet forums, covering the same time span, were examined. An Internet forum is a dedicated web application facilitating asynchronous discussions, usually organized by user-created topics, and threads. All four investigated forums were monitored by forum administrators, who have the authority to moderate and delete any thread and post on the forum. The four forums, Pim

Fortuyn Forum, Indymedia, FOK!forum!, and Marokko Community, were chosen because they each cover a specific region of the political and cultural landscape. The Pim Fortuyn Forum is one of the main populist right-wing forums. Indymedia is an international left-wing network of participatory journalists and activists, which offers activist news but also functions as a discussion platform. FOK!forum! is part of FOK!, which was originally focused on youngsters, but can now be considered as a general forum for everyone. Finally, the Marokko Community, which is part of the community site Marokko.nl, is the largest discussion platform for young Dutch Moroccans. The parent company, Marokko Media, maintains on its website that Marokko.nl has 45,000 unique visitors per day, which together post 50,000 messages a day. It has been claimed that Marokko Community was frequented by Mohammed B. in the months before the assassination (Benschop 2005). In the days after the assassination, an unusual number of autochthon Dutch members were active on this forum.

To assess how the relationship between the forums, blogs, and the traditional mass media can be interpreted, research was also done on the reporting of five major Dutch newspapers: De Telegraaf, Trouw, de Volkskrant, NRC Handelsblad, and Het Parool. These newspapers cover the entire spectrum of the mass press in terms of elitist versus populist, and right wing versus left wing. A selection of articles was made using a LexisNexis search for 'Theo van Gogh' for the first three days after the assassination. This search generated a total of 251 articles.

Although this is by no means an exhaustive study of the mediated public discussions following the assassination, it is sufficient for our meta-theoretical objectives. It allows us to reflect on the way in which the concepts of public sphere and multiple public spheres can be used to understand the medium-specific contribution of forums and blogs to public debate. The first two sections of this chapter evaluate the notion of the public sphere, while the third part examines the concept of multiple public spheres.

Public sphere as critical rational debate

Can the notion of the public sphere, as originally conceptualized by Habermas, be used to understand the specific contribution of Internet forums and blogs to public communication? Let us start with the forums. In principle, forums seem to be particularly equipped to facilitate inclusive, critical rational public debate, which, according to Habermas, forms the basis of a real public sphere (Habermas 1989). Forums enable everyone with an Internet connection to initiate and participate in public debate on a national or even international level. Moreover, as most forums allow the participants to make contributions under a nickname, they obscure many of the social markers which in offline discussions may unjustly benefit or discredit the opinions of speakers.

Yet, if we examine the forum discussions in the aftermath of the assassination, most of them appear to be neither inclusive nor critical rational. The messages on FOK!forum! discussed in the introduction section are in this sense typical. The majority of the posts simply expressed anger or sadness without much further reflection. Politicians as well as other participants in the online debates were frequently called 'idiots', 'suckers', and 'hypocrites', while Muslims, or more specifically Muslim fundamentalists, were labeled 'fascists', 'losers', 'murderers', and 'criminals'. It is important to note that most forum threads were dominated by small groups of five to ten participants.

These observations are largely confirmed by various empirical studies on forum discussions, which consistently find that only a small proportion of forum participants engage in public debate. It has been argued that most people use forums for entertainment or personal expression, rather than debate. Furthermore, research points out that when public discussion does evolve, it is far from rational and should rather be characterized as emotional and irreverent (Barber 1998; Davis 1999; Delli Carpini and Keeter 2003; Hurwitz 2004; Margolis and Resnick 2000).

Particularly problematic from a Habermasian public-sphere perspective is that the public on the forums investigated here can be characterized as rather homogeneous regarding ideology. The discussions on the FOK!forum!, and especially on the Pim Fortuyn Forum, were predominantly marked by the opinion that the assassination demonstrated that the multicultural politics of the government had failed, and that radical Muslims entail a grave danger to Dutch society. Most contributors on Indymedia, by contrast, asserted that the assassination was a symbol of the polarisation of societal relations to which Van Gogh had contributed heavily. Finally, on the Marokko Community relatively many participants argued that the assassination was the work of an individual madman and had little to do with religion. Hence, the respective forums were far from inclusive. This becomes particularly evident when considering the reporting in the five national newspapers, which each provided a platform for a larger variety of opinions than could be heard on any of the forums.

Taken together, the forum discussions clearly fall short of the criteria of the public sphere, as originally conceptualized by Habermas. There were, however, a few signs which showed that some of the forums were more favourable to critical rational public debate than others. In particular, Indymedia turned out to be a platform for more critical rational arguments. One of the participants on this forum, for example, extensively analyzed the role of the media in the aftermath of the assassination, which, according to her, should have been more critical of the role played by Van Gogh in the negative publicity on Islam and Dutch Moroccans in the previous years.[2] Although these kinds of arguments subsequently evoked several emotional and aggressive reactions, even on Indymedia, they do indicate that at least some forums incidentally meet the norm of critical rationality.

Also noteworthy were the discussions on *Marokko Community*, which were more inclusive than the ones on the other fora, as both critics and supporters of the multicultural society expressed their opinions here. For example, in a typical discussion on *Marokko Community*, one member with the nickname *aliyaah* claimed: 'When Theo van Gogh started to criticize the Jews, all doors were closed to him??? He was not allowed to practice anti-Semitism? And now that Muslims are put in the wrong by him, now there is ... freedom of speech??' Quickly someone else with the handle *Peej* responded by arguing: 'Theo has criticized and ridiculed all religions (especially their orthodox parts). This happens to be allowed in the Netherlands, where the constitution and the penal code count as the legal framework, and not a few old religious books.'[3]

Even though the discussions on *Indymedia* and *Marokko Community* still do not meet the ideal of inclusive, critical rational debate, they do suggest that Internet forums can, under specific conditions, facilitate this ideal. The discussions on *Marokko Community* were more inclusive precisely because the enraged critics of the multicultural society sought the confrontation with Dutch Muslims, whom they held responsible for the assassination. The critical rational character of some of the posts on *Indymedia* is no coincidence either, as this forum has a rather strict editorial policy. The administrators of this forum remove 'racist, fascist, sexist, and homophobe posts' as well as 'conspiracy theory nonsense, provocations, and other disinformation'.[4]

The observation that Internet forums can, under particular conditions, approximate the public sphere ideal has also been made by Lincoln Dahlberg in his examination of *E-Democracy.org*. *E-Democracy* is a volunteer-based project, which tries to make 'use of the Internet to improve citizen participation and real world governance through online discussions and information and knowledge exchange'.[5] Since its conception in Minnesota in 1994, several local discussion forums have been created in the US, UK, and New Zealand. To accomplish fruitful public political debate and a genuine exchange of information and knowledge, the *E-Democracy* project has employed a combination of rules and guidelines, as well as 'forum management to structure deliberations towards the ends intended'. These efforts seem to have paid off as this project, according to Dahlberg, in many ways approximates the public sphere conception: it has 'stimulated reflexivity, fostered respectful listening and participant commitment to the ongoing dialogue, achieved open and honest exchange, and provided equal opportunity for all voices to be heard' (Dahlberg 2001).

Despite such examples, the overall majority of the discussions investigated here, even on *Indymedia* and *Marokko Community*, did not come near these normative ideals of the public sphere. Consequently, we must conclude that in general the deliberations on Internet forums cannot be considered a digital extension of the Habermasian public sphere.

Blogosphere as public sphere

What about the blogs? In contrast to the forums, blogs are first and foremost a platform for individual authors. While many blogs offer their readers the opportunity to comment on a blog post, they do not allow them to start main blog posts on their own. Consequently, blog discussions are usually dominated by the point of view of the blogger, supported by most of the commentators. As Geert Lovink has made clear, the homogeneous character of blog discussions is the result of the implicit rules of conduct to which bloggers adhere. He argues: 'Adversaries will not post on each other's blogs. At best, they quote and link' (Lovink 2008, 21). In this sense, blogs seem to be even less of an egalitarian platform of public debate than web forums, which would lead us to the conclusion that they are even less well equipped to facilitate the public sphere.

However, this assessment should be reconsidered when we look at blogs as a collective of cross-linked blog entries. As various new media theorists maintain, together blogs can generate a lively public debate by commenting on, and linking to, newspaper articles and other blogs. On the basis of this claim, these theorists subsequently contend that blogs constitute a blogosphere, which serves an important function in public debate by being able to hold the traditional mass media accountable for its mistakes and inaccuracies (Gillmor 2004, 237; Lovink 2008, 7; Tremayne 2007, 263-265). Henry Jenkins even maintains that 'bloggers will be jousting with mainstream journalists story by story, sometimes getting it right, sometimes getting it wrong, but always forcing a segment of the public to question dominant representations' (Jenkins 2006, 216-217).

Yet, if we examine the blogs in the hours and days after the Van Gogh assassination, a somewhat different picture emerges. First, it must be noted that the number of blogs commenting on the assassination is relatively small. Even if we take into account that part of the blogs have disappeared since or could not be retrieved through Google Blog Search, 51 blogs is not that many, set against the estimated 30 million blogs which existed worldwide by the end of 2004. Moreover, there seems to have been little debate between blogs; none of the examined blogs actually discussed claims made by other blogs, even though some provided links in the so-called blog roll. Neither did the blogs comment much on the mass media reporting. A few blogs did provide links to newspaper articles but gave no further comments.

The only exception in this regard was *GeenStijl*, which strongly criticized various prominent columnists and newspapers for cooperating with the political establishment. Particularly remarkable was that this right-wing shocklog, usually critical of any multiculturalism, took the producers of two television programs to task for the way they had selected young Dutch Moroccans to appear on their respective programs. The blog accused the producers of adopting a stereotypical approach and of being only interested in radical Moroccans, who concurred with the assassination.[6] However, *GeenStijl*, which has been partly owned by the right-wing newspaper *De Telegraaf* since 2006, is not a regular blog. It is effectively a mass medium in its own right, run by a professional staff of at least a dozen editors. The rest of the examined blogs did not criticize other media, but simply gave personal expressions of anger, frustration, and despair. In form and content, these blog posts were not very different from what could be found on the forums. They certainly did not collectively function as a critical check on the mass media reporting.

The discrepancy between the observations in the literature and our analysis seems for a large part due to a difference in focus. New media theorists have primarily examined a small number of American high-traffic blogs, which are devoted to political issues and frequently challenge mainstream media (Lovink 2008, 260). Time and again the same examples are discussed in which bloggers have succeeded in correcting a national newspaper or a high profile television show. The vast majority of personal blogs is excluded in this type of research, since only a few blogs actively monitor other media.

In sum, theoretically, forums as well as blogs can, in different ways, contribute to the public sphere, as originally conceptualized by Habermas. In principle, forums are highly egalitarian platforms for diverse opinions, since they are open for everyone to participate in a public discussion or start a new one. While blogs are in theory more homogeneous, they may also function as a collective linking and monitoring platform, enacting critical checks on the reporting of mass media and other blogs. Yet, in practice, neither the blogs nor the forums seem to fulfil their public sphere potential. There are certainly examples of blogs and forums which come near the public sphere ideal, but the overall majority does not.

Of course, we could abandon the Habermasian normative criteria of inclusiveness and rationality and adopt a more lenient definition of the public sphere. Recent examples of such an approach can be found in Brian McNair's *Cultural chaos* (2006, 136-143), and Yochai Benkler's *The wealth of networks* (2006, 11, 177-178). Although this strategy allows them to arrive at a more optimistic assessment of the influence of online communication on public debate, the concept of the public sphere also loses its critical and normative force as a consequence; it practically becomes a synonym for any form of public communication.

We may conclude that the concept of the public sphere, both as a normative and a descriptive concept, does not really help us to assess the contribution of forums and blogs to public debate. If we hold on to a strict normative definition of the public sphere based on the criteria of inclusiveness and rationality, we inevitably have to dismiss the mass of blogs and forums for failing to live up to this ideal. But if we choose to abandon these criteria, and opt to employ the public sphere primarily as a descriptive concept, we can no longer use it to evaluate online communication in terms of its contribution to democracy and diversity.

Multiple public spheres

Is the concept of a multiplicity of alternative public spheres more helpful? On the basis of this notion, it has been argued that the Internet is particularly important as an instrument for the emancipation of subordinated social groups. The Internet permits, according to John Downey and Natalie Fenton, 'radical groups from both Left and Right to construct inexpensive virtual counter-public spheres' (Downey and Fenton 2003, 198). This argument has especially been based on the use of networked ICT by social activists. Research shows that the Internet facilitates the internal communication of social movements, as well as the organization of protest campaigns (Arquilla and Ronfeld 2001; Bennett 2004, 130-131; Castells 2004, 83, 154-158; Van de Donk et al. 2004, 4-6; Keck and Sikking 1999, 96). The question is whether a similar claim can be made concerning the forum and blog discussions in the aftermath of the assassination, which primarily involved individuals who were not part of a social movement.

At first sight, blogs especially seem fit as platforms for the development of a multiplicity of alternative public spheres. As we have noticed in the previous section, blog discussions are often characterized by participants who strongly concur with the blog owner's opinions. In this sense, blogs can be interpreted as alternative platforms on which specific groups debate public issues in their own circle. However, precisely the hierarchical character of blog discussions is problematic from an alternative public spheres perspective. As we have already noticed, it seems to make blogs primarily a platform for individual expression, rather than for the development of a collective point of view. This obviously undermines the potential of blogs as instruments for the emancipation of subordinated social groups. In addition, it must be noted that most blogs, except for GeenStijl, only had a few commentators. Thus, in a quantitative and qualitative sense, it is questionable whether blogs can facilitate the development of multiple public spheres.

As it turns out, the forums correspond better with the notion of multiple alternative public spheres. In contrast to the blogs, the forums, with their egalitarian architecture and thousands of visitors daily, can potentially serve as platforms for the expression of group interests and opinions. As already became clear in the previous section, the forums did indeed seem to function as such, since they primarily drew participants who interpreted the assassination likewise. Finally, important to note is that most forum discussions were characterized by emotional and heated discourse. While this type of discourse is problematic from the original Habermasian perspective, scholars working from the perspective of multiple public spheres have pointed out that such discourse can fulfil an important emancipatory role. It allows for the participation of groups who do not master the critical rational discourse used by politicians, intellectuals, and journalists who dominate mass media discussions (Dahlgren 2001, 39; Fraser 1992, 120-122; Papacharissi 2004, 266).

In the investigated forum discussions, emotional and heated discourse was specifically important because it allowed a variety of groups to articulate their specific identities and discuss the social tensions resulting from the assassination in their own terms. Particularly *Marokko Community* provided fertile ground for such discussions. For example, a day after the assassination, one member with the handle *ffeiza* claimed that 'Now, you really hear what the Dutch think about the Moroccans. Today at work we had a vicious discussion: All Moroccans should piss off. Your religion is nonsense. This is what my boss told me.' Quickly, however, another member pointed out that *ffeiza* made the same mistake as people who blamed the entire Moroccan community for the murder of Van Gogh: 'if a few "Dutch people" say something, it is not immediately representative for the whole country.' Someone else added: 'I don't know whether these statements are representative of how the Dutch think about the Moroccans. I rather think that these are just emotions that are released after such an event.' Yet, another argued: 'This is not that bad. At least he is still discussing with you. It is always better than 7 bullets and a knife in your body.' To which *ffeiza*, in turn, responded, 'I'm not talking about what is better: bullets or discussing. I'm purely talking about the fact that a person can smile at you for two years and then, after something happens, say these kinds of things'.[7]

While these kinds of exchanges correspond with the notion of alternative public spheres, this is certainly not to say that all of the statements on the forums constituted a positive contribution to public debate. While some of the discussions, such as the above example from *Marokko Community*, challenged cultural stereotypes, a large part of the investigated forum exchanges consisted of hateful messages. Particularly on the *Pim Fortuyn Forum*, many xenophobic statements could be read.[8] One message on this forum, for example, claimed: 'Islam is the plague for a free society; consequently, Islam does not belong here. This madness is a disease, which must be totally eradicated.'[9] Although less frequently, and somewhat less extreme, intolerant messages could also be found on the *FOK!forum!* and *Marokko Community*. The only exception was *Indymedia*, which has an explicit editorial policy against 'racist' and 'fascist' texts.

Similar observations have been made by Albert Benschop in his research on the online communication leading up to the assassination of Van Gogh. Benschop, who largely focused on forums, concluded: 'We have seen how radicalised Islamic youngsters used the Internet to hatch their networks of hatred and disseminate their hostile message. This gave rise to a climate for violent jihad, in which the murderer of Theo van Gogh could be recruited.' On the opposite end of the political spectrum, Benschop observed the online activities of 'right-wing extremist, neo-nationalist and neo-nazi groupings': 'With their xenophobic, islamophobic and racist statements they created a climate of hatred of foreigners, long before the murder of Van Gogh' (Benschop 2005). These concerns resonate with Cass Sunstein's argument that 'the Internet creates a large risk of group polarization, simply because it makes it so easy for like-minded people to speak with one another – and ultimately to move toward extreme and sometimes even violent positions' (Sunstein 2001, 199).

The concern over extremism hints at another analytical problem, which challenges the concept of multiple public spheres as a tool to understand the contribution of Internet forums to public debate. The concept is based on the assumption that the various social groups first develop their opinions, interests, identities, and organizational links within their own circle, and subsequently influence the larger public debate as played out in the mass media. Yet, if we examine the debate on the assassination, it becomes clear that none of the forums had much of a direct impact on the debate in the mass media. Although some of the newspapers did give short impressions of the more radical statements on forums such as *Marokko Community* and the *Pim Fortuyn Forum*, they did not discuss these statements any further. [10]

Moreover, none of the forum discussions produced any agreement between the participants about a shared interest or a particular course of actions which should be followed. This was certainly not due to a lack of initiative. Various contributors to the *Pim Fortuyn Forum* and *Indymedia*, which on other occasions served as a platform for organizing protests, made appeals for cooperation. For example, some of the participants on the *Pim Fortuyn Forum* called upon fellow members to join a protest of several right-wing organizations against the murder. This protest was supposed to serve as an alternative to the official manifestation organized by the Amsterdam municipality, which had drawn over 20,000 people. Even though a few of the forum members showed some interest, the majority did not even bother to respond. The following day, *de Volkskrant* reported that the alternative protest had not been a success as the police had far outnumbered the protesters. [11] Other calls for joint action did not produce any major results either.

Conclusion

This article has shown that the concepts of the public sphere and alternative public spheres, frequently used to understand the influence of the Internet on public debate, only have limited value when we examine particular forms of online communication in the context of actual societal conflict. More specifically, the investigation demonstrated that these concepts could only capture part of the different roles played by forums and blogs in the debate following the assassination of Theo van Gogh.

Some of the forum discussions certainly approached the public-sphere ideals of inclusiveness and critical rationality, whereas *GeenStijl* appeared to fulfil the promise that blogs enhance the rationality of public debate by providing a critical check on the reporting of the mass media. However, the majority of the forum and blog discussions did not in any way match the normative criteria of the Habermasian public sphere.

More or less similar conclusions can be drawn concerning the notion of multiple public spheres. At first sight, blogs seem to correspond with this concept, but on closer inspection it becomes highly questionable whether they facilitate the expression of group interests and opinions. Forums were even more ambiguous. Clearly, they provided a platform for the articulation of specific cultural identities. Yet, at the same time, forums facilitated the dissemination of hateful messages. Moreover, it became clear that they largely function in isolation from the discussion in the mass media, which does not conform to the idea that alternative public spheres enable subordinated groups to participate in the general public debate.

As most of the forum and blog discussions fall short of the criteria of either the public sphere or of multiple alternative public spheres, holding on to these concepts effectively leads us to dismiss and ignore the vast majority of online communication. Yet, as the concerns of Benschop and Sunstein about online extremism already indicate, the more or less isolated discussions and statements on the forums and blogs do seem to have a significant social and political impact, albeit much less direct and more diffuse than has so far been theorized. The challenge is to find out how this diffused influence exactly works. To meet this challenge and develop new conceptual tools, we need to do further research on the different forms of online communication in the context of social conflict.

A number of questions ought to be addressed. Firstly, our examination showed that many forum discussions revolved around cultural identity struggles. Can this also be observed in other cases? And under which circumstances can this facilitate the transcending of social stereotypes? According to Mark Poster, electronic communication in general, and online communication specifically, displaces the modern 'rational, autonomous individual' with 'one that is multiplied, disseminated and decentered, continuously interpellated as an unstable identity' (Poster 1995, 57). This suggests that online communication does not fixate identities but constantly transforms them. Is this also true for forum and blog discussions in situations of social crisis? And is there a difference between forums and blogs regarding identity interpellation?

Secondly, what is especially missing so far is information about the offline activities of the debate participants. To what extent do contributors maintain offline connections? Contrary to Benschop's analysis of the terrorist network in which Mohammed B. had been active, our investigation showed few indications that people developed offline relationships. Does this imply that most online exchanges are rather isolated from the traditional forms of social and political association, such as clubs, social movements and political parties? And, if this is indeed the case, how does this affect the public debate?

Notes

1. 'Theo v. Gogh doodgeschoten', *FOK!forum!*, 2-11-2004, http://forum.fok.nl/topic/ 622123/2/25; 'Theo van Gogh vermoord (deel 14)', *FOK!forum!* 2-11-2004, http://forum. fok.nl/topic/622354.
2. 'Commentaar op moord Van Gogh', *Indymedia*, 3-11-2004, http://indymedia.nl/nl/2004/ 11/22761.shtml.
3. 'Vertel mij eens....', *Marokko Community*, 3-11-2004, http://forums.marokko.nl/archive/ index.php/t-403666.html.
4. 'Spelregels van Indymedia NL', *Indymedia*, http://indymedia.nl/nl/static/help.policy. shtml.
5. 'About', *e-democracy*, 3-4-2004, http://www.e-democracy.org/about.html.
6. 'Bedankt Van Jole cs.', *GeenStijl*, 2-11-2004, http://www.geenstijl.nl/mt/archieven/ 002829.html; 'Omroepen op zoek naar kutmarokkanen', *GeenStijl*, 2-11-2004, http:// www.geenstijl.nl/mt/archieven/002832.html.
7. 'Frustaties tussen Marokkanen en Nederlanders', *Marokko Community*, 3-11-2004, http:// forums.marokko.nl/archive/index.php/t-404038.html.
8. The *Pim Fortuyn Forum* was created in the honour of the openly gay, populist right-wing Dutch politician Pim Fortuyn, who was murdered in 2002 by an animal rights activist. Fortuyn was highly critical of Islam, which he called a 'backward culture'.
9. 'Theo van Gogh vermoord', *Pim Fortuyn Forum*, 3-11-2004, http://www.pim-fortuyn.nl/ pfforum/topic.asp?ARCHIVE=true&TOPIC_ID=30391&whichpage=3.
10. 'Uitingen van woede op websites', NRC Handelsblad, 2-11-2004; 'Ook op internet zorgen na moord op Van Gogh', *Het Parool*, 3-11-2004; 'Uitingen van woede heersen op web-sites', *Trouw*, 3-11-2004; 'Wanhoop en woede op webforum', NRC Handelsblad, 3-11-2004; 'Condoleance.nl stroomt vol met racisme', *de Volkskrant*, 3-11-2004.
11. John Schoorl, 'Voor de kaalkoppen is de maat al heel lang vol', *de Volkskrant*, 4-11-2004.

References

Arquilla, John, and David Ronfeldt, eds. 2001. *Networks and netwars*. Santa Monica: RAND.

Barber, Benjamin. 1998. The new telecommunications technology: Endless frontier or the end of democracy? In *A passion for democracy: American essays*, ed. Benjamin Barber, 258-280. Princeton: Princeton University Press.

Benkler, Yochai. 2006. *The wealth of networks: How social production transforms markets and free-dom*. New Haven: Yale University Press.

Bennett, Lance. 2004. Communicating global activism. In *Cyberprotest*, eds. Wim van de Donk, et. al, 123-146. London: Routledge.

Benschop, Albert. 2005. Chronicle of a political murder foretold. *SocioSite*. http://www.so-ciosite.org/jihad_nl_en.php.

Boomgaarden, Hajo, and Claes de Vreese. 2007. Dramatic real-world events and public opinion dynamics: Media coverage and its impact on public reactions to an assassina-tion. *International Journal of Public Opinion Research* 19 (3): 354-366.

Castells, Manuel. 2004. *The power of identity*. Malden: Blackwell Publishing.

Dahlberg, Lincoln. 2001. Extending the public sphere through cyberspace: The case of Minnesota E-Democracy. *First Monday* 6 (3). http://www.firstmonday.org/issues/is-sue6_3/dahlberg/.

Dahlberg, Lincoln. 2005. The Habermasian public sphere: Taking difference seriously? *Theory and Society* 34: 111-136.

Dahlgren, Peter. 2001. The public sphere and the Net. In *Mediated politics*, eds. Lance Bennett, and R.M. Entman, 33-55. Cambridge: Cambridge University Press.

Davis, Richard. 1999. *The web of politics: The internet's impact on the American political system*. New York: Oxford University Press.

Delli Carpini, Michael, and Scott Keeter. 2003. The Internet and an informed citizenry. In *The civic web: Online politics and democratic values*, eds. David Anderson, and Michael Cornfield, 129-153. New York: Rowman & Litttlefield Publishers.

Donk, Wim van de, et.al., eds. 2004. *Cyberprotest*. London: Routledge.

Downey, John, and Natalie Fenton. 2003 New media, counter publicity and the public sphere. *New Media & Society* 5 (2): 185-202.

Fraser, Nancy. 1992. Rethinking the public sphere. In *Habermas and the public sphere*, ed. Craig Calhoun, 109-142. Cambridge, MA: MIT Press.

Gillmor, Dan. 2004. *We the media: Grassroots journalism by the people, for the people*. Cambridge: O'Reilly.

Habermas, Jürgen. 1989 [1962] *The structural transformation of the public sphere: An inquiry into a category of bourgeois society*. Cambridge, MA: MIT Press.

Hacker, Kenneth, and Jan van Dijk. 2000. What is digital democracy? In *Digital democracy: Issues of theory and practice*, eds. Kenneth Hacker and Jan van Dijk, 1-9. Thousand Oaks: Sage.

Hajer, Maarten, and Justus Uitermark. 2008. Performing authority: Discursive politics after the assassination of Theo van Gogh. *Public Administration* 86 (1): 1-15.

Hurwitz, Roger. 2004. The ironies of democracy in cyberspace. In *Democracy and new media*, eds. Henry Jenkins, and David Thorburn, 101-112. Cambridge, MA: MIT Press.

Jenkins, Henry. 2006. *Convergence culture: Where old and new media collide*. New York: New York University Press.

Keck, Margaret E., and Kathryn Sikkink. 1999. Transnational advocacy networks in international and regional politics. *International Social Science Journal* 51 (159): 89-101.

Knapp, James A. 1997. Essayistic messages: Internet newsgroups as an electronic public sphere. In *Internet culture*, ed. David Porter, 181-200. New York: Routledge.

Lovink, Geert. 2008. *Zero comments: Blogging and critical Internet culture*. London: Routledge.

Margolis, Michael, and David Resnick. 2000. *Politics as usual: The cyberspace 'revolution'*. London: Thousand Oaks.

McNair, Brian. 2006. *Cultural chaos: Journalism, news, and power in a globalised world*. London: Routledge.

Papacharissi, Zizi. 2004. Democracy online: Civility, politeness, and the democratic potential of online political discussion groups. *New Media & Society* 6 (2): 259-283.

Pantti, Mervi, and Liesbet van Zoonen. 2006. Do crying citizens make good citizens? *Social Semiotics* 16 (2): 205-224.

Poster, Mark. 1995. *The second media age*. Cambridge: Polity Press.

Rheingold, Howard. 1993. *The virtual community: Homesteading on the electronic frontier*. Reading: Addison-Wesley.

Tremayne, Mark, ed. 2007. *Blogging, citizenship, and the future of media*. London: Routledge.

Interfacing by material metaphors

How your mailbox may fool you

Marianne van den Boomen

Operating a computer is quite easy nowadays. We all click our way through our *desktops*; we *send mail*; we save *documents* in *folders*. We barely realize how these actions are framed by metaphors. Our first association with 'cleaning a desktop' has probably more to do with deleting unused icons and files on our PC than with polishing our material desk. We have no problem with the dominant office metaphors, even when they blend with metaphors from other settings, such as home, menu, or window.

Operating these metaphors usually goes smoothly. But, as we all know, sometimes things go wrong. Sometimes our actions do not yield the expected results, and our computer suddenly becomes a black box. In this chapter I aim to trace what happens when we operate our PC, and how metaphors enable or disable our access to the machine. I will take a look at the user interface and show how it may fool us with its icons, begging the question: what exactly are icons? Are they signs, are they tools? With a little help from Peirce, Heidegger and Hayles, I will end with a plea for the development of a theory of material metaphor.

A computer is no coffee machine

An ordinary PC is in fact an extraordinary apparatus. It is not only a physical machine, able to perform labor, i.e. to transform energy and raw material into a product or an event; it is also a symbol-processing machine (Hayles 2002; 2005). As a symbol-processing device, it translates its internal physical states into machine code as well as human code – code readable by humans. The latter is usually represented on the screen by the graphical user interface (GUI) with its icons, menus, and windows. Here, the PC articulates itself as a set of tools for the production, reproduction and modification of data products (texts, images, soundtracks). At the same time the PC is also a toolmaking machine, able to create new tools (programs, scripts, plug ins) which can be fed back into the very same machine. This makes the PC a much more complex device than just a set of tools.

At first sight, tools and products are clearly differentiated on the user interface. Products exist as mutable data objects (files); and tools exist as executable sets of commands (programs), or as interfacial signs (icons, buttons, menus). However, at a deeper level these tools and products are intricately nested into each other. Executable programs also consist of sets of files; interfacial signs are representations of executable commands, and thus they are, in the last instance, also files. This complex machine of nested files becomes even more complex when hooked up in a network with other computers, thereby also enabling transference of tools and products to other machines in the network.

Yet, users stick cognitively to the assumed clear division between tools and products. After all, means and ends, tools and products, are ontologically quite different, as is the case with a coffee machine: there is a clear difference between the button for cappuccino and the cappuccino itself. We never mistake the button for the coffee. But a computer is no coffee machine. And it is actually quite common in computer praxis to mistake the button for the product itself. This is due to the fact that we cannot have the product without the tool. We cannot read a text document without a word-processor program; we have no access to our mail without a mail program.

In order to work with this compound, and differentiate whenever necessary, the usage of the keyboard and the mouse is decisive; these hands-on devices are indispensable parts of the user interface. However, the visual screen with its metaphorized tools and products seems to attract all the attention. The screen seems to integrate, supersede and cannibalize all other parts of the user interface. This engulfing mechanism is not limited to computer usage as such; the screen pops up as a dominant metaphor for digital media in general, in ordinary speech as well as in new media studies (Turkle 1995; Johnson 1997; Bolter and Grusin 2000).[1] This may be explained by the ability of the GUI to translate and articulate all other components into visual representations, thus rendering irrelevant what remains invisible, and rendering unthinkable what remains unmetaphorized.

The visual tools on our screen thus seem to work as metaphorical stand-ins for complex machine processes. After the metaphorical translation of machine code into human code, there seems to be no way back. Metaphorical sign-tools acquire a life of their own, cannibalizing everything else that might be there. By showing they hide, by translating they substitute.

This mechanism is especially at work in computer icons. These small pictures are shortcuts to specific software commands in order to yield some result through the combination of human and machine actions. However, machine actions are rendered invisible wherever possible. Icons cloak their reference to software instructions and machine acts; instead, they pretend to refer to particular 'places' on a computer (My Documents, My Network, mailbox, folder) or to particular 'things' (file, program). Sometimes it is not even clear whether an icon refers to a place, a file, or a program. Take for instance your mail icon. What does it stand for? 'Well, my e-mail of course.' But what exactly is implied in the conceptual shortcut 'my e-mail'; does it refer to a specific program running? Or to a place on your computer, the mailbox, where your mail resides? Or to a set of files, sent to you as e-mail messages? Or perhaps to all of these in one?

Usually, when your mail just works as expected, these questions are irrelevant – who cares? But sometimes these questions pop up, as in the following story. It shows how different references may converge or diverge, leading to a lot of user bewilderment.

Somewhere around 1997 a friend of mine had problems with her brand new broad-band connection. She asked me to have a look at her computer. When she clicked on the mail icon an empty inbox showed up.

'See, no mail. And I'm sure I have mail; I forwarded some from my office. That man who did the installation yesterday said everything was working – just click and go, ma'am. But where is my mail?'

'Okay,' I said, 'First, are you sure you are online?'

She pointed vaguely at the wires, still hanging chaotically all over the place, swirling to her desk. I hoped they were okay, but I did not mean the cables. There was a connection icon on her desktop, displaying a telephone device.[2] Fortunately, its settings turned out to be correctly configured; a double-click established the connection with her Internet provider. And after clicking the 'get mail' button in her mail program her mail streamed into her inbox.

'That's it,' I said. 'You first have to connect, with that icon.'

My friend was puzzled. 'That telephone icon? I used that to dial up with my modem, but now I have a permanent connection, just like I have at work. There I always see my mail immediately, without having to click on anything. I don't even have such a telephone icon there.'

I explained that apparently her computer at work was configured that way. 'That telephone icon stands for any kind of connection, be it by phone line or cable. But you can bypass it. It is possible to connect automatically to your provider as soon as you start up your computer. And also to fetch your mail as soon as you start your mail program. We can arrange that, if you like.'

And so we did.

That was all. A clear, comprehensible problem; just a small conceptual error. Yet, the story is illustrative of how human-computer interaction works, how it often fails to work, and how this relates to conceptual reifications, material configurations, and hidden steps in between.

Basically, my friend took the metaphorized icons literally. She took the mailbox icon for the mail itself, and the telephone icon for using the phone itself. For her, the mailbox icon was not referring to a process, a string of commands set in action in order to obtain a computed result; rather, it functioned as a key to a specific place, her inbox, where she expected her mail to be, immediately. The icon was not read as a reference, but as the immediate referent itself. The icon had superseded and cannibalized all references, transferences and network labor involved. A shortcut indeed.

It is important to note this is not unique to my friend's computer use. It is a general feature of iconicity. Computer icons function by iconic condensation: a condensation of reference, referent, and meaning into one visual metaphorical sign, thereby substituting all involved complexities with a stable icon. Hence, the inclination to take the icon for a specific *state* (result, place, or thing) instead of a referential button able to invoke a performative *process* is very strong. In fact, this is part and parcel of the very function of icons: shortcutting and condensing the signifying and executing processes. Icons can only carry out their signifying *and* executing job by concealing the involved complexities, substituting them with stable entities.

Hence, the mail icon hides the nested processes it refers to: executing the mail program, including its configurations for a particular Internet connection, a particular mail account, and particular incoming and outgoing mail servers located at an Internet service provider. Instead, the icon represents a specific result (received mail) located at a specific place (the mailbox), as an ontologized entity. The same holds for the telephone icon: it conceals that it is referring to the execution of a connection program, including its configurations and settings. Instead, it represents the contiguous telephone device.

This concealment of software and hardware processes cannot be seen as coincidental 'non-representing'; it is a necessary and deliberate act against representation. I propose to call this act of deliberate concealing *depresentation*. We could then say that computer icons do their work by representing an ontologized stable state, while depresenting the procedural complexity. This is the task we have delegated to icons. And this is why we are seduced, indeed compelled, to take icons literally – that is, to ontologize them, to condense and collapse them into their own inextricable iconic ontology, their *icontology*.

Signs, iconicity and indexicality

This begs the question: what kind of signs are computer icons? Peirce's semiotics (Peirce 1873) seems typically apt to solve the riddle of the icon, not only because it unfolds an explicit vocabulary on *iconicity*, but also because Peirce's notion of *indexicality* enables a non-essentialist analysis of the relation between signs and the world outside language and signs.[3]

Peirce's concept of indexicality does not pertain to just any reference a sign can make to an external object. Peirce distinguishes three basic relations a sign can have to the object it refers to: iconic, indexical and symbolic. The *icon* refers to its object by *resemblance, similarity or analogy*, for example the portrait of a person, a traffic sign with a picture of a hollow in the road, or the map of a country. The *index* refers to its object by an *existential, physical or causal* connection, for example smoke indicating fire, a fingerprint identifying a person, a sundial indicating time. The *symbol* refers to its object arbitrarily, that is, by *habit, convention or law,* for example the flag of a country, the logo of a company, or the alphabet for phonemes.

These categories are not mutually exclusive; in a symbol there may be something indexical and something iconic. For example, a traffic sign is always a symbol, as it is taken up in a system of laws and conventions regarding the use of forms and colors for these signs. However, a particular traffic sign may be indexically referring to a nearby hollow in the road, and it may do so by an iconic image resembling a hollow. Peirce's classification also accounts for the fact that signs circulate and may change by use. Icons may become symbols, for instance when the iconic picture of Che Guevara is printed on a T-shirt, signifying not so much the person Guevara but radical left sympathies. Likewise, symbols may be reiterated as an index; a yellow letter M is a symbol referring to the brandname McDonald's, but as a sign on a pole it is indexical for the nearby hamburger outlet.

Peirce's dynamic triad may be able to account for the interaction between state, process and system at work in computing semiosis, especially when it comes to computer icons. At first sight, computer icons seem not to be Peircian icons at all, but rather Peircian symbols. After all, they are all arbitrary; what a specific icon stands for we have to learn by collateral experience. But at second sight, computer icons rather seem to be Peircian indices: they all refer causally and physically to a set of software instructions to be executed.

Meanwhile, on yet another level icons may articulate other relations since they can refer to their object in three ways: by resemblance (iconic), by existential relation (indexical), or by convention (symbolic). On this level the mailbox icon would be a genuine Peircian icon, since its relation to its displayed object is based on an analogy between postal mail and e-mail. The telephone icon would be an indexical sign: its representation is not based on analogy but on an existential (though outdated) relation with the telephone device. And the icon for Microsoft's Internet Explorer, the stylized 'e', would then be a Peircian symbol, since the image is arbitrary and conventional.

From one perspective, then, all computer icons can be seen as symbolical or indexical signs, and from another perspective they may be icons, indices or symbols. The latter concerns *how the object is represented* by the sign, the former pertains to the *external existence of the object.* In Peirce's terminology, these are different kinds of objects. He called the first one the *immediate object* – the object as represented by the sign – and the second one the *dynamical object* – the object as it exists in the world. This dynamical object cannot be expressed by the sign itself, it can only be indicated, and its connection to the sign has to be learned (Peirce 1909).

This differentiation between objects enables us to flesh out how computer icons work. As we have seen, desktop icons refer to an act of executing machine code. From this perspective, all desktop icons are indexical: they refer to existential, physical chains of causation, to machine processes to be executed. Their dynamical object is thus machinic code. Whatever their immediate object as expressed in the sign may be (an iconic mailbox, an indexical telephone device, a symbolical logo), their dynamical object is code.

But as we have seen, computer icons not only refer to machinic code but also to human code – readable symbols and metaphors. Hence, a computer icon indexically refers to machine code, and symbolically it refers to human code (e.g. 'mail', 'connection'). In that regard, computer icons can be considered Peircian indices (referring to the dynamical object of machine code), wrapped in Peircian symbols (referring to the dynamical object of human code), while they are only contingently iconical (if they use pictorial resemblance for representation).

Yet, in the praxis of signification this gets inverted: computer icons establish themselves as primarily iconic. While they are rarely genuine Peircian icons, they all exhibit what I have called 'icontology' – reified iconicity. They do so by equating and substituting the sign with its immediate object of reference, thus negating the indexical and symbolical references to the dynamical object.

In order to understand the strange double dynamical object of computer icons – simultaneously machine code and human code – I propose a third kind of object: a symbolic future object, a not yet actualized object, an object to become, in short: a *virtual object*. This object is not represented in the sign, neither is it the indexical, actual execution of machine code. It is what might be actualized by the joint venture of human acts and machine processes. It is not just your mail program running, it is that you might have received mail. It is not just your browser running, it is the web out there where you may find or do something. It is where machine possibility and human effort come together. It is where signs become tools for unknown and unprogrammed virtual objects.

Tools ready-to-hand and present-at-hand

This introduces another problem: how can signs become tools? At first sight tools are fundamentally different from signs. Signs are marks able to qualify, refer to, or represent other signs and things in the world; tools are things in the world able to shape and transform other things. But as Heidegger (1927) pointed out, tools exist Um-zu (in order to); their being-in-the-world always *refers* to a possible (may we say 'virtual'?) work to be done, taken up in a system of other equipment (*Zeug*) and labor. Heidegger calls a tool we just use *ready-to-hand* ('Zuhanden'); it fits with the acts of our hands, and the goal in our minds. It aligns seamlessly with its Um-zu and does not call for further reflection – we do not think about a hammer, we just use it. But when a tool does not function according to its Um-zu, for example when it breaks down, it suddenly becomes a strange separate object. Then it is not ready-to-hand anymore but *present-at-hand* ('Vorhanden'): open to questions about what is the matter with it. We then have to reconsider our engagement with the object, repair it, replace it, or change our goal altogether.

Though computer icons cannot break down like a hammer, they may function as ready-to-hand or present-at-hand. They are ready-to-hand tools when they yield the expected result. We then take their icontology for granted and need not think about them as tools or as signs; we just click and go. But when a click fails, the icon is no longer ready-to-hand but present-at-hand, raising questions about whether the equipment chain is broken somewhere, or whether we just misinterpreted the sign. In Peircian terms: this raises questions about its reference to the object, which seemed to be unproblematically immediate when ready-to-hand, but exposes its dynamical and virtual mediations when suddenly becoming present-at-hand.[4] From this perspective the transformation of the computer icon from an integrated ready-to-hand sign-tool into a decomposed present-at-hand object is not a disturbing inconvenience, but an opportunity. An opportunity to investigate how digital equipment works, how it refers to other equipment and code, how it conceals its indexical dynamics, how it can fool you, and how you can counter this. As Winograd and Flores (1985) put it: 'Breakdowns serve an extremely important cognitive function, revealing to us the nature of our practices and equipment, making them present-to-hand to us, perhaps for the first time. In this sense they function in a positive rather than negative way.'

Conceptual metaphors

My friend, looking for her mail, would probably have found little comfort in Heidegger's ready-to-hand and present-at-hand tools, or Peirce's immediate and dynamical objects. We are all seduced by the immediate object of the sign and tend to remain trapped in its icontology. We take computer icons as condensed sign-tools, without being aware of the constitutive parts. While this can partly be explained by what I have called icontology, this does not explain why, even in a situation of being stuck with a present-at-hand sign-tool, the sign and the tool part still tend to stick together. What kind of glue keeps them together? For an answer to this question, we have to zoom in on the mechanism of metaphorical substitution encountered earlier.

The shortest definition of metaphor is: something which stands for something else. While all signs in fact stand for something else, metaphors are special, since they do so in a double sense. Metaphorical signs condense two references by transferring and incorporating qualities from one object of reference into another. Hence, metaphors are mechanisms of transference (from one to another) and condensation (one within another). This transference can be accomplished by words, but equally so by images (Forceville 2008) and physical objects (Gutenplan 2005). By assigning concepts to words, images and material objects, these ontologically different things are able to blend conceptually.

According to the so-called conceptual theory of metaphor (Lakoff and Johnson 1980; Lakoff 1993), metaphors can be analyzed as sets of conceptual correspondences across semantic domains, with an underlying basic conceptual metaphor which can be abbreviated as Y IS X, or TARGET DOMAIN IS SOURCE DOMAIN (Lakoff 1993). Might this be useful to analyze our riddle of the sign-tool icontology?

Analyzing the mailbox icon as a metaphor would yield E-MAIL IS POSTAL MAIL as basic conceptual metaphor, and the cross-domain mapping would look like Table 1.

SOURCE DOMAIN: postal mail	TARGET DOMAIN: e-mail
mailbox	inbox of mail program
letters, packets	messages, attachments
sending and receiving	send or get mail button
sorting, disposing	distribution to folders, deleting
[postal distribution system]	[mail-server network at ISPs]
[delivery by postman]	[consulting a mail server; fetch mail command]

Table 1: Cross-domain mapping for the conceptual metaphor E-MAIL IS POSTAL MAIL

All elements match well, except the last two in the list. These entities are indeed involved in the conceptual transference, but they are also exactly what is hidden in the iconic metaphor. They are and are not part of the conceptual mapping; they are what I have called depresented, while the other correspondences are represented as such on the interface. Note that this depresentation does not pertain to just unused parts of the conceptual domains. Unused parts would be 'stamps' in the source domain and 'viruses' in the target domain – these associations are simply ignored, they have no cross-domain correspondence, and they are not necessary to establish the metaphor of e-mail. But the aspects 'postal distribution system' and 'delivery by postman' in the source domain do have a counterpart in the target domain – they are indispensable for a successful transference. E-mail is only mail when it is also distributed and delivered. Yet, these acts are not represented in the metaphor connecting/condensing the source and target domain. Lakoff and Johnson's model of conceptual metaphor thus gives an account of how the mailbox icon connects postal mail with e-mail on the level of the interface and human conceptual cognition, but it ignores the connections to software and machinery. It explains the human code, but not the machine code: the indexical, dynamical operations involved, such as a connection with an Internet service provider, a mail client consulting a mail server, and the subsequent transport of mail to the user's PC.

Schematized (see Figure 1) this model of metaphor consists of an input (source domain) and an output (target domain), mediated by a cognitive human mind which is able to read the metaphorical mailbox icon as immediate object, thus connecting the source and the target. The necessary machine mediations – indexical references to dynamical objects – are invisible, hidden in a black box of software and machinery. Without a properly functioning dynamical black box, the output of the virtual object ('my e-mail') will not come about.

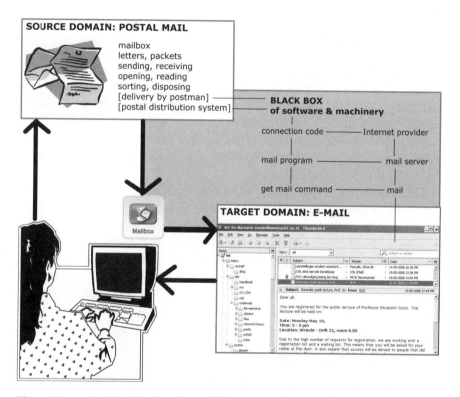

Figure 1: Input-output mechanism of the conceptual metaphor E-MAIL IS POSTAL MAIL

What is ignored in this model is that the metaphorical icon needs not only human reading but most of all *action* to invoke the transference – not only action by the user (configuring, clicking) but especially action inside the machine and the network. Meanwhile, the user is only able to read the icon as far as this action is depresented and blackboxed. As we have seen, that is what the icon does by 'icontologizing': equating the sign with its immediate object, effacing its material indexical relations to dynamical objects, pretending it stands immediately for the virtual object in the target domain.

We may conclude that the classic, conceptual theory of metaphor in fact mirrors this icontology, as it focuses primarily on the interfacial relation with the immediate object, the object as represented/metaphorized by the sign. Though this underscores once more how a sign can conceal and supersede its tool-being, it still provides no proper explanation for how the compound of sign and tool gets glued together. What we thus need, on top of the theory of conceptual metaphor, is a theory of the processual materiality of metaphor. To my knowledge, there is no such theory yet. In the last section I will tentatively gather some possible building blocks for such a theory.

Material metaphor

What is needed is a theory of metaphor which not only maps transferences between different semantic domains – from concept to concept, as does the conceptual theory – but also between different ontological domains: from concepts to objects, from software instructions to visual icons, from signs to tools. Such a theory should provide an account of the involved material indexicality of sign-tools, of their relation to the dynamical objects inside the black box, and the relation with the hoped-for virtual object.

Katherine Hayles's (2002) notion of material metaphor is a promising starting point. Hayles defined material metaphor as the instance of metaphor where the metaphorical transference does not take place between semantic concepts, but between symbolic signs and material apparatus. Like all metaphors, material metaphors condense two references, yet they do not blend two conceptual references; rather, they blend a conceptual reference with a material indexical reference. Hayles proposed the term in the context of her medium-specific analysis of electronic literature. In this field written words can do more than just signify or represent – they may, as material metaphors, be able to perform acts: dance, move, dissolve, mutate, tear apart, destroy previously read words, etc., according to the underlying software code.

This kind of e-textual performance can be seen as a radicalization of Austin's speech act theory. Austin (1962) pointed out how verbal statements such as 'I promise' or 'I baptise this ship' are not just constative utterances but performative speech acts. By being uttered (in a specific context), such utterances *do things in the world*, they accomplish a change in a state of affairs. In a similar vein e-text is able to perform 'digital speech acts'. Though Austin's speech act theory pertains primarily to language and Hayles's material metaphor primarily to digital literature, there seems to be no reason to confine material metaphor to the domain of words and texts. Just as images and physical objects may be invoked as conceptual metaphors, they may be invoked as material metaphors. Whenever an image or an object functions as a symbol *and* is able to entail a change of affairs when enacted in the proper context, it can be considered a material metaphor. Take, for example, the planting or capturing of a flag – this not only *signifies* colonization or victory, it *evokes* it by the very act of planting or capturing.

Material metaphors are ubiquitous in ordinary computer interfaces. They exist as sign-tools, as icons and hyperlinks, as pixeled buttons and switches which can indeed be switched on and off. Such material metaphors condense iconicity and indexicality by blending immediate and dynamical objects into one sign-tool. The mailbox icon is a material metaphor, able to invoke indexical material acts, changes in the material machinery of the computer and the network. Conceiving the mailbox as material metaphor thus reveals what is depresented in the conceptual metaphor. While the conceptual metaphor can explain what happens inside the head of the user, the material metaphor leads us to the hands of user, and from there to and through the interface, right inside the black box of digital machinery.

Not that the black box will become transparent. Most parts of this black box will remain in the dark, since we humans are practically blind in this digital domain. We have delegated the relevant intentional acts to code, which we can execute but which we cannot grasp directly. We are simply not equipped with a perceptual or cognitive apparatus to read the digital, to read patterns of numbers and infer their meaning or effects. However, we do have partial, mediated access to the digital. We have this possibility because machinic calculations and translations can be ontologized and represented to us as readable signs, that is as material metaphors. We are able to read and act upon parts of the code, as far as these are represented as a sign-tool. This may be done by icons, but also by textual configuration menus ('mail server settings'), hyperlinks or other metaphorized commands ('get mail', 'send mail').

While these material metaphors mostly go by unnoticed, ready-to-hand and icontologized, they are however 'near at hand'. An analysis of both their conceptual iconicity and their material indexicality may turn them into keys to the black box, able to close and conceal, but also able to open and reveal. A full-blown theory of material metaphor may thus provide analytical apertures in the digital black box, enabling us to peek inside.

In order to develop such a theory, a very heterogeneous set of analytical tools and concepts should be assembled. Though Peirce, Heidegger, Lakoff, and Hayles may be strange bedfellows, I consider their joint forces necessary for this endeavor. The ongoing proliferation of cross- and intermediations induced by digitality results in more and more material-semiotic assemblages in the form of icontologized virtual objects. They could and should be hacked analytically.

Notes

1. For example Sherry Turkle's metaphorical book title *Life on the screen: Identity in the age of the Internet* (1995). In Steven Johnson's *Interface culture* (1997) the computer interface

equals the screen with its visual metaphors. Even in Bolter and Grusin's *Remediation* (1999) the basic principles of mediation – immediacy and hypermediacy – are both defined as 'styles of visual representation' (272). See for other examples of screenic hegemony the chapters by Nanna Verhoeff and Ann-Sophie Lehmann. See for a further deconstruction of the notion of indexicality the chapter by Frank Kessler.

2. Average Internet users nowadays would perhaps not even understand the telephone metaphor as network connection icon, not being familiar anymore with dial-up Internet accounts. A telephone icon nowadays usually stands for another application: voice over IP.

3. Cf. Saussure's structuralist semiology, in which only two ingredients of the sign are distinguished: signifier (material embodiment of the sign) and signified (mental concept, produced by the differences in the chain of signifiers, arbitrarily connected to a signifier). In Saussure's linguistic conception of the sign, any notion of reference to something outside language is disabled. While this precludes the pitfalls of claiming essentialist, natural correspondences between words and things, it also excludes any conceptualization of possible relations to a world outside human language.

4. Cf. Latour's distinction between *intermediaries*, which just transmit, and *mediators*, which transform, translate and modify meaning while processing: 'A properly functioning computer could be taken as a good case of a complicated intermediary (...) But if it breaks down, a computer may turn into a horrendously complex mediator' (Latour 2005, 39).

References

Austin, John Langshaw. 1962. *How to do things with words*, eds. J.O. Urmson and Marina Sbisà. Cambridge, MA: Harvard University Press.

Bolter, Jay David, and Richard Grusin. 2000. *Remediation: Understanding new media*. Cambridge, MA: MIT Press.

Coward, Rosalind, and John Ellis. 1977. *Language and materialism: Developments in semiology and the theory of the subject*. Boston: Routledge & Kegan Paul.

Forceville, Charles. 2008. Metaphor in pictures and multimodal representations. In *The Cambridge handbook of metaphor and thought*, ed. Raymond Gibbs. Cambridge, MA: Cambridge University Press.

Freadman, Anne. 2004. *The machinery of talk: Charles Peirce and the sign hypothesis*. Stanford: Stanford University Press.

Gutenplan, Samuel. 2005. *Objects of metaphor*. Oxford: Claridon Press.

Harman, Graham. 2002. *Tool-Being: Heidegger and the metaphysics of objects*. Chicago: Open Court Publishing.

Hayles, N. Katherine. 1993. Virtual bodies and flickering signifiers. *October* (66): 69-91.

—. 2002. *Writing machines*. Cambridge, MA: MIT Press.

—. 2003. Translating media: Why we should rethink textuality. *The Yale Journal of Criticism* 16 (2): 263-290.

—. 2005. *My mother was a computer*. Chicago: University of Chicago Press.

Heidegger, Martin. 1954. The question concerning technology. In *The question concerning technology and other essays*, 1977, ed. William Lovitt, 3-35. Harper Torchbooks.

Heidegger, Martin. 1927. *Sein und Zeit*. Tübingen: Max Niemeyer Verlag.

Johnson, Steven. 1997. *Interface culture: How new technology transforms the way we create and communicate*. New York: Basic Books.

Lakoff, George. 1993. The contemporary theory of metaphor. In *Metaphor and thought*, ed. Andrew Ortony, 202-251. Cambridge, MA: Cambridge University Press.

Lakoff, George, and Mark Johnson. 1980. *Metaphors we live by*. Chicago: University of Chicago Press.

Latour, Bruno. 2005. *Reassembling the social: An introduction to actor-network-theory*. Oxford: Oxford University Press.

Lucy, Niall. 2001. *Beyond semiotics: Text, culture and technology*. London, New York: Continuum.

Manovich, Lev. 2001. *The language of new media*. Cambridge, MA: MIT Press.

Peirce, Charles Sanders. 1873. Of logic as a study of signs. In *Writings of Charles S. Peirce*, 1981, ed. Peirce Edition Project, Vol. 3.82, Bloomington: Indiana University Press.

Peirce, Charles Sanders. 1888. A guess at the riddle. In *Collected papers of Charles Sanders Peirce*, 1932, eds. Charles Hartshorne, Paul Weiss, and Arthur W. Burks, 365-367. Cambridge, MA: Harvard University Press.

Peirce, Charles Sanders. 1904. A letter to Lady Welby. In *Collected Papers of Charles Peirce*, 1958, ed. A.W. Burks, Vol. 8.328. Cambridge, MA: Belknap Press of Harvard University Press.

Peirce, Charles Sanders. 1909. A letter to William James. In *The Essential Peirce: Selected philosophical writings*, 1998, ed. Peirce Edition Project, Vol. 2.498. Bloomington, Indianapolis: Indiana University Press.

Saussure, de, Ferdinand. 1983 [1916]. *Course in general linguistics*, eds. Charles Bally and Albert Sechehaye. La Salle, IL: Open Court Publishing.

Tilley, Christopher. 1999. *Metaphor and material culture*. Oxford: Blackwell Publishers.

Turkle, Sherry. 1995. *Life on the screen: Identity in the age of the Internet*. New York: Simon & Schuster.

Winograd, Terry, and Fernando Flores, eds. 1985. *Understanding computers and cognition*. Norwood: Ablex Publishing.

Hidden practice

Artists' working spaces, tools, and materials in the digital domain

Ann-Sophie Lehmann

The construction of digital artworks demands a wide range of expertise. Conception, production and technology are closely intertwined; existing technologies have to be adapted to new artistic concepts, and new technologies inspire and create new meanings and contexts. In order to realise a work of art – be it an installation in a gallery or museum, or an online work – an artist has to be engineer, programmer, graphic designer, and hardware constructor all at once or has to have access to others who are able to shape technologies and materials as required. In the case of Daniel Rozin's *Wooden Mirror* (1999) for example – a work that produces the reflection of any person facing it by slightly shifting the polished wooden blocks of which the surface of the mirror is constructed – the cameras, motion sensors, software and wooden blocks were all custom made (Bolter and Gromolla 2003). In a sense, the construction of such complex, interactive works returns the digital-media artist to an era before the pre-manufacturing of artist's supplies. Before the invention of metal paint tubes in the 19th century, before standard-sized canvasses or marble blocks were available, artists depended on custom-made materials and workshops with trained assistants, just as the media artist today might depend on programmers and engineers to provide custom-built technology. Even when artist and programmer are the same person, for example the net.art practitioners Jodi (http://text.jodi.org) or Olia Lialina (www.artlebedev.ru/svalka/olialia), the procedures of art making are no less intricate or complex.

Thinking about the versatile practice of new media artists leads to the question of what this practice might look like. One way to find out is by studio visits or reading and watching interviews with artists (as can be done in the wonderful online archive of artist's talks compiled by the Tate Gallery, London: www.tate.org.uk/onlineevents). Another way is to look at the ways media artists represent their own practice. Throughout history, artists have taken care to display, advertise and explain their art-making skills in genres specifically created for this purpose. Some of the first representations of artists at work may be found in illuminated manuscripts, and in the early Renaissance, the representation of St. Luke painting the Madonna became a way to depict artistic practice and skill. Within a century the Christian iconography of the painting evangelist evolved into the independent self-portrait at the easel, and the atelier scene. Both genres were still widely popular in the 19th and early 20th centuries, adapting their specific iconography to changing artistic practices and new technologies. Because today's multifaceted media artist as described above might also be interested in the public display of her versatile skills, one could expect a continuation of the iconography of 'the artist at work' into the digital age. But is practice represented in the age of digital art? Do artists draw attention to the processes and procedures underlying their work? The question about a contemporary iconography of the representation of artistic practice raises more general questions about the spatial, material and theoretical aspects of this practice: what kind of materials and tools are used to construct media art, and how do artists employ these tools and materials in their creative spaces? How are these creative spaces defined and located, and can they and the creative processes within be visualised?

My first tentative answer to these questions is negative – digital modes of production do not appear to favour the representation of the artist at work because the very process of making is rendered invisible by the medium itself. However, this hypothesis must be tested first. In order to determine whether or not representation of practice is absent in the creation of digital art, this article will reflect on four aspects relevant to the question at stake. Beginning with a brief review of representations of artistic practice in the pre-digital era, a more thorough analysis of the location and designation of creative spaces in the digital era will follow. The representation of digital tools and materials used by media artists will then be focused on, incorporating a brief comparison with the representation of practice in a field related to media art – computer graphics and animation.

The representation of artistic practice and creative spaces in the pre-digital era

In the pre-photographic era artistic practice was represented in genres displaying artists working in their workshops. Needless to say, these scenes are not objective representations of generic practices, but carefully staged scenes designed to entice the viewer in the display of artistic skill. At the same time, these scenes served to invest an artist's working space with near magical qualities. The careful presentation of the 'artist at work' with brushes and paints (or their equivalents) in a studio space adorned with models, preliminary sketches and unfinished works evoked the aura of creation (Lehmann 2006; Pardo and Cole 2005). The images suggested that these spaces not only contained the materials and tools necessary to make works of art, but also housed the inspiration and genius necessary to conceive them. Furthermore, the images enhanced the mystery of artistic creation

Figure 1: The Workshop of Jan van Eyck, *etching from the series* Nova Reperta *by Jacobus Stradanus, 1555*

through an interesting pictorial paradox. On the one hand, atelier scenes allow us to witness the act of creating a painting, seemingly instructing the viewer in the actual making of pictorial illusions. Yet while we observe the processes of painting – paint being mixed, a brushstroke applied – the acts displayed before our eyes are far too complex to be copied purely based on the visual information provided. Showing art making therefore does not necessarily give away the artist's secret. On the contrary, the display of skill makes the process of creation appear all the more mysterious.

After 1900 photography and then film would replace the painted depictions of the artist at work. The latter provided more information about art making as it recorded the creative process over time. Yet these films – like Hans Cürlis's series *Schaffende Hände* from the 1920s, Hans Namuth's *Jackson Pollock* (1951), Henri-Georges Clouzot's *Le mystère Picasso* (1956) and many art documentaries made since – do not escape the paradox described above and display a 'fetishization of the actual moment of creation' (Hayward 1988, 8). To this day, especially the studio space lends itself to the idealisation and mystification of practice. Even with the artist dead and gone, the deserted studio continues to breathe the aura of creation and is treated as a shrine, with the material remains as relics. The recent transfer of Francis Bacon's entire studio contents from London to Dublin and the exhibition of Perry Ogden's beautiful photographs of Bacon's chaotic workshop as works of art in their own right are perfect examples of the cultural value attached to the traditional creative environment (for a visual impression, see www.hughlane.ie/fb_studio).

It can be concluded that the representation of practice was – and still is – closely tied to the aura of materials and spaces. This 'materialist' notion is incorporated in the very naming of the artist's space: the term atelier derives from the Latin *atele*, which referred to the wooden shavings in a carpenter's workshop. These wooden scraps and other litter from his studio (cigarette buds, lost socks, old cloth) are at the heart of the work of Jedediah Caesar. Caesar collects debris in boxes, fills these with liquid resin and then saws the transparent cubes into thin slices. The results are beautiful, archeological samples of the studio, which embody as well as question the representation of material practice.

The designation and location of creative spaces in the digital era

New media have led to the formation of new creative spaces; spaces that seem to have caused a dislocation of the materiality of the traditional working space. In order to situate digital artistic practice and its representation, this section will attempt to trace and outline the physical, metaphorical and theoretical appearances of these new spaces.

Beginning with the designation of the new spaces, it is remarkable that in new media art practice, a working space is frequently referred to as a laboratory rather than a studio or atelier – traditionally, the spaces of the production of art and science have been separated since the Renaissance (Alpers 1998). Often abbreviated as media lab or design lab, the new working space is a sharp contrast to the traditional concept of the studio. Obviously, this shift owes much to the essential role of technology in new media art. Also, the notion of creation associated with the traditional studio might be less appealing than the notion of experiment associated with the laboratory. Yet the laboratory, just like the studio, carries its own traditional set of connotations, which are deemed highly problematic by some scholars. Bruno Latour has criticised the laboratory as the ultimate black box; as a place where experiment and invention are kept from public view, and only finite results are allowed to emerge after having been carefully wrapped in impenetrable layers of scientific reasoning (Latour 1987). Although the artist's laboratory has come to signify the cross-disciplinary link between art and science and could therefore symbolise a partial opening of the black box, the production and making of art still seem to be hidden behind the walls of the lab. Consequently, there is no equivalent to the traditional depiction of the atelier described above, no laboratory-iconography representing the work that goes on inside.

This obscuring of creative practice is matched by an apparent reluctance to describe the technological processes behind digital artworks with words. In recent overviews of new media art, very little attention is paid to the actual production of the artworks discussed (Greene 2004; Paul 2003; Stallabrass 2003).

Although net.art plays with digital technologies and addresses their impact on art, society and politics, the actual technologies and procedures behind the individual artworks remain obscure. Artists simply 'draw links between sites'; 'build online artworks'; or present 'a sophisticated piece of programming' (Stallabrass 2003, 27-29). When artists themselves refer to their own practice, we get a notion of their presence behind the computer, yet we have no idea what they actually do with the computer. In a 1997 interview net.art pioneer Vuk Cosic describes how he has neighbouring studios with Heath Bunting, Alexei Shulgin and Olia Lialina, emulating the studio set-up of Picasso and Braque in early twentieth-century Paris: 'We steal a lot from each other, in the sense that we take some parts of codes, we admire each other's tricks', and the Belgian duo Jodi wrote in the early 1990s: 'it is obvious that our work fights against high tech' (Stallabrass 2003, 34, 38). The 'drawing' of links and 'building' of sites, the comparison with Braque and Picasso, the fight against 'high-tech' all draw on traditional terminology and metaphors. The vocabulary for the description of the technological aspects of new media art practice on the other hand is limited. So how do we imagine the code-tricks Cosic mentions? How do we differentiate between high- and low-tech if technology is neither a verbal nor visual issue in the self-reflection of practice and in the critical analysis and public presentation of art works? Maybe technology is still considered dull to the wider public? The result being that 'techno-talk' is kept to a relatively small, artistic community that possesses sufficient technological understanding.[1]

Interestingly, the notion of the laboratory with its metaphorical connotations of secrecy and highly specialised technological processes, in combination with the textual silence surrounding these processes, contradicts a vital yet somewhat utopian ideal proclaimed by scholars of new media culture and theory like Henry Jenkins and Pierre Lévy. This ideal envisages new media as open-source, enabling technologies, which facilitate and inspire the participatory production of culture.[2] The contradiction between the 'black boxing' of artistic practice and the ideal of a participatory culture might be due to the mechanisms of the art market – above all the demand for originality – to which eventually even the most non-conformist artist may succumb. In order to solve this conflict, open the 'black box of practice' and represent the new media artist at work, a means to facilitate the description and visualisation of the technologies used in art practice must be found.

In addition to the symbolic and physical shift of the site of production from open studio to closed laboratory, new media have had a profound impact on the notion of space. In general, new media initially seemed to emphasize the traditional division of space into metaphorical and/or virtual spaces on the one hand and actual, physical spaces on the other. More recently, scholars like Katherine Hayles (2002) and Mark Poster (2004) have argued that the inherent dichotomy of real and non-real spaces should be discarded in favour of a model that is based upon Michel Foucault's concept of heterotopias, sites 'that have the curious property of being in relation with all the other sites' (Foucault 1986). This model suggests that through new media, virtual and physical spaces intersect each other simultaneously, continuously creating new spaces, all of which co-exist in a non-hierarchical structure.

New media artworks are a perfect illustration of these new spatial heterotopias. In new media art works – as George Legrady, theorist and practitioner in the field of digital media, wrote as early as 1999 – metaphorical and virtual spaces always intersect with physical spaces: 'In the process of interacting with the digital world, we can consider real space as the site where our bodies come into contact with the technological devices by which we experience virtual space' (Legrady 1999, 105). Legrady describes the embodied visual or sensual experience of the viewer when looking at new media art in physical spaces like museums but also on computer screens. The artworks themselves are, as he emphasises, immaterial, however: 'Artists who create in digital media can produce works that do not require embodiment in a physical object. These works are free from the constraints of materiality as they exist as numeric data' (ibid., 106). Legrady argues that the artwork, 'free from the constraints of materiality', arrives at an intersection of the virtual and the real when it is being viewed and experienced. In his argument, Legrady puts the immateriality of the artwork first, but what about the other end of the process, the initial making of the art work? Before becoming what Legrady calls 'immaterial', there must have been a form of interaction between the maker and the digital building blocks of the artwork under construction, equally embodied as the experience of the viewer of the finished piece. It follows that the artwork only seems to be immaterial in between making and viewing, while the processes of production (when the artwork is made) and perception (when the artwork is experienced) imply materiality through human contact. Just as the act of perceiving is bound to a physical location, so the physical interaction between the artwork and its maker must have a location of some sort, somewhere within the heterotopia of intersecting virtual and physical spaces.

Where then could the creative space of the new media artist be located, and how do artists describe it? An artist of the Amsterdam KKEP collective (www.kkep.com) once told me about the process of making a collaborative piece in the early years of the Internet. While she was in Amsterdam and her collaborator in New York, they would work in the 'natural' shifts dictated by the time difference and send their work back and forth to one another via the Internet. Not only did they get twice as much work done as they would have in the same time zone, they also profited from the creative input of the different environments they lived in. I interviewed Joanna Griffin, who works with the visualisation of satellite data, at the Utrecht Impakt Festival 2004 about her ideal working space. She described it as 'a place where I can plug in my computer and make coffee'.

In both cases, the physical location of the artist overlaps with the creative space to a certain extent, yet the latter is obviously much more than somewhere to plug in the computer and make coffee. The creative space is much more difficult to mark out. Can it be found at the desk, in front of the computer, or rather at the intersection of the physical and the machine world, the human-computer interface? Is it the computer itself, like the practice of case-modding suggests, creating visual spectacle by turning the outside of the computer into a personalised artefact (Simon 2007); is it inside the computer where software programs like Photoshop, Maya or Paint mimic the artist's studio with its traditional tools and materials; or is it in the virtual space beyond the machine? Or is it in all these places at the same time: an oscillating creative space; an artistic new media heterotopia?

While the last option, the oscillating creative space, is the most likely answer, this space is at the same time the least tangible and concrete. More insight into the possible structure of this creative working space may be gained from the field of computer science. In order to design collaborative virtual environments, much research has been carried out into the spatial experience of users who engage and work with digital technologies. A basic outcome has been that users move about in multiple, simultaneous and hybrid spaces. Letting go of the spatial dichotomy between (pure) physical and virtual spaces provides a parallel with the theory of the digital heterotopia as described by Poster. Computer science, however, needs to move beyond theoretical concepts in order to translate the spatial hybrids back into concrete designs. During this process, the new spatial conditions (which, as illustrated above, tend to evade exact positioning) need to be redefined outside the restrictive terminology of geographical location. In order to do so, Paul Dourish, Professor of Computer Science at the University of California, Irvine, introduced the distinction between space and place in his call for a social design for collaborative virtual environments (Dourish 2001). This concept, borrowed from the social sciences, allows for a non-geographical definition of the new spatial situation because it adds yet another layer to the hybridisation of digital and physical space: the flexible meaning of spaces in their form as place. According to Harrison and Dourish, spaces are part of the material out of which places can be built. Dealing with physical structure, topology, orientation and connectedness, spaces offer opportunities and constraints. Places, on the other hand, reflect cultural and social understandings. Places can also have temporal properties; the same space can be different places at different times (Harrison and Dourish 2001, 73).[3]

Dourish's differentiation between space and place also helps to identify the creative working space of the artist: it is a socially and culturally shaped place, created from the hybrid fabric of virtual and physical spaces. On a conceptual level, this definition brings us closer to the whereabouts of the artist at work in the digital domain. But it still does not help to visualise this place. On the contrary, the oscillating, creative virtual and physical space/place seems to resist representation even more than it evades verbal description, maybe because there is no fixed space left to depict anymore.

The visibility of digital tools and materials

While the creative space seems to defy representation, there are other ingredients of the art-making process that do not. These are the tools and materials of the new media artist in or at the computer. Just like the creative space, tools oscillate between a physical and virtual presence, because the keyboard, mouse, pen – or in the case of touch screens the hand itself – are tangible devices translating movement into digital action on the screen. Most of the time, the virtual part of the tool is represented by an icon referring to a familiar device of non-digital origin, like the brush, pen, eraser or spray-can; in other cases the specificity of a digital action has been related to icons previously alien to the studio like for instance the lasso or the magic wand.[4] The physical tool can operate a variety of different, even opposing, virtual tools. For example, the mouse controls the eraser as well as the clowning device in a paint program. Yet in spite of their hybrid structure and seemingly simplified functions, the tools demand a user just as skilled and sensitive to their creative potential as do 'traditional' tools, as Malcolm McCollough pointed out in his important study, Abstracting craft (1996). Recently, Richard Sennett argued along the same lines in his manifesto for a re-evaluation of craftsmanship (2008).

Digital materials are more evasive than tools because they have no physical component but are entirely virtual. Yet even in the virtual domain, they oscillate between two shapes. On the surface, they resemble artistic material of the physical domain (images, paint, brushstrokes, colour, etc.). On a different level they are software, part of software, or in their purest form, code. A simple example is the HTML code attached to colour shades. The fact that digital tools and materials are ultimately represented in such forms could turn them into an interesting element of the hypothetical representations (so far) of the new media artist at work. However, where the brushes and palettes, chisels and rulers, marble slabs and paint tubes, paper and charcoal of pre-digital artists figure prominently in the (self)-portraits discussed above, there is no comparable elevation of their digital counterparts discernable yet. It is indeed hard to imagine a depiction of a mouse or a brush icon being done as lovingly and romantically as, for example, the tools in François Bonvin's Attributes of Painting where palette and brushes symbolise the creative process.

Taking into account the recognition of digital craft and craftsmanship, it could be merely a question of time until digital tools are used in representations to evoke the magical aura of artistic creation.

In this context, we may observe that digital tools and materials have not shed the iconic or symbolic bond with their precursors, as the media theorem of the 'horseless carriage' syndrome would have it. On the contrary, the current development of design software strives for an ever more perfect imitation of the materiality and tangibility of traditional artistic tools. The desire for a reconciliation of

Figure 2: François Bonvin, Attributes of painting, *late 19th century (Courtesy Barber Institute of Fine Arts, Birmingham)*

the senses of vision and touch, separated by the digitalisation of creative processes, is present in the amazingly precise imitation of artistic materials, from different sorts of digital canvas to virtual oil-paint that actually needs to dry, to applications simulating the direct/immediate touch and feel of virtual paint and brushes in 3D environments (for example, Baxter et al. 2004).

These developments in the design sector push towards the frontier of what Jay David Bolter and Richard Grusin have called the myth of 'transparent immediacy' (Bolter and Grusin 1999). In this ideal and never completely realisable state, the user could become ignorant of all traces of mediation and 'handle' digital materials and tools directly. One might ask if the continuous effort to recreate traditional materiality in virtual environments does not restrain the development of tools and materials of an essentially digital nature, without precursors in the non-digital domain. So far, the metaphor of the painter's, sculptor's or architect's tools and materials proves to be much harder to shake off than that of the creative space where the tools and materials are handled, which easily gave way to new forms of hybridisation.

It is interesting to see how digital tools, now they have become tangible and have re-appropriated, as it were, the aura of traditional creation, also become attractive for representation. I will illustrate this with two examples; one is an educational application, the other an artwork.

The *I/O Brush* is a multimedia tool for children, developed by researchers in the MIT Media Lab. It is an oversized brush with a wooden handle and bristles that incorporates a small camera. With the brush, the children are able to film a certain structure or surface and then 'paint' with this image on a digital canvas (the application is reminiscent of the 'image-hose' in paint programs). The central notion is the effortless incorporation of real-world materials into digital art projects. In the articles describing the *I/O brush* (Ryoaki 2004) and on the MIT website (http://web.media.mit.edu/~kimiko/iobrush), photographs and short films show the fun and ease with which the children use the ingenious combination of digital technology and tangible tool. Watching the little artists at work, the viewer is immediately convinced of the success of the brush.

Fugure 3: Child working with I/O Brush

Daniel Rozin's art project *Easel* (1998) functions in a comparable way. A computer screen is set on a painter's easel so that it appears as a traditional canvas. On the 'canvas' gallery visitors may combine and modify live video images and material from the Internet with a digital device mimicking a brush. Rozin describes his work as 'a group made of two pieces that build on the concept of painting with video. The pieces in this group are truly interactive as the visitors are encouraged not only to incorporate their image into the piece but to actively paint and change the whole appearance of the piece, becoming the artists themselves' (http://smoothware.com/danny/neweasel.html). It is essential to this concept that Rozin's artwork is neither just the easel with the digital canvas, nor the various

Figure 4: Computer animator at work

works the eventual users will create. The work of art is the sum of the whole interactive process of creating images.

In both cases, the focus lies on image-making, and the visuals explaining the *I/O Brush* and *Easel* present us with the creative engagement of users: a child handling the brush, a gallery visitor painting. These representations, which are obviously related to the iconography of the painter at his easel and the depiction of the artist at work in the art documentary discussed above, form part of a visual tradition I want to call 'showing making'. The difference is that they do not show the creators of *I/O Brush* or *Easel* at work, but those who interact with the finished product. We see how intricate technologies have disappeared behind the metaphor of painting, enabling others to use them within the familiar frame of traditional artistic practice. The creative practices of those who constructed these technologies remain hidden.

The *making-of* in computer graphics and animation

So far, the search for the representation of artistic practice in the digital domain has been rather unsuccessful. Yet there is an area of digital image-making where processes of production are almost excessively represented: the field of computer graphics and computer animation. Here, 'showing making' has even been defined as a separate genre, the making-of. As a genre the making-of is much older than computer graphics, but through the use of digital image manipulation in film, it has gained tremendously in popularity (Hight 2005). This is due to the new form of image creation. Artificially created photo- and hyper-realistic images captivate viewers because they have no indexical equivalent in the real world. Things, people, places that never existed, or do not exist anymore (e.g. dinosaurs), and events that never took place or are impossible to film in the real world may be visualised with the help of a computer (cf. Jones 1989, Moskovich 2002). As such, these spectacular visuals seem to undermine the paradigm of indexicality associated with photography and film.[5]

A way to appeal to the fascination and apprehension caused by computer graphics is to show how these images were generated. This can be for explanatory as well as commercial reasons. In a traditional making-of, the viewer gets a peek 'behind the scenes', listens to the director's erudite commentary, watches actors being interviewed on the set and witnesses hilarious bloopers. The making-of of computer-animated scenes looks rather different. It is much more static. Most of the time we see animators or technicians sitting in front of computers, displaying skilful manipulation of tools and digital materials while the images they create come into being on a screen. Glancing over the shoulder of computer wizards, we might witness the different stages of a spectacular stunt, like the 'bullet time' effect in the *Matrix Trilogy* (Wachowsky Brothers 1999-2002) or the building of an underwater anemone in *Finding Nemo* (Stanton and Unkrich 2003) on its way to photorealism, from wire-frame animation to a full-coloured and shaded sequence. The formal set up of these making-ofs bears a close resemblance to the iconography of the atelier scenes discussed above.

The genre also answers to the same visual paradox. Practice is displayed without giving away the secret of the actual 'how to'. Showing the computer animator at the screen does not deconstruct visual illusion. If this were the case, we would probably not enjoy watching making-ofs. Yet, regardless of their promise to reveal the making of illusion, the genre does not destroy but rather enhances the pleasure of looking. Part of this pleasure is achieved because we learn about the amount of work and skill invested in the creation of illusionist imagery. This knowledge causes the viewer to admire the dexterity and competence of the maker(s). Knowing how much effort has been invested in its creation might also heighten the desire to become immersed in the image (Hediger 2005). Moreover, the stimulation of awe is of economic value as the making-of is a way to display the power to shape technology ('only we can create these images').

Hidden practice

Although a fixed mode to represent practice does exist, new media artists generally do not use the making-of to reflect on their practice. This might be for a number of reasons, such as the commercial aspect and the predetermined appearance of the genre. But predominantly, an artist might not employ the visual strategies of the making-of because it is so closely tied to the creation of photorealist or at least figurative imagery. This is also the reason why the making-of can seamlessly tie back into the visual vocabulary of the painter in front of the easel. Mimicking reality and creating visual illusion profits by showing or showing off practice, be it in the 16th or in the 21st century. Yet today's new media creative practices encompass infinitely more strategies than the representation of realistic computer-generated imagery. Artists who operate within this set of paradigms seem to prefer not to represent themselves (at work) at all.

To summarise, the process of artistic practice seems to be rendered invisible by a variety of factors: the metaphor of the laboratory; the difficulties in describing and visualising the procedures of data programming; the hybridisation of creative space; and the multiplicity of artistic practice within this space. Practice itself does become visible, but only in certain instances, dissociated from the artist. It appears in the digital tools mimicking analogue predecessors, in digital materials like software and data, or in interactive art-works engaging the viewer/user. However, the embodied representation of the artist at work only resurfaces when creative practice remediates traditional modes of art making, like the affirmative creation of realities in computer graphics and animation.

Two conclusions are possible. Either the representation of artists at work has become obsolete in new media art practice and the mystification of artistic creation has finally been discarded, or the representation of practice has become just as hybridised as the space in which it takes place. It has been shown above that the representation of practice can mystify or even fetishize the creative act. At the same time, 'showing making' counteracts mystification because it can reveal the intricate interactions between actors, technologies, tools and materials, making artistic creation and visualising procedures comprehensible. As such, the potential of the genre is much too exciting to be abandoned. Most likely, creative practice in the digital domain is still in search of representation.

An earlier version of this essay appeared in *Computers and the history of art* vol. 3, eds. A. Bentkowska-Kafel, T. Cashen, and H. Gardiner, Chicago: Intellect Books 2009.

Notes

1. An exception is Olia Lialina's article 'A Vernacular Web. The Indigenous and The Barbarians', http://art.teleportacia.org/observation/vernacular.

2. For a critical discussion of the ideal of participatory culture, see the chapters by Mirko Tobias Schäfer and Eggo Müller in this book.
3. Michel de Certeau defines space and place in an opposing manner, see the chapter by Sybille Lammes in this book.
4. So far, little research has been conducted on the history and development of tool metaphors for paint programs. For a general overview see, Alvey Ray Smith (2001). On the sometimes confusing, metaphorical relation of computer icons with computer processes, see the chapter by Marianne van den Boomen in this book.
5. This complex issue is a frequently discussed problem in new media studies, see the chapter by Frank Kessler in this book. See also William J. Mitchell (1992), Barbara Savedoff (1997) and Lev Manovich (2001).

References

Alpers, Svetlana. 1998. The studio, the laboratory, and the vexations of art. In *Picturing science, producing art*, eds. Peter Galison, Caroline A. Smith, 401-417. New York: Routledge.

Baxter, William, Jeremy Wendt and Ming C. Lin. 2004. IMPaSTo: a realistic, interactive model for paint, NPAR '04: *Proceedings of the 3rd international symposium on non-photorealistic animation and rendering*. ACM June 2004.

Bolter, David Jay, and Richard Grusin. 1999. *Remediation: Understanding new media*. Cambridge, MA: MIT Press.

Bolter, David Jay, and D. Gromala 2003. *Windows and mirrors: Interaction design, digital art, and the myth of transparency*. Cambridge, MA: MIT Press.

Cole, Michael, and Mary Pardo eds. 2005. *Inventions of the studio: Renaissance to Romanticism*. Chapel Hill: University of North Carolina Press.

Couldry, Nick, Anne McCarthy eds. 2004. *Mediaspace: Place, scale and culture in a media age*. London: Routledge.

Dourish, Paul. 2001. *Where the action is: The foundation of embodied interaction*. Cambridge, MA: MIT Press.

Foucault, Michel. 1986. Of other spaces. Diacritics 16 (1): 22-27 (also at http://foucault.info/documents/heteroTopia/foucault.heteroTopia.en.html).

Greene, Rachel. 2004. *Internet art*. London: Thames and Hudson.

Harrison, Steve, Paul Dourish. 2001. Re-place-ing space: The role of space and place in collaborative systems. *Computer supported cooperative work: Proceedings of the 1996 ACM conference on Computer supported cooperative work*, 67-76. Boston, Massachusetts.

Hayles, N. Katherine. 2002. Flesh and metal: Reconfiguring the mindbody in virtual environments. *Configurations* 10 (2): 297-320.

Hayward, Philip. 1988. Echoes and reflections: The representation of representation. In *Picture this: Media representations of visual art and artists*, ed. Philip Hayward, 1-26. London: John Libbey.

Hediger, Vinzenz. 2005. Spaß an harter Arbeit: Der Making of-Film. S. 332-341. In *Demnächst in ihrem Kino: Grundlagen der Filmwerbung und Filmvermarktung*. Marburg: Schüren Verlag.

Hight, Craig. 2005. Making-of documentaries on DVD: *The Lord of the Rings* trilogy and special editions. *The Velvet Light Trap* 56 (3): 5-17.

Jones, Beverly. 1989. Computer imagery: Imitation and representation of realities. *Leonardo: Journal of the International Society for the Arts, Sciences and Technology*. Supplemental Issue: Computer Art in Context: 31-38.

Latour, Bruno. 1987. *Science in action: How to follow scientists and engineers through society*. Cambridge, MA: Harvard University Press.

Legrady, George. 1999. Intersecting the virtual and the real: Space in interactive media installations. *Wide Angle* 21 (1): 104-113.

Lehmann, Ann-Sophie. 2006. Wat de hand weet: De kunstenaar aan het werk. In *Ateliergeheimen: Over de werkplaats van de kunstenaar vanaf 1200 tot heden*, eds. Mariette Haveman, E. de Jong, Ann-Sophie Lehmann, and Annemiek Overbeek, 120-141. Amsterdam: Kunst en Schrijven.

Manovich, Lev. 2001. *The language of new media*. Cambridge, MA: MIT Press.

McCullough, Malcolm. 1996. *Abstracting craft: The practiced digital hand*. Cambridge, MA: MIT Press.

Mitchell, William J. 1992. *The reconfigured eye: Visual truth in the post-photographic era*. Cambridge, MA: MIT Press.

Moskovich. Julia. 2002. To infinity and beyond: Assessing the technological imperative in computer animation. *Screen* 43 (3): 293-314.

Paul, Christiane. 2003. *Digital art*. London: Thames and Hudson.

Poster, Mark. 2004. Digitally local communications: Technologies and space. Paper presented at conference *The global and the local in mobile communication: Places, images, people, connections*. Budapest. (http://www.locative.net/tcmreader/index.php?cspaces;poster).

Ryoaki, K., S. Marti, H. Ishii. 2004. I/O Brush: Drawing with everyday objects as ink. *Proceedings of the SIGCHI conference on Human factors in computing systems*, 303-310. Vienna, Austria.

Savedoff, Barbara. 1997. Escaping reality: Digital imagery and the resources of photography. *Journal of Aesthetics and Art Criticism* 55 (2): 202-214.

Sennett, Richard. 2008. *The craftsman*. London: Allen Lane.

Simon, Bart. 2007. Geek chic: Machine aesthetics, digital gaming, and the cultural politics of the case mod. *Games and Culture* 2 (3): 175-193.

Stallabrass, Julian. 2003. *Internet art: The online clash of culture and commerce*. London: Tate Publishing.

Smith, Alvey Ray. 2001. Digital paint systems: An anecdotal and historical overview. *IEEE Annals of the History of Computing* 23 (2): 4-30.

Wilson, Steven. 2002. *Information arts: A survey of art and research at the intersection of art, science and technology*. Cambridge MA: Harvard University Press.

About the authors

Marianne van den Boomen is lecturer-researcher at the Department of Media and Culture Studies at Utrecht University. Her research focuses on media philosophy and metaphors.

Marinka Copier is assistant professor at the Department of Media and Culture Studies at Utrecht University. Her research focuses on games, (role) play cultures and education.

Isabella van Elferen is assistant professor at the Department of Media and Culture Studies at Utrecht University. In her research she seeks links between media, music, and philosophy.

Frank Kessler is professor of media history at the Department of Media and Culture Studies at Utrecht University. His research focuses on early cinema, emerging media and theoretical reconsiderations of the dispositif.

Erna Kotkamp is lecturer-researcher at the Department of Media and Culture Studies at Utrecht University. She conducts research on the methodology and design of e-learning software in relation to learning theories.

Sybille Lammes is assistant professor at the Department of Media and Culture Studies at Utrecht University. Her main research subjects are related to games and digital cartographies as socio-spatial cultures.

Ann-Sophie Lehmann is assistant professor at the Department of Media and Culture Studies at Utrecht University. Her research is concerned with the history, theory, and practice of image making in old and new media cultures.

Jos de Mul is professor of philosophical anthropology at the Erasmus University of Rotterdam. His versatile work includes many publications about the philosophical dimensions of new media cultures.

Eggo Müller is associate professor at the Department of Media and Culture Studies at Utrecht University. Television as medium, popular culture and participation are his main research areas.

David B. Nieborg is PhD student at the Amsterdam School for Cultural Analysis (ASCA) and lecturer at the University of Amsterdam. His publications explore the interaction between commercial game culture, technology, marketing, and military communities.

Eva Nieuwdorp is teacher-researcher at the Department of Media and Culture Studies at Utrecht University. She is writing a PhD about pervasive games.

Thomas Poell is lecturer-researcher at the Department of Media and Culture Studies at Utrecht University. His research mainly deals with historical questions of media and democratization.

Joost Raessens is associate professor at the Department of Media and Culture Studies at Utrecht University. His main research interests are playful identities, serious games and the playful use of media.

Douglas Rushkoff is a writer and professor of media culture at New York University's Interactive Telecommunications Program and a founding member of Technorealism. His research focuses on media, society, and change.

Mirko Tobias Schäfer is assistant professor at the Department of Media and Culture Studies at Utrecht University. His research focuses on participatory culture and culture industries.

William Uricchio is professor and director of comparative media studies at MIT and professor of comparative media history at Utrecht University in the Netherlands. His research considers the transformation of media technologies into cultural practices.

Nanna Verhoeff is associate professor at the Department of Media and Culture Studies at Utrecht University. Her research concentrates on emerging media, in particular on historical as well as contemporary screen media as sites for virtual mobility.

Imar de Vries is assistant professor at the Department of Media and Culture Studies at Utrecht University. His research areas include mobile telephony as ideal communication and media archaeologies.

Berteke Waaldijk is professor of language and culture studies at Utrecht University. Her research concentrates on the history of gender, culture and citizenship.

Index

A

Abu Ghraib 193
access 136, 142
accumulation 149-150, 155
actor 9-10, 121, 128-129, 162-163, 169
actor network 161-162
actor-network theory 162, 168
advertising 45
aesthetics 15, 95, 101-102
affordances 10, 12, 15, 84-85, 137, 144, 151, 153, 155, 194
afilmic 192-193, 195
Age of Empires 223, 229
agency 13, 25, 121-124, 126, 128, 130-131, 151
agent 13, 23, 121, 124, 126, 130-131, 144
Agent Smith 121
Ahrendt, R. 130
Aibo 151, 157
Aktenzeichen XY 52-54, 56
al Qaeda 38
Alberti's window 201
algorithm 139
amateur culture 59
American Idol 50
America's Army 11, 36, 141, 145
America's Most Wanted 51-52
analog/digital 136, 138
Anderson, D. 160
Andrejevic, M. 50-51, 55
animation 193, 215, 268, 277-279
anime 145
anonimity 110
anthropology 9

anthropomorph 122, 124, 173
Apoptygma Berzerk 121-122, 127-130
apparatus 11, 21-23, 25, 27, 29, 31, 33, 83, 86, 88, 104, 210, 212, 220, 253, 262
  apparatus theory 21
  gaming apparatus 21, 26, 32
application 210
appropriation 9, 13, 15, 147-148, 150-153
Apter, M. 205
arcade hall 37
archive 135, 193
archiving 13, 149-150, 155
Argent Dawn 159
Aristotle 175
Arnold, M. 85
art 98, 270
  digital art 268
  net.art 271
  new media art 267, 270, 272
artificial intelligence 121
artwork 267
attention deficit disorder 177
attention economy 176
attention span 177
attraction 110-111, 115
Attributes of Painting 274
audience 139, 175, 179
  active audience 50-51
augmented reality 200
aura 96-99, 103, 268-270, 275
Austin, J.L. 262
authenticity 41, 45, 96, 187-188
authorship 55, 114, 137, 145, 181